DI   M. McCumiskey.   .99

Perspective

A handbook of Chris

CW00745768

M.A. Chignell

Edward Arnold

First published in Great Britain 1981
by Edward Arnold (Publishers) Ltd
41 Bedford Square, London WC1X 3DQ

Edward Arnold (Australia) Pty Ltd
80 Waverley Road, Caulfield East,
Victoria 3145, Australia

Reprinted 1982, 1983, 1984, 1986, 1987

British Library Cataloguing in Publication Data

Chignell, M.A.
   Perspectives: a handbook of Christian responsibility
   1. Christian ethics
   I. Title
   241   BJ1251

   ISBN 0-7131-0614-X

Acknowledgments:

My warmest gratitude to many friends, but especially to Barbara Windle, without whose expert and meticulous help this book would never have been written, and to Doreen Sides, whose interest and competent typing of the manuscript has been an encouragement to us all.

M.A.C. March 1981

The Publishers wish to thank the National Council of the Churches of Christ in the USA and Thomas Nelson, New York for permission to use verses from the Revised Standard Version of the Bible, copyrighted 1946, 1952 © 1971, 1973.

Set in 10/11 pt Century
Printed by Richard Clay Ltd, Bungay, Suffolk

Contents

All chapters include relevant biblical passages and a section on Christian attitudes today; each ends with a full discussion and work programme. All biblical quotations are from the Revised Standard Version, *except where otherwise stated.*

Preface: To the Student

Moral ideas are the scaffolding of life. It is a horribly complicated scaffolding. A great deal of it is undoubtedly useless, and becoming more so as the building develops. . . . The scaffolding (however) must be approached with the greatest care. . . . You need revolutionary people to prevent obsolete pieces from obstructing the workmen; you need conservatives so that the whole thing doesn't collapse all of a sudden.
Pierre Ceresole (Founder, International Voluntary Service), USA 1909

This book is designed to help you undertake a course on the theme of Christian Responsibility, whether called by that name or Christian Perspectives on Personal and Social Issues or Christianity and Contemporary Society. As the title indicates, this book is written from a Christian outlook, but two points need to be clear at the start.

First, many people act and think in a morally responsible way and yet do not necessarily call themselves Christian. People of other faiths also have very strong and noble moral codes. The book is not meant to suggest therefore that ethics belong to the Christian alone. But an all-inclusive account of morality would take a volume of enormous size; instead I have geared this book to the demands of the majority of the examining boards.

Second, even among Christians there are widely differing points of view about many of the great issues studied here. You will see this particularly when you come to look at such themes as abortion or pacifism. Although I have tried to deal fairly with these various strands of Christian conviction, some people may think insufficient weight has been given to their individual standpoint. However, the syllabuses are so broad and the many topics so vast that each section of the book has to be comparatively short and is not meant to be comprehensive. The aim is to start you thinking, discussing and then deepening your study of the particular subjects which most interest you. The whole thing will come alive through debate and wider investigation.

The appropriate Old Testament and New Testament teaching

will be considered within Sections A, B and C. There are more biblical references in Section A—The Individual—and many of the items are dealt with at greater length than those in B and C. This is because in some respects Section A is more relevant to daily living. We must first realize what it means to be a responsible individual before we can hope to become active members of the community or see ourselves as world citizens. I have had to condense the material in B and C, so that the individual student can have maximum scope for further research.

Some teachers and students may prefer to study Section D first. In it a number of relevant biblical ideas have been set out directly, partly because there are syllabuses which deal with these themes, but also because it is difficult for the religious and/or Christian person to start working out a moral code without a basic background knowledge of biblical teaching. So Section D attempts to summarize and clarify some of the complex issues with which the Old and New Testaments deal. Of course, it has been impossible to present all the various interpretations of the biblical text. The fact that there are so many different Christian denominations in this country alone (Roman Catholic, Church of England, Free Churches and so on) amply illustrates how Christians have always strongly defended their right to declare their personal position in matters of faith and belief. While at one time there was little communication between the different churches, there is now a real desire (the ecumenical movement) to move towards some kind of unity, but not uniformity. We can agree to differ and respect each other's point of view. So whether you or your teacher agree or disagree with some of the interpretations in this section, I hope that the text will stimulate lively discussion. The views expressed are not intended to be simply accepted or rejected, but to provide a focal point for debate. Unless we start to think about what we believe and learn to share our thoughts with others in a spirit of honesty and tolerance, we cannot enlarge our own horizons and become truly adult people.

I hope very much that the book may also be of use to many Religious Education classes who are not taking any examination at the end of their course. As a teacher I have discussed all the topics raised in this book with a wide variety of non-examination students and have had my own thinking stretched and broadened by this enlivening experience.

Section A — The Individual

Introduction

His capacity for rational thought

As far as we know, animals live by instinct and are totally involved in the present. Even building nests, feeding their young and storing food for the winter are instinctive means of survival. Human beings, on the other hand, are capable of getting outside their immediate circumstances, by reflecting or thinking about how their past decisions got them where they are and how they might be able to change the situation if it is undesirable.

His capacity for moral choice

According to the Bible one of the characteristics which distinguishes man from the rest of the animal kingdom is his capacity for moral choice. Adam is shown as being able to respond in trust and obedience to God's wishes and later as withholding that response. The Genesis parable also states that mankind is commissioned to rule the earth as God's representative and it implies that man is given power of reason; that is to say, he can think about his actions before he does them and reflect afterwards upon their consequences. Man is therefore treated as a being who is capable of taking responsibility both for himself and for others. So, when Cain in jealousy murders his brother, God questions him about Abel's whereabouts. His violent cry 'Am I my brother's keeper?' is really a guilty protest of irresponsibility which has echoed down the centuries of human history.

His formulation of rules of behaviour

Because humans are able to think about the consequences of their words and actions (although often they do not exercise this ability), they have been capable of working out rules of behaviour to which the majority of people in the community must conform if that particular community is to survive. From the study of ancient civilizations and modern-day primitive societies, we can see how laws, customs and traditions have grown up and how different have been ideas about sexual rites, marriage contracts, the ownership of property and the rights of the ruling class or king. Despite

1

cultural differences, however, every society has recognized an elementary law of right and wrong. Courage, loyalty and honesty, for example, are all qualities which any community values if it is to remain intact. And the world's great religions, of course, have laid down quite definite moral codes which their followers must live by if they are to be faithful members. As moral beings we may judge the rightness or wrongness of an act by the effect it has upon another person. Thus to lie, cheat, steal and bully are all harmful because they destroy trust and someone else's well-being; whereas an act of kindness or good neighbourliness is creative because the recipient benefits by it.

The importance of a moral code
A moral code matters both for the individual and for his community, but to be a workable code it must be neither too rigid and unalterable, nor too weak and flexible. What is important is that each individual goes through the hard process of thinking out for himself what is really worthwhile in the business of living, not just from a selfish point of view but also for his community. This process should continue for the whole of life, but to begin to think for oneself and to form one's own judgments is a sign of adulthood.

To reach this kind of independent and responsible way of thinking is not easy and it involves the development of certain skills, such as learning as much about a problem as possible, being able to express in words what one thinks about any issue, listening patiently and respecting other people's opinions, and entering into discussion with them so that some kind of agreement may be reached. We also need to recognize what is true or false, what can be supported by logical argument, what is unfair or prejudiced both in our own thoughts, words and actions and in what others think, say or do. Thus, in the end we may arrive at a stage where we do not simply accept as right that which we have been told is right either by our parents, or our teachers, or 'experts' in particular fields of study or national leaders, nor do we accept as right that which our contemporaries say and do, or what we read in the newspapers and see on television. All these factors can help us in formulating our own opinions, but in the end the decision is our own and we take responsibility for it.

One philosopher has described authentic living, i.e. the real and genuine article, as the state of being able to make individual, personal moral choices; and inauthentic living, i.e. false, sham or pseudo, as allowing others to make choices for us, or being too easily influenced by all sorts of outside forces, such as the mass media. Using the term in this rather special way, we might say that authenticity is perhaps another way of describing the chief characteristic of a mature and responsible human being.

Parliamentary legislation
In 1969 two important pieces of parliamentary legislation changed the age of majority from 21 to 18. At the age of 18 you can now vote, can marry without your parent's consent, be a blood donor, make a will, buy or sell a house, give valid receipts and act as a trustee. In other words, you can legally make important and lasting decisions. Before these Acts of Parliament were passed, there was much discussion as to what constituted a mature person and whether an arbitrary age could be set for reaching such maturity. It was recognized that people functioned and developed at different levels. One person may be physically grown up, but quite childlike in his or her emotions; another may be very adult in his or her intellectual approach but sexually unawakened. In the end it was agreed that 18 was as good an age as 21 for establishing some legal age of majority, when a person was judged as being responsible for his or her behaviour. According to the law of the land, other ages have also been fixed, such as compulsory education between 5 and 16, and after the age of 17 a young person can be tried in a magistrate's court.

A sense of responsibility
In the following sections of this book, we shall discuss what is involved in having a sense of responsibility, not only as an individual but also as a member of the community and the world at large. Some of the many problems which arise in life will be looked at from different angles in order to help the reader think about them deeply, discuss them with others and so perhaps come to some conclusions of his/her own.

Discussion and work
1 Discuss the statement that animals live entirely by instinct, but human beings have the ability to live by reason and to make moral choices. Think of examples of unreasonable behaviour. What factors other than reason influence our decision making?
2 Various factors influence people in making moral decisions:
  (a) fear of punishment;
  (b) desire for praise or reward;
  (c) enlightened self-interest—in other words, if you do me a good turn, I'll do you one in return;
  (d) respect for law and order;
  (e) genuine interest in and concern for the welfare of others.
What usually motivates you in making decisions? Does the

motive vary according to the importance of the issue to be
decided?

3 How far do the factors listed above correspond with the stages of
our moral development from infancy to moral maturity?

4 Do you think a single age of maturity can be established? How
would you define maturity?

5 There are various laws relating to the age when a person may
consume alcohol with or without food, own a firearm or license a
motor vehicle. Do you know what these ages are? If you could,
would you change them?

1 Family life

We must start with the family because that is where life begins
and unless we are tragically deprived children, our earliest memories are linked with our relationship to our parents and possibly
our brothers and sisters. The origins of family life must go back
to the basic sexual attraction between men and women and the
equally important fundamental human need for love and security.
Also, in primitive days an individual would not have had much
chance of physical survival on his own. He needed to live within
the framework of the family, clan or tribe. In this short section
there is no time to look at other cultural ideas about the family constitution, as we have to consider our own 20th-century ideas and
their Jewish/Christian backgrounds. But different approaches
have been tried. Some societies have been matriarchal in structure, with the woman taking the dominant role.

In the Old Testament

Family life was of very great importance to the Jew and still is. The
Old Testament gives specific instructions about family loyalty
and dependence. The Fifth Commandment, 'Honour your father
and mother' (Exodus 20:12), is addressed to the adult members
of the community. It instructs them to care for their elderly parents in a society that had no welfare state to provide retirement
pensions and supplementary benefits. The theme of honouring
one's parents runs throughout the Old Testament, being specifically mentioned in Proverbs 23:22—25 and Ecclesiasticus 3:1—16.
Agricultural or nomadic societies calculated their prosperity by
the number of children, especially sons; in those sparsely populated times the high infant mortality rate and the fact that women
often died in childbirth robbed the clan of essential members. However, for the Hebrew the first-born son and the firstlings of the
flock were always regarded as God's possession and the human

4

boy had to be 'bought back' or 'redeemed' by a suitable substitute. The concept of animal sacrifice could seem repugnant to us (although we ourselves sacrifice millions of animals each year in scientific experiments), but the idea which lies behind the redemption of the first-born is important. It is a way of saying that, although the family is very significant and human life is also valuable, loyalty and service to God are even more precious. In fact a person must see his priorities clearly and must always put God first.

In the New Testament

When we turn to the New Testament we read in Luke's gospel that Jesus was a dutiful son to his parents, although on one occasion he surprised them by staying behind in Jerusalem to listen to the famous rabbis discussing religious topics, thus asserting his independence on a matter of vital spiritual significance to him (Luke 2:41—52). When he grew to manhood he was obviously much concerned about his mother. By this time Mary was presumably a widow since Joseph's name is never mentioned (Mark 6:3). Jesus was always angered by the exploitation of widows (Mark 12:40), was sensitively aware of their needs (Luke 7:11—17) and, when dying, asked his best friend to look after his mother in his place (John 19:25—27). Jesus bitingly condemned the lawyers who allowed a selfish son to neglect his duties to his parents on the pretext of some legal hypocrisy (Mark 7:8—13) and he reproved his disciples because they foolishly tried to prevent mothers bringing their children for his blessing (Mark 10:13,14). He clearly loved children, taught that they must be valued in their own right as persons (Mark 9:36,37) and even used a child to symbolize the quality of life which an adult must possess if he is to be a citizen of the Kingdom of God (Mark 10:14,15). Although it is not certain what Jesus meant by this, it is probably fair to say that a child's outstanding quality is its receptiveness and dependence. It does not ask to be brought into the world and it is the duty of its parents to cherish and uphold it until the child itself passes through childhood to a stage of relative independence and strength.

Jesus always stressed that human beings need both to give and to receive love and, in many respects, mankind has a dependent status and a dependent nature. This should not, however, lead to domination, exploitation or subservience, but to active partnership and inter-relationships. In terms of the family it means that parents must accept real responsibility for their children as people in their own right and not as extensions of themselves. Having brought children into the world, they have a deep obligation to give them all the care, love and attention that is possible to help

5

them develop fully. Children in return also have a profound duty to respond to their parents in love and trust (where these qualities are justified), and to be loyal and caring, treating their parents also as people in their own right who have needs and difficulties.

Paul gives some good advice about family relationships in his letter to the Colossians and also to the Ephesians (although some scholars are not sure whether Paul is really the author of the latter). Children are told to be obedient to their parents because that is pleasing in the Lord's sight, but parents are also instructed not to drive their children to resentment as this will make them feel frustrated (Colossians 3:19—21). The new idea here is that Paul recognizes that children have rights as well as parents. In fact the whole passage (Colossians 3:18—4:1) stresses that the under-privileged, whether wives, children or slaves, are all entitled to just consideration and fair treatment.

In the 20th century
The institution of the family has become a matter for debate in the 20th century because of the emancipation of women and the economic status enjoyed by many young people. Nowadays, the woman may be unwilling to give up the kind of freedom she enjoyed before she had a child. Both parents may now go out to work, so that the man does not necessarily hold the purse strings. When young people become financially independent through earning high wages, they can then leave home. In earlier times girls normally left home only to get married. On occasion, educational differences between parents and children can create such barriers that the two generations are no longer able to communicate with each other. The term 'nuclear' family is sometimes used to describe the small family group of father, mother and children; the term derives from the word nucleus—a kernel, around which something may grow. An 'extended' family includes grandparents, uncles, aunts, cousins and other relatives. Up to the first half of this century, family units were usually extended families in which help was available in times of difficulty and crisis. Now, owing to the introduction of birth control methods and economic pressures, the family unit is very much smaller and is often under considerable strain. Many old people are no longer cared for in their own houses but are placed in Residential Homes or, if completely unable to look after themselves, in geriatric wards of hospitals.

Alternatives to the family
Various alternatives to the traditional view of family life have been tried in this century, particularly in Israel and China. It is interesting that the two races who have placed great significance

and importance on the family above all other considerations, have been those which have been willing to look at alternatives. In Israel the Kibbutz ideal arose out of strong practical considerations. It was a question of survival. Furthermore, the Russian and Polish Jews who emigrated to Israel took with them the ideals of equal sharing and working for oneself, as opposed to having servants.

In the Kibbutz everyone is equal. The women share in the work on the farm and village and therefore the children are cared for by a communal 'mother'. From infancy to adolescence the children live, eat, sleep and learn with their own age group in the care of trained nurses and teachers. They spend time with their parents in the evening after work and on the Sabbath. However, this way of life has proved too rigid for many Jews and different types of community living have developed, either in a kind of co-operative farmers' settlement or in a shared farming village. In both cases each family lives in its own homestead whilst sharing the marketing and buying of supplies. Latterly, some Israelis have seriously criticized the Kibbutz concept. Many young people have found it extremely difficult to break away from the dependence which such a close-knit community offers, while others have reacted strongly against it. They have refused to live and work on the Kibbutz because they want to have money, possessions, independence and a real family home of their own.

In China communes were started in 1958. The children are cared for collectively so that women may be freed for work. The recent emancipation of Chinese women was in some respects a great step forward from the old system, although the rigours of life have meant that the peasant woman has always had to work desperately hard with her husband in order to survive. But such is the pressure of increased population in modern China that the authorities are attempting to limit couples to one-child families. The precious single child would then undoubtedly be brought up by its parents.

In Russia, where family life has always been very strong, the authorities also experimented with communes—both to free women for work and also to educate children according to certain Marxist principles. But in both China and Russia the commune idea seems to have lost favour.

In Western Europe and the United States there have also been breakaway movements amongst young people who have wanted to live a community life. On the whole, these communes have not been long lived. The oldest and most successful form of communal life has, of course, been carried on in the great religious houses and institutions of both East and West, but these were never set up in competition with, or as a universal alternative to, family life in the normal sense. What these religious houses did confirm was that men and women who entered a particular order accepted the authority and discipline of that order from a sense of personal conviction, which ensured the smooth running of the establishment.

Jesus and the Christian viewpoint

Jesus was not uncritical of the family, and we too have a responsibility to consider present-day concepts clearly and objectively. Jesus pointed out that there was a higher loyalty than that of the family. When his mother and brothers came to visit him, he startled his hearers by saying that everyone who heard the word of God and obeyed it was his family, pointing to a deeper relationship than the natural blood tie. There is such a thing as affinity of purpose and outlook (Mark 4:31–35). Bringing in the kingdom of God was all-important to Jesus and those who joined him in this endeavour were part of his spiritual family. It is against this background that we must look at several other sayings which seem to strike a harsh note. On one occasion, he pointed out to the crowd which was following him, the great cost of discipleship (Luke 14:25–27, Matthew 10:37–38) by saying that a man must put his loyalty to the kingdom above all else. (N.B. when Jesus uses the word 'hate', we should not take it too literally, as there are several Old Testament passages in which 'hate' is used in the sense of 'loving less'.) At another time a would-be disciple asked for permission to give his father a decent burial before himself joining Jesus. The man was probably confident that Jesus would agree that he should fulfil one of the most sacred of all Jewish obligations. In his reply Jesus tested the man's sincerity, just as he further challenged another man who wanted to go home to say goodbye to his family before following Jesus (Luke 9:59–62).

Perhaps the trouble with our modern concept of the 'nuclear' family is that we expect far too much of this self-contained unit. It is somehow supposed to provide everything a person needs. By contrast, in the Old Testament the extended family or clan or tribe was also vitally important, and in the New Testament Jesus talked of the great spiritual family of believers (note especially Mark 10:29–31). Both these biblical concepts recognize that the family finds its proper fulfilment by being part of a larger unit. What makes the family a viable structure is that it has the potential to express and to meet the deepest longings and desires in people, that is the desire to love, to care, to cherish and to share one's life with others.

From a Christian point of view there has needed to be much

rethinking about the family because Christians have accepted the prevailing ideas of the subordinate role of women which existed not only in medieval times but right up to the end of the 19th century. Considerations of family tradition, wealth, financial bargaining and the idea that women and children were the property of the husband and father have all made the family a restrictive place. Today some of the problems are different. We have struggling one-parent families and homes where children have plenty of pocket-money but little care and attention; we also have the conflicts which women face in choosing between their careers and their commitment to their children. Those people, however, who can consciously decide to have a child ought not to shirk the responsibility involved in bringing up that child during its formative years. We will discuss in Section B the difficulties which arise in the community when family life goes wrong. For the moment, it is enough to say that the impersonal nature of modern life and the vast increase in population both highlight the importance of the family. In 20th-century cities the individual has greater need than ever for the sense of belonging and identity which a rightly balanced, loving family unit can provide.

Discussion and work

1 Look up and discuss the relevant biblical passages quoted above. How radical do you think Jesus was in his approach to the family? Compare also his idea of God as a loving father in the parable of the Prodigal Son (Luke 15:*11—32*).
2 Discuss the differences between family life today and in the Victorian era when fathers ruled with a rod of iron (or, at least, a hard strap) and mothers had to cope with successive children.
3 Discuss the Victorian proposition that 'children should be seen and not heard'. What implications does this attitude have for the parent/child relationship? Was this approach conditioned by the fact that mothers could employ paid staff to look after their children?
4 In the past, in many wealthy families, children learned to care more for their 'nannies' than they did for their mothers; what is a modern equivalent to this situation?
5 Women have fought for the right to go out to work and be financially independent, but many sociologists and psychologists have pointed out that a child needs a constant relationship with either its mother or its father for at least the first few years of its life, and that baby minders, crèches etc. are not an adequate substitute for the personal, warm, tender relationship which a parent can give to its child. Do you think employers should be willing to give either the mother or the father a length of time off

work, but with a view to reinstatement afterwards, to enable this very important period in a young child's life to be catered for?

6 Dr Mia Kellmer Pringle has suggested that there should be two types of marriage, one for those who want to live together and share each other's life styles and the other for those who want to have children. The second marriage, where another life is involved, should be a commitment for at least 15 years. Do you think this is a fair proposition? Having decided to have children, do you think a couple should endeavour to give their child a stable family background for at least the first 15 years of life?

7 What qualities do you think are needed in bringing up young children? Do you think there should be training sessions for parents to meet this need?

8 Discover what you can about Kibbutzim in Israel and communes in China. What can you find out about the existence of British communes? What do you think are likely to be the major differences between the Jewish, Chinese and English systems?

2 Friendship

Life may begin with the family but it certainly does not stop there. The advantage of a loving, stable background, where there are creative relationships between parents and children, is that the children learn to go out from the close family unit to explore and make relationships with other people. If there has not been a secure background, then the child or young person finds it more difficult to form the right kind of independent relationships with others outside the family. Some of the tensions which can arise in a home may come as a result of the parents' disapproval of the kinds of friendships entered into by their sons or daughters.

In the Old Testament
The Old Testament makes some specific points about the value of friendship. The story of David and Jonathan is probably the classic example of two men whose friendship for each other surmounted suspicion, ambition and treachery. Saul was king, David his musician. David had married Michal (Saul's daughter) and had sworn a covenant of friendship with Jonathan (Saul's son), who had legally adopted him as his brother. But Saul became jealous of David's valour in battle and planned his death. Both Michal and Jonathan took David's part. Although Jonathan was his father's heir, he felt convinced that David would somehow become the next king. Despite this, Jonathan saved David's life and remained steadfast in his friendship (1 Samuel 19—20). When Saul and

10

Jonathan were killed in battle, David lamented over them in an elegy which is probably one of the oldest pieces of poetry in the Old Testament (2 Samuel 1).

An example of friendship between two women, Ruth and her mother-in-law, Naomi, is given in the story told in the book of Ruth. On the death of her husband, Ruth chose to remain with her mother-in-law rather than return to her own homeland 'for where you go I will go, and where you lodge I will lodge; your people shall be my people, and your God my God' (Ruth 1:*16*).

A further remarkable story of friendship is found in the book of Jeremiah. The prophet had spoken out so strongly against the policies at the court, that the king had weakly agreed to his imprisonment in a muddy well. Jeremiah would most certainly have died but for the fact that he was rescued by an Ethiopian eunuch, a black man in the king's service. The eunuch must have risked a great deal to save his friend (Jeremiah 38:*1—13*).

As one might expect from the Wisdom literature, there are sayings about friendship both in Proverbs (18:*24*) and Ecclesiasticus (6:*6—16*), where the qualities of true and false friendship are spelt out. The writer believes that like is attracted to like: 'Whoever fears the Lord makes true friends, for as a man is, so is his friend' (*Jerusalem Bible*). This is not always true, of course, as inexperience can lead us into friendships which at a later date, we regret and recognize as having been formed on a superficial basis.

In the New Testament

In a famous passage (John 15:*11—15*), Jesus called his disciples his friends and gave them the specific commandment to love one another as he had loved them. 'Greater love has no man than this, that a man lay down his life for his friends.' The basis of friendship, therefore, as Jesus saw it, was the *mutual* trust, loyalty and love which might exist between people even though they were considered unequal in certain respects. In the 1st century AD, there were clearly marked distinctions between man and woman, adult and child, master and servant/slave, and there were racial tensions between Jew and Gentile. These factors made friendship between members of different categories very difficult. Even so, friendship could exist where each appreciated the innate worth of the other person, regardless of the fact that one was superior or inferior according to the social roles of the time.

Paul often talked about friendship or brotherly love when writing to the different congregations he had founded or for which he felt a particular responsibility. For him, brotherly love was the hallmark of the Christian, as is shown in his letter to the Ephesians (4:*25—32*), especially the words 'do not let the sun go down upon your anger'. Paul was advising his readers to make up quarrels immediately, rather than to leave the dispute until it became harder to forgive or admit faults. That Paul practised what he preached is shown by the way he forgave John Mark for his desertion (2 Timothy 4:*11*) and by his love for Luke and Philemon. This quality of brotherly love and friendship was all important to the young, tiny, struggling Christian community when individuals depended upon each other for hospitality, financial support and courageous identification under persecution.

In today's society
We live in a culture where there is far greater equality between the sexes, between generations, teachers and pupils, employers and employed, and between people of different social background and race. Nonetheless, great barriers and injustices still remain and divisions split our society and our world into opposing interest groups. Just as in New Testament times when friendships helped to bridge the gulfs that separated people, so today the qualities of true friendship are of the utmost importance. A friend must be honest, tolerant, sympathetic and appreciative of the other person's point of view and character. Friendship cannot exist where there is a conscious feeling of superiority on the one hand and deception or flattery on the other. We usually enter into a friendship because we want to do so. It will be based therefore on some kind of mutual attraction or regard, on several common interests and even on a similar outlook or purpose in life. It should be free of constraint, of jealousy, envy and competitiveness.

It is perfectly possible to be friends with one's parents and teachers even though age and experience are not equal. The generation gap is soon closed and when a young person becomes an adult these differences are not important. Life is greatly enriched by friendship with people who are not only our immediate and obvious contemporaries but who may belong to quite different spheres, whether through education, talents, upbringing or nationality.

Friendship can lead to 'falling in love', although usually it has nothing to do with sexual attraction. It is easier today for people of the opposite sex to be friends with each other because of the greater freedom which women enjoy, but such friendships have existed in the past. Where the two members of a marriage partnership are not just lovers but also real friends, they have the happy basis of a truly fulfilled relationship.

Discussion and work
1 Read and discuss the passage in Ecclesiasticus. Do you agree

with all that is written there? If not, why not?

2 Do you think it is possible to be friends with one's parents? What are some of the problems which a difference in age can make between two friends?

3 What specific qualities of friendship would you look to give and receive?

4 What does being honest with one's friends mean and entail?

5 What do you understand by loyalty to your friends?

6 What problems of friendship might arise between two people of the opposite sex?

7 What famous examples of friendship from fairly modern history have most impressed you and why?

3 Sexual loving and marriage

Background to our present problems

Before the 20th century, in a world where there were insufficient human beings, the great need was to beget offspring for the preservation of the family, the tribe and the race, particularly as infant mortality was high and the average life expectation low. Thus it happened that at other times in history and in other cultures, a boy or girl might be married soon after puberty or menstruation to begin the fathering or bearing of children. Material wealth, however, has enabled us to adopt a different attitude. We require young people to stay at school until they are 16. We have passed laws for their protection by, for example, making sexual intercourse illegal before the age of 16 and by defining an age of majority. We have created a 'teen' age, which our psychologists have given the name of adolescence, the period when the child grows up to become a man or woman. In creating this modern teenage we have tried to understand and even isolate the problems encountered by young people. In some respects, however, social pressures have made life unbearably complicated for the adolescent and nowhere is this more apparent than in the realm of sexual feeling. Furthermore, institutional Christianity has traditionally accepted sexual inequality and has therefore been slow to clarify our present dilemmas.

We have to be clear about our facts. The awakening of sexual feeling is normal and necessary. In the animal kingdom it results in mating and procreation, i.e. begetting of offspring, but human beings go through this awakening process in different ways and even at slightly different ages. To feel attracted to another person, to want to make physical contact, to hold hands, to kiss and embrace is all part of people's ability to communicate with each other and to use their physical being to express emotional and psychological facets of their personality. Sexual love grows out of sexual attraction, although attraction does not necessarily lead to love. Sexual love is a deepening and intensifying of the desires for contact, finding final expression in the mutual giving and receiving which is experienced in sexual intercourse. Although they are often confused, sexual love is not the same as sexual lust. Love sees the other as a person; it involves an unselfish attitude of respect and appreciation. Lust never sees a person, merely an object which is a means to the end of satisfying desire.

Changing ideas

Before the emancipation of women, most people thought that the feminine nature was sexually passive. The man would normally take the initiative in the relationship and finally at intercourse lay his seed in the bed of the womb, hoping it would bear fruit in the coming of a child. A barren woman was a disgrace because people might believe she had not been able to care for the seed within her. Many medieval paintings illustrate quite clearly the current idea that the male seed contained the perfect human being in minute form. This belief explains the conviction that masturbation and homosexual practices were sinful and debased. All such acts wasted the precious seed which contained the fully formed human. We know now that there is an equal biological contribution from men and women in producing a child. We are also aware that there are too many people on our planet and that although the seed and the ovum can result in another human being, they are not sacred in their own right. They are only potentially significant and important as the means of bringing into the world another person. It is also true that women are not necessarily passive at all. In some matriarchal societies (where the woman was dominant rather than the man) it has been the woman who has taken the lead in mating. For various biological, emotional and psychological reasons, the female is different from the male, but perhaps not so different as previous generations have supposed.

Being clear about the facts is the first step towards facing our problems in a responsible manner. And these problems are largely of our own creation. On the one hand Christians have said that marriage is for a lifetime, that sexual intercourse belongs only to marriage and therefore a young person must wait until he/she finds the right partner with whom to live permanently. On the other hand young people become sexually aware and responsive to sexual attraction some years before marriage is either legal or socially and economically viable, i.e. workable. These problems are worse now than at the turn of the century because our society

14

exploits sexual attraction as a means of selling goods, or as a sure way of entertaining. Young people are constantly exposed to sexual matters through television, newspapers, magazines and other kinds of literature. They can no longer grow up innocent because nothing is left to the imagination and romantic love may even be derided as mere fantasy.

Old Testament teaching

In seeking for some answers to our difficulties we must first look at the biblical background to our cultural ideas. The Genesis parable of the creation of mankind regards sexual attraction in a very positive way. Adam was overjoyed when he awoke and found Eve beside him. The actual Hebrew words are even stronger than the English translation suggests: 'This at last is bone of my bones and flesh of my flesh'. The fact that woman is taken out of man's side symbolizes the strong sexual urge of men and women to become one flesh, this being the biblical way of describing sexual intercourse. Thus the writer of the Genesis parable sees sexual attraction as part of God's creation and therefore good.

Jewish society was patriarchal in structure; that is to say the man was the head of the family, the woman his possession. As the Hebrews looked on God as the clan father of his people, so the man was the dominant figure in society, although women were not insignificant. The patriarchal sagas show women playing an important role in the tribal history of Israel and they obviously exerted a great deal of influence as we can see by the story of Jacob and his four wives! Marriage was regarded as a solemn and binding contract, although divorce was permitted (Deuteronomy 24:1—4). One of the best descriptions of the cultural context of Jewish marriage is found in Ecclesiasticus 26:1—23, written originally in Hebrew and later translated into Greek by the author's grandson in 132 BC. Another writer in the book of Proverbs (31:10—31), gives us an alphabetical poem on the perfect wife. The Old Testament regards a girl's virginity before marriage and faithfulness after as absolutely essential. She is her husband's possession and must not have been 'defiled' by another. She is also the bearer of his children and the mainstay of his family. At one time adultery was punished by stoning (Leviticus 20:10), although this was not enforced in Jesus' day (John 8:1—11).

New Testament teaching—Jesus

When we turn to the New Testament we find that Jesus' teaching about marriage arises out of a question put to him by the Pharisees (Mark 10:1—12). Moses had permitted divorce if the husband found 'some indecency' in his wife. The matter was much debated at the time because two famous rabbis had disputed about the meaning of 'indecency' or 'unseemly'. One said it must entail sexual infidelity, while the other claimed it could be some trifling fault. When Jesus was asked what he thought about divorce he refused to be drawn into rabbinical controversy about the letter of the law. He went back to what he understood to be God's original intention. His comment on two people becoming one flesh was 'What therefore God has joined together, let not man put asunder'. Afterwards his disciples questioned him further. In Jewish law a man could divorce his wife by a note of dismissal but a woman had no legal rights. A man could not commit adultery against his own wife by having sexual intercourse with another woman. If he had intercourse with another man's wife, he committed adultery against the husband, not against his own wife. Jesus, however, put women on the same footing as men by saying that a man could commit adultery against his wife by divorcing her and marrying another, just as a woman could commit adultery by divorcing her husband or being divorced and marrying another.

The terms adultery and fornication are technical ones. The first describes an act of sexual intercourse between a married person and someone other than the wife or husband. Adulterers are breaking their marriage vows of sexual fidelity. Fornication means the act of sexual intercourse between those who are not legally married and who are therefore not breaking the marriage contract.

Jesus was at all times interested in motives not merely in actions. Remembering this we may possibly interpret his teaching in the following way. He clearly stated the principle behind true marriage according to his understanding of human relationships. While he emphasized the act of union itself, he did not refer at all to the child, the possible outcome of sexual union. He did not say that divorce was always wrong but he saw marriage as a permanent, exclusive relationship. He clarified the disciples' ideas by stressing the fundamental sexual equality between men and women. In a further passage (Matthew 5:27–28) Jesus again highlighted inner motivation. More often than not, lust was the basic cause which led to adultery and divorce (Matthew 5:31,32) should only take place on the ground of unchastity. In other words he seems to be saying that a marriage should only be dissolved when it is no longer the true union of which the sexual act is a symbol. If men and women cease to feel sexual love for their partners and have intercourse with others, then the relationship is no longer a real marriage and divorce is possibly the only solution.

Matthew records (19:10–12) that Jesus distinguishes three reasons for not marrying. Some may be eunuchs (i.e. sexually impotent) from birth; others may have become eunuchs as a result of surgery; a third category may actually choose to be eunuchs so as to dedicate themselves to the kingdom of heaven. He obviously does not mean that they are self-castrated but that they have committed themselves to celibacy (the unmarried state, in which one refrains from sexual intercourse) for the sake of the kingdom. That he himself was celibate is not surprising in view of the urgency of his task and the short period available to him; he must have sensed his lack of time right at the beginning of his ministry. That he advocated celibacy for his disciples is simply not proven. Although Paul was celibate Peter was not, nor were some of the other apostles or 'the Lord's brothers', who apparently travelled around with their wives (1 Corinthians 9:5). The verses from Matthew mean, in other words, that in Jesus' view some might choose to sacrifice personal happiness for the kingdom's sake. This saying therefore in no way devalues marriage as does the insistence upon a celibate priesthood.

New Testament teaching — Paul
Paul wrote to his friends at Corinth about a specific problem affecting the Christian congregation there at that time. It is not Paul's fault, but that of succeeding generations of Christians, that advice meant for one occasion should have been interpreted as binding for all time. The apostle believed that the end of the world was soon to come. Jesus would return in glory and establish his kingdom on earth. This view was shared by Paul's Christian contemporaries but was later modified when events did not turn out as expected. Himself a celibate, Paul resolved not to marry, probably for the sake of his work as well as for temperamental reasons. He advised the men and women at Corinth, a notably cosmopolitan and bawdy city where sexual licence and vice were commonplace, that it was better not to marry if this course was at all possible. If passions were strongly aroused, however, Paul advised people to get married and be faithful to husband or wife. He also spoke out against separation and divorce and gave some wise counsel about mixed marriages. The early church fathers used this letter in support of their belief that the unmarried state was more glorious than marriage and that sexual passion could only be sanctified by marriage and the begetting of children. In other words marriage was a necessary control to prevent men and women from falling into the sin of immorality.

Paul had the insight to realize that men and women are equal in sexual loving (1 Corinthians 7:4), but this fact is sometimes overlooked because he did rate marriage as a second best by saying 'I wish that all were as I myself am', i.e. celibate (1 Corinthians 7:7).

17

The Ephesian letter (which certainly contains many of Paul's ideas) compares the marriage relationship to that of Christ and his church:

> Wives be subject to your husbands as to the Lord. For the husband is the head of the wife as Christ is the head of the church, his body, and is himself its Saviour. . . . Husbands love your wives, as Christ loved the church and gave himself up for her . . . so husbands should love their wives as their own bodies (Ephesians 5:21–33).

The writer is speaking as an enlightened man of his time, raising the marriage state to the highest ideal he knows. But living as he did 2000 years ago, he could not be expected to think that men and women were socially equal. Nevertheless, he put forward the new idea that women had rights as well as men and should be treated with love, even sacrificial love and respect.

Christian attitudes today
It is against the background of this influential biblical material which later formed Christian tradition, that we have to re-examine our present attitudes.

On the question of a celibate priesthood many would argue that while some men may wish to take a vow of celibacy others may not, and that it is unnecessary and wrong to insist on this vow being essential to the priestly vocation. By implication it downgrades the sexual relationship of mutual love and support found in marriage. With the exception of Roman Catholicism, the Christian church including the Eastern Orthodox and the Anglican communions has found that married priests are doubly effective, not only because of their understanding of marital problems, but also because of the support they receive from their wives.

Sexual equality: The vast majority of Christians are now convinced that there is really no religious justification for thinking that men and women should not be equal in their relationship with each other, neither being subservient. In past times when child-bearing and child-minding made most women financially dependent upon their husbands, women were not free to develop in other ways and some might therefore have appeared to be intellectually inferior. Some psychologists have argued that the biological differences between men and women necessarily meant that they had different sexual codes. In their view a woman's whole emotional make-up was more deeply involved than a man's in the act of lovemaking, because a single occasion of intercourse could result in nine months pregnancy, childbirth, breast-feeding and childrearing. Men were therefore more casual and even promiscuous in their approach to sex. In theory at any rate, the use of modern contraceptive methods has freed women from the inevitable results of sexual intercourse. They are now able to be as casual, promiscuous or faithful in their sexual behaviour as men have been. But it would be tragic if the use of contraceptives led to casual and promiscuous behaviour and the downgrading of sexual experience rather than the rediscovery by both sexes of their fundamental sexual natures. Men also can be deeply emotionally involved in sexual intercourse, can share as far as possible in their wife's labour, be present at the birth of their child and support their family as fully as possible. And a woman who practises birth control can be just as lovingly committed to her husband and her children, if she has any, as generations of housebound women before her.

Birth control: Roman Catholic theology distinguishes between natural birth control and what it defines as artificial birth control. Natural methods include abstaining from sexual intercourse and only having the full relationship at a 'safe' period in the woman's menstrual cycle, when there is less likelihood of conception. 'Artificial' methods are those available through modern medicine. According to Roman Catholic doctrine, the latter methods are against the law of God and therefore sinful. Nevertheless very many lay people, both Catholic and Protestant, practise birth control through the use of modern contraceptives, even if it causes some Catholics a conflict of conscience. Such modern Christians believe that sexual intercourse is an expression of sexual love and need not be primarily for the purpose of having children. Just as it is perfectly right to seek artificial aids if sight or hearing fail, so it is right and proper to seek aids to limit the size of a family when health, money and other considerations make this essential. The physical union between husband and wife is life-giving in the deepest sense, even when there is no question of a child, because it expresses and symbolizes all that is involved in the total commitment of two people who are in love with each other. This emphasis is in line with Jesus' own comment as reported in Mark 10:8. It is also right to add that some married people, having had their family, go through a sterilization operation which enables them to continue with their love-making without the need for contraceptives.

What is more controversial, however, is the use of contraceptives by two people who are not married. In the past the Christian church has insisted that all sexual intercourse should be confined to the marriage relationship, that girls especially should be virgins before marriage and that premarital and extramarital sex was sinful (1 Thessalonians 4:1—8). Fear of unwanted pregnancies made women very careful about sexual relationships before marriage, although the seduction of the young and innocent by the unscrupulous of both sexes has always happened. Fear of venereal disease has also kept many from the casual sex encounter, even though the use of prostitutes has been a constant factor in any culture with strong marriage traditions. But if contraception, abortion and medical care can now broadly deal with all these former preventives to sexual relationships outside marriage, what should be the responsible attitude today?

The Christian affirmation
In this rather overwhelming welter of changing circumstances, opinions and ideas, the Christian can affirm three things. First, to exploit and misuse the body is a mistake. The whole person is involved in sexual activity; sexuality is part of our being. To treat sexual desire simply as a bodily appetite is to misunderstand our true natures. The basic human need is to love and be loved and this need will not be met by the gratifying of temporary sensual pleasure. The body is the outward expression of the self, not something apart. The sexual instinct, like the religious instinct and the instinct of self-preservation, has to be recognized, understood and harnessed in the service of the total personality.

Second, the Christian affirms that he will always be guided by love and respect for the other person. He or she can thus see all activity, whether physical, sexual, emotional or psychological, as reflecting consideration for the other. In this way sex is not divorced from love but always expressed in the context of love. As sexual love-making expresses the total commitment of each partner, it demands the security of a permanent relationship. Only so can love truly grow and understanding of the other come to full maturity.

Third, the Christian will wish to ensure that the young and innocent are given the protection they need. In May 1980 the *British Medical Journal* reported that in 1974 and 1975, more than 7000 school girls below the age of 16 became pregnant each year. The difficulties arising from pregnancy at such an early age were many: the pregnancy itself was more likely to be complicated so that the mortality rates were higher; acute depression could follow and so the risk of attempted suicide was also higher than among adults; research had also shown that many girls of this age were unable to establish a proper relationship with their child and some baby battering ensued. Another serious consequence of such early pregnancies was the disruption of education. The article suggested that doctors should point out the possible medical consequences of sexual activity at such an early age and family-planning programmes should be directed specifically to the needs of the young. With

20

such warnings, not only from the medical profession but also from other responsible bodies, society as a whole should become more aware of how destructive current trends can be. Young people must be given a chance to grow up emotionally before they are expected to cope with full sexual experiences and take mature sexual decisions.

Finally, it must be stated that a minority of Christians have also declared their belief in the rights of homosexuals of either sex to enter into deep and permanent relationships with each other on the basis of mutual trust and love. New light on heredity patterns and biological factors suggests that some people are born homosexual and therefore their condition is not a 'perversion' of which they can be 'cured'.

Discussion and work

1 It has been said that casual sexual encounters 'harden the arteries of tender feeling'. What do you think is meant by this and do you agree with the statement?

2 One of the arguments used to support virginity and celibacy before marriage is that sexual experience before marriage makes a person lose the sense of wonder and mystery which should be there in sexual love. Do you agree?

3 Read the Anglican marriage service and discuss it in class. The service has recently been modernized. What are the changes in wording and why have they been introduced? What do you think is good about the service? Is there any emphasis in it with which you would disagree?

4 Do you think that people who have had sexual intercourse before marriage should have a church service? Why do you think many people prefer a church service even if they are not practising Christians?

5 What different words are used in a Registry Office wedding?

6 What kind of ceremony or service would you like for your own wedding, assuming you want to get married?

7 Do you agree with the statement that the practice of premarital intercourse makes it harder to maintain fidelity in marriage?

8 The sexual impulse can be creative or destructive. The Christian view is that it affects the total personality. Discuss ways in which it is a force that can be used for good or evil.

9 Discuss the statement 'It takes more than love to make a marriage. It is a moral act to make a unique kind of union that is enduring and exclusive.'

10 Do you think there should be sex education in school? What form do you think this should take? Is knowing the biological

facts any kind of sufficient preparation for the sort of experiences which come later?

11 Would you consider 'living together' a good preparation for marriage? Do you think the lack of total commitment in such a relationship would impose extra strain on the two people involved?

12 In the traditional marriage, the wife kept house, minded the children and supported her husband in everything, whereas the man earned the money and made all the major decisions. Society expected them to do everything together whether they really wanted to or not. A more modern approach is that there should be a greater interchange of roles, so that the woman can take up some kind of activity beyond home-making, thus giving her an opportunity for a different kind of personal growth. The man would then share in the household chores and child-minding. They might take separate holidays and even consider an exclusive friendship outside marriage with someone of the opposite sex.

Compare and discuss these ideas of marriage, showing what you consider to be the Christian concept.

4 When things go wrong

(a) Divorce

Marriage is still immensely popular, but the success of a marriage depends upon many factors. There must be deep love which includes sexual attraction. There must be openness and trust, based on the courage to be honest about difficulties and problems. There must also be a certain compatibility about important issues, such as the use of money, leisure activities and friendships outside the marriage relationship. As women can now have the same educational opportunities as men, can achieve economic independence, and can plan when and if they have any children, there is much more chance of an equal relationship than ever before. But everything depends upon what the two people, as individuals, bring to the interdependent relationship, what they are hoping to get from marriage and what they are both able and willing to give and receive.

Often people are damaged by their childhood and they then come to marriage with impossibly high demands which cannot be met. Sometimes there are deep divisions because the two people do not really know each other before they get married; having built up a picture of an ideal person, they are then deeply disappointed because their expectations are not realized. Sometimes one partner is cruel, possessive, dominating and the other's life is made intolerable. In the past the woman suffered greatly because the man had so much power over her. In marriage she became his property and all her wealth or lack of it was his also. We live in a more enlightened age; even so, a power struggle can go on if the husband attempts to keep as much control as he can and the wife fights to achieve a different status. But when a marriage really breaks down there is now the possibility of divorce.

The legal situation

Up to 1844 all marriages in this country were religious ceremonies. After this date it was possible to have a civil marriage, which took place in a Registry Office. In 1857 Parliament abolished the prerogative, i.e. the exclusive right of the Church's court to grant a divorce. They set up a civil court and legalized divorce on the grounds of adultery. In 1937 the Matrimonial Causes Act extended the grounds for divorce to include cruelty, desertion for three years, and incurable insanity, as well as the existing ground of adultery. The Matrimonial Causes Act of 1973 (which came into operation in 1974) consolidated various enactments including the Divorce Reform Act of 1969, and the Nullity of Marriage Act of 1971. At the present time it is illegal to petition for divorce within three years of marriage, except in cases of extreme hardship. The only ground for divorce for either party to a marriage is that the marriage has broken down irretrievably. There are five supporting facts which a petitioner can present: adultery; unreasonable behaviour (e.g. mental or physical cruelty, insanity); desertion for a continuous period of at least two years; living apart for a continuous period of two years is also ground for divorce provided that both parties consent to a decree being granted; if the other party withholds consent, the couple must have lived apart for a continuous period of at least five years for divorce to be allowed.

The law also deals with the financial relief available to the married parties and their children.

The church's position

The Christian church is divided in its opinions about divorce. There are some who are totally opposed to it, believing that marriage is indissoluble. On compassionate grounds they might agree to a judicial separation, but there can be no question of remarriage. There are others who believe that Jesus allowed divorce for adultery and that therefore marriages can on occasion be dissolved, although they ought to be permanent. Finally, some Christians acknowledge that there are various reasons why a marriage may break down irretrievably and that once this has happened divorce can be the only solution. After divorce a Christian may feel free to enter into a second marriage when, learning from past mistakes, there is a better chance of creating a truly loving and permanent relationship.

The Roman Catholic and Anglican communions do not permit remarriage of divorced people in church. (The Roman Catholic church's laws about the nullity of a marriage are not discussed here because they do not affect the legal situation in this country.) The Free Churches have always been less strict in this matter and there are movements in the Anglican church to change existing procedures. Unlike a Roman Catholic priest, an Anglican clergyman may ask his bishop's permission to marry a divorced person in church. Probably there are a few clergymen in every diocese who are prepared to conduct such a ceremony, which is allowed by civil law even though it is against the law of the church.

Many Christians today are very concerned about the increase in the divorce rate, especially amongst young people. Some statistical evidence does suggest that young people who marry at the age of 18, without parental consent, run a greater risk of divorce than those who marry later. A survey ('Marriage in Britain 1945—1980') published in May 1980 gave the divorce levels in Western society as ranging from 22% of all marriages in England and Wales, to 40% in the United States. But if divorce rates were high so were the cases of remarriage. If the present rate continued, one in five men and women born in about 1950 will have married for the second time by the age of 50. However, the survey's author, Dr Jack Dominian, saw two trends which may lead to a fall in divorce rates. One is that fewer marriages are enforced by premarital pregnancy, and the other is that the average age for marriage is beginning to creep up.

In the International Year of the Child (1979), the Family Action Group of the Order of Christian Unity issued a report entitled 'Torn Lives', which was described as a child-centred approach to divorce. The group found that an increasing number of children are suffering, or will suffer, from the break-up of their parents' marriage. At the time of writing, the number involved was running at the rate of 200,000 a year. The report also pointed out that the number of divorce petitions had risen from 54,000 in 1968 to 170,000 in 1978; and 40% of second marriages now fail, so that 'the situation is far more serious and complex than many people realize'. One of the most serious psychological effects of divorce was that children grew up to be completely cynical about the possibility that marriage might be a permanent relationship.

24

The biblical background

As always, we must try and assess the situation as realistically as possible; this approach is very important when we look at the biblical material.

Old Testament teaching reflects a type of society which, in some ways, was quite unlike our own. A divorced woman, especially if she was no longer young, could be destitute. Stable marriage and family life were essential to any sound community existence. So the prophet Malachi could write:

> ... the Lord was witness to the covenant between you and the wife of your youth, to whom you have been faithless, though she is your companion and your wife by covenant. Has not the one God made and sustained for us the spirit of life? And what does he desire? Godly offspring. So take heed to yourselves, and let none be faithless to the wife of his youth. For I hate divorce, says the Lord the God of Israel... (Malachi 2:*14—16*).

The need to protect defenceless women and children was a major factor in the Old Testament prohibition against divorce. But in our society women are not necessarily financially dependent upon their husbands, nor are there always children involved.

In the New Testament

Jesus concentrated on the act of union which constituted a true marriage and warned against the dangers of another person breaking up that relationship (Mark 10:*6—9*). He also spoke of the lust which can often cause a marriage to disintegrate (Matthew 5:*28*). Selfish and irresponsible sexual behaviour with someone outside the marriage can totally destroy trust. It can also indicate a real breakdown of the partnership. According to Matthew (5:*32*) Jesus said that sexual infidelity was the only legitimate cause for divorce. He also apparently disapproved of remarriage and considered it to be adultery, but his comments on adultery could be interpreted as a way of laying stress on men's and women's sexual equality, not as a definition of adultery itself.

Paul condemned divorce (1 Corinthians 7:*10—11*) but he was also writing in a society where women were completely dependent upon their husbands for all means of support; it was imperative that they and the children should be protected. Paul did not believe that a husband should divorce his wife because he was a Christian and she was not, or vice versa. If, however, one partner desired separation because of religious differences, the couple should be allowed to separate (1 Corinthians 7:*12—16*).

Paul believed that the end of the world was coming shortly, when humanity would have to be transformed from an earthly to a heavenly existence; hence his preference for celibacy. What really mattered was union with Christ and illicit sexual unions harmed the disciples' relationship with Christ (1 Corinthians 6:*16—20*).

Jesus and Paul both considered that marriage was terminated by the death of a partner.

Christians today
Valuable though the New Testament teaching is, it is clear that Christians have interpreted the relevant passages according to their own understanding of Jesus and Paul. The new factors in our own circumstances insist that we look at the matter in the light of our own experience and understanding of the nature and demands of love. When some theologians have claimed that Jesus was putting forward a new law on the indissolubility of marriage, other Christians have argued that rigid adherence to the ideal of an unbreakable life-long commitment may cause untold suffering and hardship. People can make mistakes. They can also be destroyed or at least badly damaged by exploitation, misuse and ill-treatment. Jesus was always concerned to protect the weak and dependent members of society, such as widows, mothers and children. However, the only law that Jesus definitely gave was the law of Love. By its very nature, it is impossible to enforce this law, just as it is impossible to enforce a true marriage relationship by rigidly keeping a vow of fidelity. Although love may partly depend on the will, the intimate closeness of marriage can only be maintained if there is spontaneous tenderness, respect and attraction.

Some Christian theologians hold that when two people become 'one flesh', their union is an indissoluble bond but this doctrine is not universally agreed. Others believe that the phrase 'one flesh' is a poetic and symbolic way of describing sexual intercourse. It really signifies the deep moral, emotional and spiritual union which takes place through the physical union. This complete giving and receiving of love creates an inner commitment which is all-important. Where that commitment is destroyed, for whatever reason, then the marriage ceases to be a true marriage and the physical act also ceases to have any significance.

Despite their different interpretations, all Christians feel a deep need to speak out against a superficial view of marriage. Individuals in an affluent society can be much more interested in personal fulfilment than they were when survival was the main priority. And personal fulfilment can become a purely selfish aim leading people to disregard the feelings, rights and needs of others. It is important to strike the balance between believing the marriage contract is unbreakable and thinking that vows are insignificant if a partner wishes to try someone new.

Discussion and work

1 Not everyone knows that when marriage gets tough and difficult there are organizations which can help, especially if consulted in the early stages. The National Marriage Guidance Council and the Catholic Marriage Advisory Service are two of them. Find out all you can about the work of the Marriage Guidance Council. It may be possible for a Counsellor to visit your school and talk about the Council's work.

2 Discuss some of the things which could go so wrong that divorce might be the only solution. Include such topics as attitudes towards money, leisure and children as well as the sexual relationship.

3 The children of a broken marriage are often the worst sufferers. Do you think parental divorce is less harmful to a child than being brought up by two people who really cannot get on with each other?

4 Discuss the statement 'People *fall* in love, but marriages are *made*, because the will as well as the emotions is involved'. If marriages are made, can they also therefore be unmade?

5 Do you think young people prepare themselves sufficiently for marriage?

(b) Unwanted pregnancies and abortion

In theory no girl nowadays need become pregnant if she does not wish to do so. In practice, unwanted pregnancies still happen for various reasons. Contraceptives are not always 100% effective; one or other partner may be ignorant of the basic need for precautions, believing that there has not been 'full' sexual intercourse when, in fact, conception has taken place. Also, of course, girls can be seduced, raped or made pregnant against their will.

Courses of action

There are usually four courses of action open to an unmarried girl or woman if she finds she has conceived. She can marry the father of the child and so give her baby a 'name'. This is not so common as it used to be, although many young people do still get married because the girl has become pregnant either by accident or design. Second, she can have the child adopted. This is a very painful process for the young mother, leaving her with a desperate sense of loss and deprivation, even though she may be convinced that she has done the right thing. Third, she can keep the child and support it herself, perhaps with the help of her parents. One-parent families are increasingly accepted in to-day's society but, even so, the mother needs a great deal of courage and determination. Fourth, she can terminate her pregnancy by abortion.

The legal situation

Until the 1967 Abortion Act it was illegal to carry out abortions in this country and many women died of severe haemorrhage or infection after a back-street operation. Under the terms of the 1967 Act a doctor may legally prescribe an abortion for the patient if he considers that the risk of abortion is less than the risk of the continuing pregnancy to:

(i)   the life of the pregnant woman;
(ii) her physical or mental health; or
(iii) that of her children; or
(iv) there is a substantial risk that if the child were born it would be seriously handicapped by physical or mental abnormalities.

The operation must be performed in a recognized hospital or other approved institution and the law advises that account 'may be taken of the pregnant woman's actual or reasonably foreseeable environment'.

The Act leaves a great deal to the discretion and judgment of the doctor, as it does not define 'risk of injury to the physical or mental state of the woman' or her children.

Opponents of abortion

A forceful body of Christian and humanitarian opinion strongly condemns abortion. It believes that the unborn child, having no means to protect itself, should be protected by law. The Society for the Protection of Unborn Children (SPUC), founded in 1967, is Roman Catholic in origin but receives support from Anglican and other Christian denominations. The aims of the SPUC are 'to uphold that human life ought not to be taken except in cases of urgent necessity . . . as children need special safeguards and care, including appropriate legal protection before as well as after birth'.

The argument against abortion is twofold. First, that at conception a child comes into being. Therefore to remove the foetus, even in its very early stages, is murder. Second, we cannot assess the potential value to the world of any unborn child, even if it appears to be unwanted, or the family history very unhealthy. Hundreds of thousands of ordinary people as well as some famous ones (Beethoven for instance) would never have lived if the Abortion Law had been in operation earlier.

Individual groups have attempted to change the law. The proposed Corrie Bill (1979—80) wanted to include the word 'serious' in the injury clauses. In effect this would have ruled out abortions where psychological and social reasons are the major influence on a doctor's decision. The same Bill hoped to reduce the age beyond which the foetus could not be aborted from 28 to 20 weeks. Doctors admit that some infants born at 23 weeks are very much alive at birth, even though they do not as yet survive.

The Church of England's Board for Social Responsibility has made it clear that it views abortion as 'a great moral evil'. If the mother's life is threatened by her pregnancy, abortion may be the lesser of the two evils, 'but the right of the innocent child admits surely of few exceptions indeed'.

The British Section of the World Federation of Doctors who Respect Human Life, also came out in support of Mr Corrie's proposals as 'a step in the right direction to the full restoration of the right to life of unborn humans'.

Pro-abortionists
The Abortion Law Reform Association (ALRA) was founded in 1936 with the aim of changing the law to permit abortion. Many who favour abortion are associated with women's liberation movements and they are supported by some sections of the medical profession. There are different categories of support ranging from those who think abortion 'on demand' is right, to those who feel that abortion is a reality and should, therefore, be legalized. Women's movements declare emphatically that a woman has the right to decide whether she will bear a child or not; that she has a right to decide what happens to her own body. For a woman to want an abortion is in itself sufficient evidence that she would be an unsatisfactory mother and that the child would be unwanted. For them, the removal of the foetus at up to 28 weeks is not 'murder' by any stretch of the imagination. Others, on humanitarian grounds, consider that even if abortion is itself an evil, it may well be a lesser evil than the misery to the mother or to the child that would result from the continuance of the pregnancy. They believe that legalizing abortion by no means debases the value of human life, but is in fact an attempt to improve the quality of life which either the mother or the child might have.

Whilst not necessarily supporting abortion, many Christian laity would dispute the absolute belief that human life begins without question at the moment of conception and ought to possess the full rights of a person from that time.

The main medical associations declared themselves against the Corrie Bill because it might compel them to turn away what they considered to be deserving cases.

The present dilemma

Concern over the high number of abortions is widespread in Christian circles. Sweden is traditionally liberal in its sexual attitude, but the Swedish church and other social agencies are currently examining the causes leading to 30,000 abortions per year. Among other factors, they believe that women are increasingly reluctant to use contraceptive pills for fear of side-effects, thus abortion is being seen as a means of birth control. Abortion as a method of birth control is also widely used in Japan. Many women, however, feel the need to pray for the souls of their 'washed away babies', which are commemorated in little named statues in shrines. In one or two cities gynaecologists, doctors and nurses gather together once a year for a memorial service to these unborn children.

To use abortion as a means of controlling the population is surely abhorrent to all Christians. The real heart of the matter is that all people should be taught and encouraged to take full responsibility as far as they can for their own bodies. If two people decide they will have sexual intercourse, then they must be aware of the possible outcome and take preventive steps if they do not wish to have a child. The crisis of pregnancy is a very profound one and whatever decision the girl or couple take, the pregnancy can never be unmade. Although the medical profession is divided about the psychological and emotional effects of abortion, the operation may be followed by severe depression. The Christian view is that sexual activity is not simply a physical hunger and thirst that can be satisfied; it is an expression of the total personality and involves another person who must be treated with respect, love and consideration. It can also involve a third person, the unborn child, to whom both the man and the woman are directly responsible.

Discussion and work

1 A number of psychiatrists believe that girls become pregnant because they want to or need to, even if they have not faced up to this need themselves. What do you think the psychiatrists mean? Do you agree with them?

2 Do you think the case for abortion after a genuine rape is different from the one in which genuine lack of knowledge produced the pregnancy?

3 Discuss the statement 'Abortion is the greatest destroyer of man in the world'. These are the words of Mother Teresa at her acceptance of the Nobel Peace Prize 1979.

4 Look at the arguments both for and against abortion and see if you can find out further information from the various organi-

zations supporting the rights of the unborn child and the rights of women. Arrange a debate on the subject.

5 Discuss the proposition 'The best course might well be not fresh legislation but the working out by the medical associations of a clearer code of practice. . . . Within the terms of the 1967 Act, surely the doctors are their own best policemen.' (*Church Times*, February 1980.) Is it right for us to depend on the medical profession to make society's moral value judgments?

6 Should each request for abortion be judged on its own merits, taking into consideration all the individual circumstances, or should we aim at a law which can be applied to every case?

5 Education

Some basic facts
'British education aims to develop individual abilities to the full and to shape those abilities for the benefit of society as a whole' (*Education in Britain*, a pamphlet prepared by the Central Office of Information, 1979). Compulsory schooling takes place between the ages of 5 and 16, although some provision is made for children under 5 and many pupils remain at school beyond the minimum age. Post-school education is sited mainly at universities, polytechnics and colleges of further and higher education. More than a third of young people received some form of post-school education in 1979 compared with a fifth in 1965.

Over 11 million children attend Britain's 38,000 schools. Most receive free education financed from public funds, but about 4% attend schools wholly independent of public financial support. Schools supported from public funds are of two main kinds in England and Wales: county schools and voluntary schools. County schools are provided and maintained by local education authorities wholly out of public funds. Voluntary schools have mostly been established by religious denominations and receive varying amounts of public finance according to type. Nearly a third of the 30,470 schools maintained by local education authorities in England and Wales are voluntary schools. In 1978 some £8658 million was spent on education which represented about 6% of the gross national product. Special education is provided for children who require it because of physical or mental disability.

Under the 1944 Education Act all children in county or voluntary schools receive religious instruction and take part in a daily corporate act of worship unless their parents choose otherwise.

This century has seen great strides forward in educational facilities. There has been much debate about the purpose of education and the sharing of privileges which were once enjoyed by a small minority, especially in the case of higher education. Now there is far greater equality of opportunity for boy and girl, rich and poor. A period of rapid change and experiment in the school curriculum and teaching methods is currently giving way to one of reappraisal. Governments, in theory at any rate, are pledged to improving the quality of education at all levels, although politics influence major decisions. Both parents and pupils, however, must exert their right to express opinions which may influence policies. Biblical insights can be of some help in formulating priorities.

Wisdom literature
The Old Testament library contains a whole category of writing known as the Wisdom literature (see p. 144). As you might expect, these books deal with the great themes of life's experiences and offer advice for successful living. The Israelite sage wrote to warn his pupils (who were boys) against those who might seduce them into wrong ways, whether the temptation was to sexual indulgence or dishonest practices. As the whole of his life was orientated to belief in God (Yahweh) and God's revealed will for his people, the Jew's educational system would inevitably be built upon religious and moral principles. The book of Proverbs clearly set out the teaching aims of the wise sayings; they were:

That men may know wisdom and instruction,
   understand words of insight,
receive instruction in wise dealing,
   righteousness, justice and equity;
that prudence may be given to the simple,
   knowledge and discretion to the youth   (Proverbs 1:*2—4*)

Later in the book Wisdom was shown as one of God's greatest gifts; men were to seek it above all else:

My son, if you receive my words,
   and treasure up my commandments with you,
making your ear attentive to wisdom
   and inclining your heart to understanding;
yes, if you cry out for insight
   and raise your voice for understanding,
if you seek it like silver
   and search for it as for hidden treasure;
then you will understand the fear of the Lord
   and find the knowledge of God   (Proverbs 2:*1—5*)

The fear of the Lord is the beginning of knowledge;
   fools despise wisdom and instruction   (Proverbs 1:*7*).

Education was a lifelong process whose ultimate aim was a more profound knowledge of the mysteries of God:

My son, from your earliest youth choose instruction,
and till your hair is white you will keep finding wisdom
(Ecclesiasticus 6:*18 Jerusalem Bible*).

A scholar was a man who grew upright in purpose and learning, pondering on the Lord's hidden mysteries, so that others praised his understanding and he was not forgotten by succeeding generations (Ecclesiasticus 39:*1—15*).

Jesus and Paul as teachers

The New Testament presents Jesus as one of the greatest teachers of all time. Following the custom among famous Jewish rabbis, he taught largely by parable, a method exactly suited to his very mixed audiences. But it is clear from the response he evoked that he always got through to people and made them think. They reacted to him either in outraged resistance and rejection, or in ardent acceptance. Very few remained unaffected by his presence or his words.

We can see from his letters that Paul also was a great teacher to his various congregations. He instructed them in matters of faith and moral conduct, seeking to emphasize spiritual values (Philippians 4:*8*). But he never separated the way one lives from the faith one has because he believed that a morally good, upright life sprang from a heart and mind that were transformed by a right relationship with God, made possible through faith in Jesus Christ (Galatians 5:*25*).

Education—a process of understanding

From this brief survey we can recognize that the Jew and Christian did not see true education as a matter of simply learning things by heart in a mechanical fashion and reproducing them in order to pass examinations. It was a process of understanding what life was all about in order to evaluate it and live it to the full and draw nearer to God, the source of all knowledge. Some psychologists might say that it is motivation—why we learn and what we want to learn—which is all-important in gaining and acquiring knowledge and making it our own. This is precisely what Jesus demonstrated.

Differing 20th- century views

The Christian church in the 20th century is, of course, not unanimous in its ideas about education. Present thinkers are aware that many mistakes have been made in the past; on occasion, schools have perhaps lost their inspiration and concentrated only on obedience. So today some very radical thinkers believe that our educational systems must be drastically changed if we are to create a new society and a new world. Training people simply to carry on as before will accomplish nothing. Some suggest that the only way to educate is to start where children are and answer their questions, not supplying them with information they are not particularly interested in knowing. Other thinkers cling tenaciously to the past and believe there should be very little change in the curriculum. They blame some of the difficulties encountered in schools at present on the fact that the timetable structure has changed, discipline is not so strict and parents have lost control. The subject of corporal punishment provides an example of how Christians can disagree. Some believe totally in its abolition, while others take literally the saying 'spare the rod and spoil the child'.

Basic Christian principles

There are, however, several aims and principles in education to which all enlightened people should be able to subscribe, especially as Christians. First, education should not be a way of moulding young people into the most convenient pattern for governmental control. Past experience has proved that it is perfectly possible to train people to accept certain attitudes even though they may be morally wrong. We have only to look at the development of such concepts as racial superiority and militarism to see how blind people can become because of upbringing and social conditioning. Education must be based on the worth of the individual child and in helping that child to the fullest development of its personality, through rational and compassionate means. It should also be concerned to equip young people with the mental, emotional or physical tools to make the most out of life. The young should be given the encouragement, training and example to develop skills and aptitudes which will enrich not only the person involved but the community, but they should not be manipulated by society for its own ends.

Second, the teacher and pupil should regard one another with mutual respect and affection. The Christian will try to be true to the insights of Jesus. It is all too easy for pupils to typecast teachers in artificial moulds of authority and not see them as people in their own right. Similarly, teachers are mistaken in their attitudes if they group children together and think only of classes or age groups or categories of behaviour. The teacher's authority is based on the fact that training and experience have given him/her certain information, knowledge, skills which will benefit

34

the child, and the most important teaching skill of all is the ability to inspire that student to explore fresh avenues and ways of learning. The teacher should never use authority to dampen or diminish initiative and enterprise, but always to encourage the gradual development of the pupils in his/her charge.

Third, education in school is only a stepping stone to the greater experience of adult life. On leaving school the pupil should have a developing awareness of man's nature and the universe in which he lives and a growing belief that he has something worthwhile to contribute to society as a whole. Christians in particular can witness to the significance and importance of man's religious instinct, one which at present goes sadly unrecognized in a secular world. For the Christian, the religious dimension to life is the essential; without it he would lose not only his perspective but even his courage and determination to bring about beneficial change.

Discussion and work

1 Discuss the propositions (a) that simply being able to pass examinations is what school is all about, and (b) that if school education does not help one to get a good job, it has been a failure.

2 What do you think should be the purpose of your education?

3 In what ways, if any, does school prepare you for adult life?

4 In what ways does the education you receive at school differ from the education you gain through your family and through contact with your own friends and contemporaries?

5 Why do you think some teenagers are unhappy at school? How far does the blame lie with the educational system if boys and girls play truant? What other factors may be involved? Why do you think some people want to leave school before the compulsory age of 16?

6 What part should Religious or Moral Education play in school?

7 What is meant by saying that the most important task of the R.E. teacher is to examine what is involved in being human in the truest and deepest sense? Would you agree that this is the R.E. teacher's responsibility?

8 Do you ever feel that your education is trying to mould you into a particular type of person and that you do not naturally fit that mould?

9 What do you most enjoy about school?

10 Do you think teachers have too much or too little authority? Does their authority enable you to get the most out of your school experience?

11 Are you giving the best you can to the school community?

12 Discuss fairly and realistically what changes you would introduce into school if you had the power to do so.

6 Work and leisure

We live in a restless and changing society. The pace of change is faster than at any other time in human history and it may go on accelerating up to the end of the century, if not beyond. When our own life span is limited, it is difficult for us to assess accurately the extent of change, but those of you who are reading this book will not remember when there was no television and your children will not remember the coming of the micro-chip! Just as the change from an agricultural to an industrial economy in the 19th century caused great social upheaval, so the change from an industrial to a technological age is proving very challenging and even, at first, disruptive. Change is always unsettling and sometimes frightening, but it can also be stimulating and exciting. Nowhere is this more true than in the basic area of work and leisure.

Definition of the terms
For the purpose of our discussion we will define work as the activity which earns a person a living. It is either paid employment or self-employment which enables a man or woman to live. One definition of leisure is free time, or time at one's own disposal. It is the opposite of work in the sense that at work one is under an obligation to fulfil some particular task for which one is employed and paid a wage. Although not obliged by others to do so, self-employed men and women usually impose upon themselves patterns of employment. The man who is a craftsman in pottery or wood, or a writer, will of necessity work out his own schedule, applying the same kind of discipline to his use of time as any other person employed by someone else. Leisure activities can be as physically and mentally strenuous as a paid job of work. They can be relaxing and creative pastimes. On the other hand they may be simple stop-gaps to pass the long hours when boredom threatens.

Previous attitudes
The division of our time into work and leisure is a comparatively new development. In primitive agricultural societies such as those we read about in the Old Testament or those still operating in parts of India and Latin America, work is a grim matter of survival. The experience of people living in harsh and barren landscapes, where it is only possible to eke out a bare subsistence, is reflected in the realistic words of the Genesis parable (3:*17–19*)

where the ground is cursed because of man's disobedience: 'in toil you shall eat all the days of your life. . . . In the sweat of your face you shall eat bread till you return to the ground . . .'.

The industrial revolution and the growth of the trade union movement

Our recent forebears knew only too well the struggle for survival. During the early stages of the industrial revolution the working classes suffered great poverty, hardship and appalling labour conditions. It was not until laws were passed in parliament, sometimes in the teeth of strong opposition, that children were prevented from working in factories and coal mines (the Factory Acts), while the Ten Hours Act in 1847 recognized that human beings had a right to leisure. Trade Unions came into being to protect the rights of workers whose only weapons were their solidarity of feeling and action. Their aims have always been to secure better wages and improved working conditions for their members. At first trade unions were not recognized, but once they were made legal, membership steadily increased. Today the great majority of unions are affiliated to the Trade Union Congress.

Since World War II, the achievements of the Welfare State have brought tremendous improvements. The health and security of employees are safeguarded by law and the general public is protected against industrial hazards (The Health and Safety at Work Act, 1975). Employees are entitled to sickness benefit if unable to work and are insured against accident. People who are laid off work through no fault of their own are rightly given redundancy payments. Workers are protected against unfair dismissal. If an employee considers he has been unjustly treated, he can appeal to an industrial tribunal (The Employment Protection Act, 1975). Everyone willing to work but unable to find employment is entitled to some kind of allowance or supplementary benefit. And at the age of 60 for women and 65 for men, all contributors are eligible for retirement pensions.

The right to work

The right to work is fundamental. This is enshrined in Article 23 of the United Nations Universal Declaration of Human Rights, 1948: 'Everyone has the right to work, to free choice of employment, to just and favourable conditions of work and to protection against unemployment.' In this country the 1968 Race Relations Act, the 1970 Equal Pay Act and 1975 Sex Discrimination Act have all helped to create a better society where racial and sexual discrimination in matters of employment are considered illegal.

The rate of wages a man or woman is paid is usually settled as the result of an agreement between the trade unions and the employers. Working conditions are also regulated by the laws of the land. When things go wrong between trade unions and employers, there are independent advisory bodies whose aim is to help create better industrial relationships.

Despite all these provisions and the concern of both official and voluntary organizations, the fact remains that much work in an industrial society is dull and repetitive. The job of tending one piece of machinery day in day out, perhaps without seeing or knowing what may be the end product of the assembly line, can be so boring as to be soul-destroying. Karl Marx used the word 'alienation' to describe the effects of labour in factories and Pope Pius XI recognized that many kinds of work could lead to the perversion of man; 'For from the factory dead matter goes out improved, whereas men there are corrupted and degraded.' The worker who is not able to participate fully in what he is producing, who uses no real skill or creativity, who is not able to feel any personal satisfaction in it or sense of community effort, is being destroyed and psychologically impoverished by his work.

In our society a repetitive, boring job is often compensated, at least in theory, by the pay packet at the end of the week. And many thousands accept the idea that boring work can be endured if one's leisure activity is pleasurable and creative.

We are, however, living in a period of increasing unemployment and nowhere is this more keenly felt than by those who leave school or places of further education and cannot find a job. Forecasters, such as the University of Cambridge Department of Applied Economics, predict a figure of 5 million unemployed by 1990. This gloomy picture is disputed by other experts but, nevertheless, unemployment is a very serious problem.

Background to current unemployment difficulties
One important reason for our present dilemma is that man's technological skill has enabled him to make machines which can do the work previously done by men and women. Thus, one technician can now supervise an entire floor in which machines manufacture the whole product from start to finish. Nowhere is this more apparent than in the invention of the micro-chip. This tiny microprocessor, a minute computer sometimes no bigger than a thumbnail, is capable of receiving, storing, processing and reissuing information; its methods are very similar to those of the human brain. As these chips become cheaper and more reliable, they can be used extensively in place of human labour, not only in the workshop but also in the office. It is not possible yet to assess the effects of the Micro-Revolution, but obviously there will be a lower

demand for certain types of labour. A group of experts interviewed for 'TV Eye' in September 1978, estimated that between 3 and 4 million people were likely to become jobless as a direct result of micro-technology. Not everyone agrees on such high figures; David Firnberg, Director of the National Computing Centre, is optimistic. He believes that 'the extraordinary new power which microelectronics make available so cheaply will surely create a whole mass of new opportunities for products and services'.

A second factor is of the utmost significance to any industrialized society; this is the diminishing world resources of raw materials and solid or liquid fuel. Some estimate that at the present rate of consumption the supply of present known resources of oil will scarcely outlast the year 2030. For oil, like coal and other solid fuels, is a non-renewable substance. Man discovers it and extracts it but he does not make it or grow it, although it is possible for him to produce some synthetic oil and synthetic fibres which can take the place of certain fast-dwindling raw materials. The initial wealth of industrialized nations has largely depended on a ready supply of both cheap labour and cheap energy, whether in the form of coal, coke, gas, electricity or oil. Now both manpower and energy are very expensive so that factories and manufacturing industries prove too costly to run and their products are priced out of the mass market.

Some biblical insights
The biblical philosophy has been that work is necessary for man's physical, emotional and spiritual well-being. The Genesis parable shows man as a gardener in Eden (2:15) and it is only when he is disobedient that work becomes a hardship not a blessing (3:17—19). The writer of Proverbs 6:6—8 treats laziness with some humour, although there is the realistic warning, repeated later in chapter 24:30—34, that work is a necessity for survival. A different view is taken by the rather pessimistic but down-to-earth preacher of Ecclesiastes:

I hated all my toil in which I had toiled under the sun, seeing that I must leave it to the man who will come after me; and who knows whether he will be a wise man or a fool? Yet he will be master of all for which I have toiled and used my wisdom under the sun. . . . What has a man from all the toil and strain with which he toils beneath the sun? For all his days are full of pain, and his work is a vexation; even in the night his mind does not rest.

The writer is protesting against the seeming injustice of life; death forces man to leave the fruits of honest hard work to someone who may waste them. But he ends with the reflection that the present here and now can give happiness and satisfaction: 'There is nothing better for a man than that he should eat and drink, and find enjoyment in his toil . . .' (2:*18—23*). The sage of Ecclesiasticus advised his pupil to be gentle in carrying out business and to behave with modesty and restraint (3:*17—31*).

Jesus told two parables which are relevant to our discussion. The first is about labourers in a vineyard (Matthew 20:*1—16*). Some of the men worked 12 hours in the blazing sun, others worked for far less time but they were not to blame for their idleness. They hung about waiting for work all day and were only employed in the late afternoon out of kindness. The parable is really about God's attitude to men, showing that he loves them all and deals with them according to his love, not according to their merits. Nevertheless, it does to some extent reflect an attitude towards work and unemployment which is still with us today; when all the men receive the same wage in the evening there is much resentment in the minds of those who had worked far longer than the others.

The second parable speaks of two sons (Matthew 21:*28—31*). The first son refused to work in the vineyard when his father asked him to do so, but later he changed his mind and went. On the other hand the second son said 'I go, sir' but did not go. 'Which of the two did the will of the father?' asked Jesus. In its context this parable underlines Jesus' criticism of those who paid lip service rather than true service to God, but the principle applies to life and work in general.

Mark implies that Jesus himself was a carpenter and worked for his family (6:*3,4*) until he gave up his job to follow his special calling of bringing in the Kingdom of God. His disciples also left their ordinary occupations to be with him during the short period of his ministry, usually reckoned to be about three years (Mark 1:*16—20*; 2:*14*). Luke tells us that Jesus and his friends were supported and helped by a group of women who were his disciples (Luke 8:*2,3*).

Although Paul travelled around the Roman world, he always insisted on working for his living and not relying on the financial gifts of his pupils, a practice which was customary in New Testament times:

> You yourselves know that these (i.e. my) hands ministered to my necessities, and to those who were with me. In all things I have shown you that by so toiling one must help the weak, remembering the words of the Lord Jesus how he said 'It is more blessed to give than receive' (Acts 20:*34,35*).

Paul was a tent-maker by trade, although we do not know quite what this entailed (Acts 18:*3*). He had to write in the strongest terms to his friends in Thessalonica (3:6–13) because some members of the congregation there, expecting the end of the world at any time, had given up work altogether. 'If anyone will not work, let him not eat . . . (they must) do their work in quietness and to earn their own living. Brethren, do not be weary in well-doing.' In biblical times there were, of course, no organizations to protect the workers from exploitation. Rulers, princes and affluent householders had absolute authority over their subject peoples and subject families and slaves. Nevertheless, the teaching of Jesus always stressed the significance and importance of every individual. This fact is even more striking when we think about its cultural setting. In later ages the inspiration which eventually led to the abolition of slavery was found in the Christian community itself. The emergence of workers' groups to safeguard their own particular interests and movements for the emancipation of women also arose from the insights of Christian thinking.

All in all the Bible suggests that work is a necessity, though sometimes a very trying burden. We should undertake it in the right spirit, co-operating with others and bearing in mind the general good. Sometimes it may be right for the majority to give financial support to the few so that, like Jesus, they can carry out some specialized task. But independence is always a good thing and those who are strong and capable should use their mind and energy to the full.

Christian attitudes to work
We find here, as in all the topics we have touched, that Christians disagree about attitudes to work and remedies for our ills. Many feel deeply concerned that the challenge of the technological revolution must be faced squarely. They recognize that the Christian church of the 19th century failed to speak out against the gross inequalities which the industrial revolution created between the few very rich and the many poor. They are determined to identify the new strong and weak groups which are being formed and to fight, together with all people of good will, for a just society.

Christian thinkers are aware that we need an adequate philosophy of work and leisure. Pope John XXIII saw the potential of work when he said 'a man should develop and perfect himself through his daily work'. But despite this ideal, man has often been degraded by work because many employers, whether in factory, farm or coalmine, have been primarily concerned to make money for themselves. The consumers' needs have been secondary to the producers' profits, while the workers' rights have been merely a matter of their wages. Some Christians, therefore, are convinced

41

that we need a different ethic, making the production of *necessary* goods and services our priority. In a world of shrinking resources, we do not want to continue primarily as a *consumer* society. Work should first enable us to live creatively, in the sense that we use and perfect our gifts and skills. Second, it should enable us to live with and for others in the sense that we join together in a corporate effort which benefits the whole.

Many Christians feel passionately that as we live in a finite world with fast dwindling resources, the industrialized nations' greedy consumption of essential raw materials only increases rather than diminishes the overall poverty of the great majority of the earth's population. They insist that we must face the question of whether or not it is right that we should go on attempting to expand the national economy. The profit motive is a false god and has no goal beyond itself. Others might say that the creation of wealth is a right and proper activity which makes possible the flowering of culture.

We certainly need to ask ourselves who is the master today, the man or the machine. We also need to ask what sort of a world we are creating. Is it a world with a truly human face in which the potential of human beings can be fully realized? We must believe that the individual can achieve something positive by the integrity of his own life and by becoming really well informed about the various alternatives open to him. The individual can refuse to be treated as a cog in the machine, although it may cost him a great deal to do so. He can resolve to be honest and hardworking, but as a Christian he will not allow himself to be exploited nor will he exploit others. He will refuse to do a job that is morally offensive to him because its basis is the unjust treatment of others. And he will consider very carefully the relationship between work and leisure, because leisure also has a part to play in the fulfilment of human personality. Like work, leisure demands that we exercise freedom of choice and it can include the discipline and companionship which are also found in work.

Discussion and work

1 Discuss the question of what work does to the worker.
2 'Without work all life goes rotten, but when work is soulless, life stifles and dies' (Albert Camus). Discuss what the writer meant by 'soulless' and how he visualized life being stifled and dying.
3 If you had the choice between a well-paid but rather boring, safe job, and a poorly paid but interesting job, which would you choose? Discuss the arguments which led to your decision.
4 How far do you think money compensates for either a boring or a dangerous job? Do you think people go into dangerous jobs

such as exploring for North Sea oil for the money or for the excitement?

5 Do you think men and women have different attitudes towards work?

6 Do you think the work a woman does in looking after her home and family is undervalued and underpaid?

7 Mass production has enabled ordinary people to buy goods, such as motor cars, which once were reserved for the very rich. But working on a car assembly line has also denied the employee the job satisfaction which is his natural right. Which do you think is more important? Must we choose one or the other? Is there no other way out of the dilemma?

8 It is known that small businesses, of which there are several hundred thousand in Britain, provide much deeper satisfaction to the work-force because workers feel more involved. In consequence, we are now seeing the start of a general movement towards greater industrial democracy. All sorts of experiments are aimed at increased worker participation, workers' co-operatives and further opportunities for workers to make decisions. Do you know any successful small businesses or any such experiments? If you owned your own business, how would you run it?

9 Traditionally our society has distinguished between 'white collar' and 'blue collar' workers. The white collar worker is employed in clerical or office jobs, whereas the blue collar worker is a manual employee. Do you accept such distinctions? Do you think one kind of work is superior to another?

Christian attitudes to leisure
The privileged few have always had the leisure to pursue creative activities of their own choosing. This was made possible in the Greek city-state culture because slaves performed all the menial tasks; in previous centuries the rich of this country had many dependents and servants. But there was always a danger that such wealth and ease would breed a terrible selfish indifference to others outside the charmed circle.

It is possible that our changing economic conditions may lead to very many people having greater periods of leisure but much less money to spend. We could well be entering a period when thousands of people will have enforced unemployment, but even if present forecasts do not come true, the attitude we have towards our time is all-important. Man possesses essential dignity. He has the ability to endow what he does with significance, therefore both work and leisure can be a means of fulfilment. From a Christian viewpoint some basic principles about the use of time may be worth considering.

First, personal fulfilment and enrichment is not attained by selfishness, but rather in service to others. As we have now a welfare state, we tend to think that all problems encountered by the sick, the aged, the lonely and the deprived can be taken care of by the professionals—the social worker or the medical team. But this highly impractical idea is one which deprives people of the pleasure of giving freely. The norm should be good neighbourliness. Opportunities for voluntary service are boundless (see p. 197), and if we have time to spare we should spend some of it in doing an action or a job for someone else which will make life a lot easier for them and create a happier neighbourhood.

Second, we should consider the sense of satisfaction which we get when we do something creative or accomplish something which has been difficult to achieve. People become engrossed in all kinds of hobbies, using their manual or mental skills in making a beautiful garden, or a beautiful piece of needlework and embroidery, or in joinery, or mending the motor-bike, or cleaning the car, or cooking a superb meal, or learning another language, craft or skill. The list is endless. The introduction of television into our homes has tended to make us passive audiences, doing little about providing our own amusements, even though it keeps us well informed about the world in which we live. So we need to examine carefully what gives us genuine pleasure. It may be going out for a drink or a meal with friends or having them to our homes so that we can talk together; it may be going to the cinema, theatre, concert or disco, or walking in the hills or pursuing some kind of sport. All these things are active, because we have taken the initiative to do them, whereas simply sitting and looking at the box can be merely letting things happen to us.

We might discover a fourth dimension to life by learning to meditate, which is a right and positive use of physical passivity. Meditation is many-sided, but its simplest experience is taking time to look at, learn and understand the marvellous complexity, beauty and rigour of our earth.

We shall have combined our work and leisure to form something worthwhile if at the end of the day we can think back and see that we have been of service to someone else, have been creative in that we have contributed something positive to life, have been active in friendship and enjoyment and have stopped to stare, to listen and wonder.

Discussion and work

1 Various ways of coping with the increasing problem of unemployment have been suggested:
  (a) the introduction of a shorter working week;

(b) longer holidays (at present the average is 15 working days plus the seven days statutory public holidays such as Christmas and New Year);

(c) more leave for further training;

(d) curtailing each person's period of active work. This would mean that people entered employment at a later age than 16 or 18 and left it before 60 or 65. (The Government Job Release Scheme permits some people to retire as much as three years early if this will enable someone else who has no job to take their place.)

What kind of programme would you work out for yourself if you only had a part-time job on leaving school? Do you think you would find any difficulties in working for three days a week with four days in which to please yourself? How would you spend your spare time?

What kind of hobbies are you interested in? What are the chief things in life which give you pleasure?

2 Many experts think that people who are willing to work will not be able to do so in the future because there will only be a limited number of jobs available. With this in mind some people suggest that everyone should be given a guaranteed income or social wage or basic economic security. They hope that this would change social attitudes, so that there would be no disgrace or demoralization in being out of work. Could you imagine such a situation in your lifetime? How do you think people would cope with it? Do you think there should be more education for leisure as well as education to help a person find work? Do you think such a guaranteed income would encourage people to be lazy? If you did not have to work for a living do you think you would be more enterprising, creative and happy or less so?

3 Discuss the extremes of being a work-addict or work-shy. Does an energetic and proper use of leisure help in any way to remedy these two attitudes?

4 Think of the elements you personally would need for a fulfilled life; how high on the list is job satisfaction? Why? What other sources of fulfilment do you consider available to you?

5 'Consider the lilies of the field, how they grow; they neither toil nor spin; yet I tell you, even Solomon in all his glory was not arrayed like one of these' (Matthew 6:29). Jesus is talking about having a perspective which frees a person from anxiety. Natural things have a grace and beauty because they are content simply to be. How might this perspective influence our attitudes towards work and leisure?

6 'My leisure is the moment when I really start living, as opposed

to the time when I have to work either at school or in a job.'
Discuss this point of view.

7 The use and misuse of money

The last section suggested that many people put up with boring
and dead-end jobs for the sake of good pay, and that many industrialists are more interested in profits than consumers' needs or
workers' rights. It is fair to say that in our particular culture the
possession of money and all the material goods, comfort and
security which it brings has been equated with happiness, hence
the extraordinary phenomenon that millions of people gamble on
the football pools each week in the hope of winning a fortune. As
money is such an important and ever-present topic, it is worth discussing what we may mean by a responsible attitude to it.

Origins of money
Ancient man measured his wealth by the head of cattle he possessed or the amount of jewellery which his wives wore. In Old
Testament times, rings or ingots, gold, silver and other precious
metals were weighed in payment for goods and services. This was a
commonsense way of easing market facilities under the barter
system. The introduction of pieces of metal stamped with an official image or superscription became possible under a more cen-
tralized government and further encouraged trading. During the
New Testament period coinage was widely used as a method of
paying taxation throughout the Roman Empire. Today's money,
whether metal or paper, is only valuable for what it represents;
unlike ancient gold and silver coins it would have comparatively
little value if melted down or pulped.

Jesus' teaching about money
In the Sermon on the Mount Jesus contrasted earthly with heavenly treasure. The former was worthless because it was imperma-
nent and because man became consumed by anxiety to retain it.
The latter was a permanent possession because it resulted from
the quality of life (Matthew 6:*19—21*). Jesus was definite that a
man could not serve two masters, God and mammon (a Semitic
word for money or riches) 'for either he will hate the one and love
the other, or he will be devoted to the one and despise the other'
(Matthew 6:*24*). Luke records two of Jesus' parables which illustrate his teaching. The first (Luke 12:*13—21*) is the story of a rich
man who decided to retire on the proceeds of his fortune and spend
the rest of his life on pleasure. Ironically, he died immediately. His

money was of no use to him. In the second story (Luke 16:*19–31*) Jesus condemned the exclusive selfishness of worldly riches. All his life the rich man cared nothing for the poor beggar lying at his gate. He only saw things in a different light when their positions were reversed after death.

The gospels recount two meetings between Jesus and rich men. Mark (10:*17–31*) tells how Jesus faced the young ruler with the supreme challenge of selling all he possessed and becoming Jesus' disciple. The young man could not rise to this demand and Jesus, saddened by rejection, warned his friends of the danger of riches. By giving a false sense of security, wealth could deaden one's sensitivity to others and distort right perspectives of what was important in life. On the second occasion (Luke 19:*1–10*) Jesus met a rich tax collector at Jericho. Moved by seeing Jesus and entertaining him in his house, Zacchaeus promised to give away half his fortune and to make full restitution for any former dishonest practices. By contrast with the first young man, Zacchaeus was not asked to give up all his wealth, but he himself recognized that he had too much and that he must use the remainder in a responsible way.

When Jesus visited Jerusalem (Mark 11:*15–19*) he was enraged by the dishonest practices of the traders and money changers in the Temple area. He thrust them out of the Court of the Gentiles; their exploitation of worshippers was completely contrary to God's will.

On an earlier occasion Jesus sent out his disciples on a training mission to see how they would get on without his personal support (Mark 6:*7–13*). He gave them some very precise instructions. They were to take no money with them but were to rely on each other and the welcome that they received from the people to whom they went and to whom they preached. The fact that it is possible to be independent of money, putting one's security in some kind of inner power for one's survival, has been demonstrated again in our own times by the story of Satish Kumar and his friend Prabhakar. They decided to walk from India on a peace mission to Moscow, Paris, London and Washington. Vinoba Bhave, a famous disciple of Gandhi, advised them to take no money with them on their journey, because money would prevent them from making contact with people. Their pilgrimage took them two and a half years but they were faithful to their commitment.

Jesus was not unrealistic, however, about the proper use of money. One day Jesus' enemies attempted to trap him into some kind of damaging admission by asking him whether it was right for a Jew to pay tribute money to Caesar. The Roman tax was hated by all good Jews as it emphasized their status as a conquered people. The silver denarii bore the name and likeness (or image) of the Emperor. On being given a coin Jesus said, 'Render to Caesar the things that are Caesar's, and to God the things that are God's' (Mark 12:13—17). Man has a two-fold duty. If governments are to do their lawful and necessary work they need the financial and social support of their citizens; but, of course, being part of a city, state or nation is not the only obligation a man has to fulfil. Genesis (1:26,27) states that man is made in the image of God. It is possible, therefore, that Jesus was suggesting that man's first offering must be of himself to God.

Further New Testament teaching

Although we can only guess at his motives, the fact that Judas sold his master for silver (Matthew 26:15) demonstrates the power of money. Its weakness and inadequacy was shown dramatically on a much later occasion when the magician Simon attempted to buy from Peter and John the ability to bestow the gift of the Holy Spirit. Peter condemned Simon harshly for his misconceptions: 'Your silver perish with you, because you thought you could obtain the gift of God with money! You have neither part nor lot in this matter, for your heart is not right before God' (Acts 8:14—24).

The early Christians, following the advice and example of their master, were willing to share all their wealth and material possessions with each other (Acts 4:32). The story of the Jerusalem community shows us in stark contrast the generosity of Barnabas as opposed to the deceit of Ananias and his wife Sapphira, who wanted the credit for giving all their money into the common fund, but who secretly kept some back for themselves (Acts 4:36—5:4). Jesus himself was sharply critical of those who gave to charity for the sake of their own reputations (Matthew 6:2—4).

Writing to his friend Timothy, Paul perhaps summed up those early disciples' views by stating that 'the love of money is the root of all evils; it is through this craving that some have wandered away from the faith and pierced their hearts with many pangs' (1 Timothy 6:10).

Christian attitudes today

It is very difficult to try to formulate rules about how we should spend our money; what some consider extravagances are necessities to others. Individuals must be free to decide their priorities for themselves. Some Christians take vows of poverty, chastity and obedience and either enter monastic orders or work in the world spending the minimum upon themselves. Others endeavour to use whatever wealth they gain or inherit for the benefit of those less fortunate and are generous in founding colleges, medical centres, libraries and other institutions. Those of us who do not experience these extremes of poverty or riches may adopt a few simple principles as a guide to individual or family decisions about money.

(a) Be organized so that you know where your money is going and do not merely let it slip through your fingers. This enables you to see whether you are being extravagant about luxuries and whether you are being generous enough in sharing some of your money with others, either through hospitality or in service.

(b) Families should discuss money honestly so that all can take their right responsibility for the family budget. The family should also be outward looking and should think in terms of sharing and service.

(c) Money must always be regarded as far less important than people. You cannot buy the things which really matter, such as love, friendship, a vocational job, a creative way of life. These depend upon the integrity and worth of people as people.

(d) We must shun all dishonest practices however plausible the arguments put forward in their favour. It is perfectly possible to be honest in business. People only allow money to corrupt them because they mistakenly believe that material possessions provide a fulfilled life.

The individual family may have very little influence on the way its local or national government uses the money received from rates and taxes. However, ratepayers' associations and other pressure groups do try to exercise some sort of control. Each person can also attempt to make known his views about the way in which the bank, government, building society, unit trust, insurance group or private company use his savings or investments. For example, some Christians who are convinced pacifists would decide not to invest money in any company who are directly or indirectly concerned with the manufacture of arms.

Discussion and work

1 Discuss the ethics of hire purchase schemes. Do you think it is better to try and save for things and wait until you can afford them than to buy them on a hire purchase basis? What are the arguments both for and against such a view?

Do you think raising a mortgage on a house comes into the same category? If not, why is there a difference?

2 Is it true that money only becomes valuable according to the way it is used?

3 Should a part of each wage or salary go into savings?

4 What percentage of an individual's or family's budget should be spent on helping others?

5 Discuss the proposition that men are better at handling money than women.

6 Is the money that you earn in any sense different from money you are given or inherit or win on the pools?

7 'Every man has his price.' What is meant by the saying? Do you think it is true?

For the whole question of the distribution of wealth in the world, see Section C and related topics.

Gambling

We cannot leave the subject of money without mentioning gambling, a legalized activity in this country. Under the 1969 Gaming Act, the National Gaming Board was set up under the Home Secretary; betting offices and bookmakers' businesses are licensed by local authorities all over the land. The many forms of gaming range from horse and dog racing, gaming clubs, football pools, bingo halls and premium bonds, to gambling on the Stock Exchange, an activity which is given the more respectable name of 'playing the market'. It is estimated that at least 12 million people do the pools every week. In 1970 the pools brought in a sum approaching £2200 million, averaging out at about £40 per annum per head of population. There is no indication that this expenditure is decreasing.

Reasons for gambling

It is true that gambling can become an obsession. When this happens people may spend all their money on their particular sport. If the gamblers have children or family commitments, then innocent people can suffer through negligence and eventual ruin. But the addicts to gambling are in the minority. In trying to understand the motives which lead people to gamble, two factors are significant. If, as we have said, hundreds of thousands of workers get no real pleasure out of their employment, they will crave both for excitement and release from this captivity. Money is a way out and a premium bond or a harmless flutter on the pools may provide the money to escape and do something different with one's leisure if not with the whole of one's life. Second, so much of our present-day society has become dull and safe that very little risk remains (except for travelling on the roads!). Many people are by nature adventurous and are prepared to take a gamble, if not with money, with circumstances and with life itself. This adventurous spirit is an essential part of man and has led to his climbing Mount Everest, landing on the moon and exploring unknown continents. Gambling with money is only one expression of the need for risk; it has become excessive in industrialized and highly organized societies because other avenues of adventurous living are closed.

Christian attitudes
Some Christians feel that the dangers in gambling are so great that it is better to abstain from it altogether. However, much money is raised for charity and church by raffles and various minor gaming activities, so that other Christians consider that a little moderate gambling may be good fun and relatively harmless, whilst they obviously condemn excessive and selfish habits.

Jesus once told a parable about talents (Matthew 25: *14–30*). Literally speaking, talents mean bags of gold or money, although they can also represent personal gifts and abilities. The story tells how a man going on a journey entrusts his wealth to his servants. Each servant is given a task or responsibility within his capabilities. The first two work to double the money left with them, although in using it they do take a risk that they might also lose some of it. The third servant is afraid and perhaps lazy—we do not know which—but he does nothing with the money. When the master comes home this servant blames his inactivity on his master's hard character. (Jesus knew that life could be very hard and even unjust at times.) But the servant is punished because he did nothing. He took no risk, not even putting the money on deposit where it could have gained some interest. The successful and hardworking servants are rewarded with more responsibility. The third servant is punished by being deprived of the opportunity for further service. The parable illustrates a saying of Jesus (Mark 4:*25*) which in essence means 'If you don't use, you lose'.

The Christian therefore acknowledges that there must be a certain element of risk if life is to have any zest and fulfilment. He can discover that zest by using his gifts and abilities in the service of others. By truly basing his life on the intangible reality of faith in God he is indeed living adventurously. The craving to gamble with money arises from a certain basic emptiness. It is very sad that people should feel obliged to fill the void in their lives with something so fundamentally unsatisfying as money gambling. Rightly viewed, the adventure of Christian living offers everyone the element of permanent challenge and genuine risk. Jesus' call is always a call to act adventurously.

For further discussion see "The fulfilled life", p. 168.

Discussion and work
1 Do you agree that gambling is basically wrong and that one should not take part in it?

2 'All life is a gamble'. How far is this true? Is it, in any case, an adequate defence of gambling?

3 To what extent is gambling governed by the 'get rich quick' motive and the desire for money? How different is this from the adventurous spirit that Jesus talked about in his parable?

4 Do you know of any people who have won large sums on the pools? Discuss what effects the win had on their lives and whether or not it brought them happiness.

8 Freedom to choose when to die

(a) Suicide

Facts and Figures
Up to 1961 it was a criminal offence to commit suicide or attempt to do so. In that year the Suicide Act was passed, without opposition; this removed suicide from the arm of the law. But it remains a criminal act, punishable by up to 14 years imprisonment, to aid or advise suicide.

According to statistics published by the Samaritans (see below) suicide is one of the most common causes of death in England and Wales. It is also estimated that it kills at least 1100 every day throughout the world, that is one every 80 seconds. In Britain the numbers are 84 a week, or one every two hours. The Samaritans also say that there is a close connection between the amount of social change taking place in a society and its suicide rate, but that the suicide rate is lessened where people have a strong religious commitment.

Although these dreadful facts paint a gloomy picture, it is also true that in Britain, unlike most other industrial countries, the rate of suicide dropped each year from 1962, when it was 6061, to 1972, when it was 4193. Many things contributed to this decline, such as the developing social welfare services, better medical resuscitation (restoring life) methods, better medical treatment for depression and the emergence of the Samaritan organization. According to medical opinion the suicide rate has been declining as the Samaritans have been growing.

Attempted suicides far outnumber fatal suicides. It is generally accepted that more women than men attempt suicide and that people aged 24–44 years are more at risk than other age groups. Attempted suicide is also one of the most common medical emergencies seen in hospital casualty wards and suicide attempts are probably running at 100,000 a year, that is one every five minutes. Of these attempted suicides, the majority admitted to hospital are suffering from drug overdose. Approximately 10% of those who attempt suicide later succeed in killing themselves.

Causes

Suicide arises from a variety of causes but usually people take or attempt to take their own lives when they are driven to the loneliness of despair. Both social pressures and personal tragedy can lead people to despair. It is also now recognized that certain types of deep depression constitute mental illness. In this state, the person concerned may be unable to make a rational decision. Some individuals are less capable of coping with crises than others. Through no fault of their own, people who have suffered an unhappy or insecure childhood, start life with a basic mistrust. They may become afraid of making mistakes and develop a sense of inferiority. Unable to communicate with others, they become lonely, lose confidence in themselves and do not develop their talents. In the end life seems to them pointless and unbearable. Many people who attempt suicide do not want to die, but they do not want to go on living in their present circumstances. In such cases the attempted suicide is a cry for help. If the victim is to recover fully, he needs compassionate help and understanding. No one should ever dismiss an attempted suicide as merely an attention seeker.

Obviously many outside factors contribute to a state of deep depression. The death of a loved one can leave the individual desolate; being made redundant without the prospect of another job can bring the very demoralizing feeling of not being wanted by anyone. People can become frightened of increasing old age and incapacity; they can worry unduly about money or the lack of it, and they may have to endure a long and drawn out painful illness which exhausts their reserves of strength. Drink and drug problems heighten depression. Heroin addicts for example, are 40% more likely to commit suicide than members of the population as a whole.

Christian attitudes

Although many ancient peoples believed that in certain circumstances it was perfectly honourable to take one's own life, the Jew and Christian have always firmly believed that all life is sacred and ultimately belongs to God. Men and women have no right therefore to 'murder' themselves, any more than they have the right to take another person's life. In the past the Christian church insisted that suicides had forfeited any hope of eternal life. They had died with their crime unforgiven and could not be buried in consecrated ground. Today, a more compassionate attitude is arising as

Christians realize the tremendous effects of social pressures on individuals. Increasing scientific knowledge has also made them more aware of the medical reasons for suicide. Coroners often arrive at the verdict that a man has taken his own life whilst the balance of his mind was disturbed. Considering all these factors, the Christian may conclude that judgment belongs only to God.

Every suicide or attempted suicide is a personal tragedy. It can bring about great suffering to the individual's family and friends. People always feel that something could surely have been done to prevent such a sad end to a life. Psychiatrists believe that about 80% of the people who kill themselves do give some indirect sign of their intentions. So it is apparently not true that people who threaten to commit suicide are always unlikely to do so. When we go through a bad time we all feel a basic need to talk to someone else about it. The trouble is that many people have no one whom they trust or to whom they can turn in a crisis. A Christian maintains that life may be rich, meaningful and joyful, especially when a person bases his thinking on spiritual values and can draw on spiritual resources. He will therefore work to establish a caring community in which individuals are supported when they are going through difficult periods in their lives, and when lonely or depressed they will find fellowship with others. On a political and social level, he will also hope to build a better society, so that people are not subjected to unbearable tensions, discrimination or fear.

The Samaritans

In 1953 Chad Varah, a Church of England priest, was appalled to discover that three suicides were taking place every day in the Greater London area. He decided to do something to help. Being the Rector of St Stephen's Walbrook, London, he installed a telephone in the church vestry and publicized the fact that anyone thinking of committing suicide could telephone him there. This was the start of the Samaritan organization. Today there are 174 centres and 20,000 carefully selected and trained volunteers offer a 24-hour service. They speak to 250,000 callers every year. They give their time and caring without payment, offering friendship to those in need of it. They do not give money to their clients. Although many people who work for the organization are Christians, many are not and there is no evangelizing. Chad Varah has written 'the only preaching the Samaritans are allowed to do is in deeds'. Very ordinary people from every age group and background become Samaritan volunteers. They need to be reliable and sympathetic and their basic skills are developed through training and experience.

At least two official enquiries into suicide have recommended increased use of the Samaritans, while their success has been demonstrated in a study of 30 towns. Where 15 towns had Samaritan centres and 15 were without, the suicide rate in the non-Samaritan centres rose by almost 20% whereas in the Samaritan towns it dropped by 6%.

Discussion and work

1 Discuss some of the situations in which individuals might be tempted to take their own life.
2 Is it important that the Samaritans do not attempt to convert people to any particular faith? Why do you think so?
3 What qualities do you think a Samaritan volunteer should have? As an adult, would you be interested in becoming one?
4 Ask a speaker from the local Samaritans to talk to your group and tell you more about their work. Their address will be found in the telephone book.
5 Discuss the following: 'Suicide is not a "problem" to be "solved", but rather a question to be answered.' Hugh Valentine, *The Friend*, March 1981.

(b) Euthanasia

The Oxford dictionary defines this word as 'gentle and easy death; the bringing about of this especially in cases of incurable and painful disease'. The issue has become one of public concern in the Western world where, despite the great advances in medical knowledge, dying can be a prolonged, painful and deeply distressing process. In fact many people would argue that advanced medical techniques now enable a patient to be 'kept alive' in the literal sense when death would be a preferable end. A life of suffering can be a living death. A life of complete helplessness can be a life of real humiliation. Under present laws a doctor, or a member of the patient's family, who helps the sufferer end his own life, risks being charged with the serious crime of murder or manslaughter.

The Voluntary Euthanasia Society

This organization, now known as Exit: The Society for the Right to Die with Dignity, was founded in 1935 under the Presidency of Lord Moynihan, a past president of the Royal College of Surgeons. It aims to bring about a change in the law 'so that an adult person, suffering from a severe illness for which no relief is known, should be entitled by law to the mercy of a painless death, if and only if, that is his or her expressed wish.' Parliament has debated this subject in 1935, 1950 and 1969, but each time the Bill proposing euthanasia has been defeated.

The Society is very clear that it is not in favour of suicide as such; it is also definitely against any suggestion of compulsory euthanasia in the sense of 'getting rid' of the old, infirm, unwanted, deformed or mentally defective person (see below). The Society urges 'that the law should allow, but not compel, doctors to help incurable patients to die peacefully at their own request. The patient must have signed, at least 30 days previously, a declaration making his request known. The declaration would be independently witnessed by two people, unrelated to the patient or to each other, who would not stand to gain by the patient's death. The patient could revoke the declaration at any time. Two doctors, one a consultant, would also have to certify that the patient was suffering, without reasonable prospect of recovery, from a physical illness that he found intolerable.'

Christian attitudes

Christians are united in completely condemning *compulsory euthanasia*. During World War II reports from Germany clearly indicated that the bodily deformed, the insane and those suffering from hereditary disease were liable to compulsory euthanasia. The Nazis justified their action by saying that it was in the interests of the common good to get rid of the less healthy members of society. In 1943 Pope Pius XII spoke for all men of good will when he expressed his great grief at what was happening in Germany: 'what sane man does not recognize that this not only vitiates [i.e. corrupts or debases] the natural and Divine law written in the heart of every man, but flies in the face of every sensibility of civilized humanity? The blood of these victims . . . cries to God from earth.'

On the question of *voluntary euthanasia*, Christians are divided. Roman Catholics take a firm stand on the sanctity of human life and reject any attempt to alter the law:

A statute authorizing voluntary euthanasia, even with safeguards, would be no more acceptable (than compulsory euthanasia) to the Christian conscience. Such a statute would injure the common good by undermining respect for innocent life, a moral idea essential for the maintenance of society's security. (N.St J. Stevas, *The Right to Life*).

On the other hand some prominent Protestant Christians have actively supported the idea of voluntary euthanasia:

I believe in the relative unimportance of death in God's plan for us. I am therefore a convinced member of the Euthanasia Society. I sincerely believe that those who come after us will wonder why on earth we kept a human being alive against his own will, when all dignity, beauty and meaning of life had vanished; when any gain to anyone else was clearly impossible, and when we should have been punished by the State if we kept an animal alive in similar physical conditions. (Rev. Dr Leslie Weatherhead)

There are two other relevant factors to be considered:

(i) *Personality changes*: It is now possible for surgeons to perform brain operations which can bring about a personality change. The powerful drugs which physicians and psychologists use to alleviate depression and other related conditions also raise questions. Some people strongly criticize attempts to treat violent criminals with drug therapy. They question whether medical treatment which brings about a fundamental personality change can reach a point at which it is almost the equivalent of taking that person's life. Pope Pius XII said:

It is not permissible for the patient to consent to medical procedures ... which will lead to the permanent destruction or considerable lessening of free will. ... Man is thus reduced to the level of a living automaton. The moral law cannot permit such a reversal of values.

(ii) *Unnecessary lengthening of life*: As medical science develops, wealthy industrial societies are faced with an increasingly ageing population. Today hospitals have special geriatric wards where people are kept alive by care and medication, but they are unable to live any kind of independent or purposeful life. Many Christians believe that if medication or surgery increases the length of life but in so doing seriously diminishes its quality, then men and women should be informed of all the possible outcomes so that they can make their own decision to accept or reject treatment. One person may decide against a cancer operation if he knows that the operation will in reality do little to arrest the progress of the disease. Another may be willing to go through the ordeal, believing that while there is life there is hope, or from the unselfish motive of furthering medical research, even if his own personal benefit is very slight.

The Euthanasia Society provides a Declaration which an individual can give to his doctor, ready for use if the time comes when the patient can no longer make any decisions for his own future. It is 'a protection against unwanted medical survival', a condition which one doctor described as the pointless prolongation of human suffering and misery arising from well meant but foolish enthusiasm for maintaining life. An example given was the case of a woman aged 104 who, although obviously dying, was given a blood transfusion. The Society stresses that the Declaration does not ask the doctor to do anything contrary to the law. 'I request that I be allowed to die and not be kept alive by artificial means and that I receive whatever quantity of drugs may be required to keep me free from pain or distress even if the moment of death is hastened.'

The great difficulty of all these problems is increased by the debate about what constitutes clinical death. Should people be kept on life-support machines when there is no further hope of *conscious* survival?

Discussion and work

1 In what circumstances, if any, do you think voluntary euthanasia could be justified? If it were made legal, what strict conditions and safeguards should be included in the law? Who should make the choice and who should carry it out?

2 What is the difference between actually ending a person's life through drug therapy or other medical means and allowing a person to die? Discuss with examples.

3 What boundaries, if any, should be put upon scientific exploration into the human personality and human life?

4 Find out from a doctor what tests are used to determine clinical death in this country and discuss any problems arising.

For further discussion on Christian attitudes to death and the after-life, see p. 173.

Section B — The Community

Introduction

Human beings cannot exist in isolation. Beginning with the family unit, we are all dependent upon one another in the ever-widening circles of school, work, neighbourhood and state. Living as we do in a country with developed industrial and welfare organizations, we do not always recognize our dependence; instead we take for granted all the services which local and central government undertake for us through various bodies. But we realize our need very acutely when, for some reason or other, our water or electricity supply is cut off or our house catches fire or we are taken seriously ill.

We also know that our relationship with others is not only necessary to our physical existence but to our personal growth. We have to learn to share, to co-operate, to work together with different kinds of people and to take responsibility not only for ourselves and our immediate friends or family but also for many others if we are to become truly adult people. If we are simply passive members of society, content to earn a wage, pay our taxes, watch television and, if we only exercise our power to choose or decide when we select the goods we buy and consume, then we are only half alive. To live life to the full we need to be active participants in our neighbourhood.

Paul saw Christians as members one of another (Ephesians 4:25—32). In one sense it was easier for the very first followers of Jesus to realize that they were interdependent and responsible. They spent their days as partners in small, caring communities, sharing all their resources and supporting each other in times of hardship (Acts 4:32—35) and persecution (Hebrews 10:32—35). In spite of all their problems, their lives were characterized by the love, joy and peace which the spirit of their master inspired (Galatians 5:22). Modern Christians, living in a different cultural setting, attempt to be both part of the worshipping community of their local church and also responsible members of the larger groups through which they are involved either in work or leisure activities. There are numerous Christian organizations which play an active role in trying to resolve the great social and moral

59

problems of our age. In addition, many Christians join non-religious bodies as part of their commitment to build a more just society.

In the following sections, we shall first be discussing the present structure of local government and the difference between statutory and voluntary organizations. Then we shall look at the many kinds of people who are in need or at risk in our community. We shall try to understand some of the problems which arise from the misuse of personal freedom or from more complex social conditions. Through all this background information we may be able to see how we too can play a creative part in our community by exercising our personal gifts and interests for the benefit of others.

Discussion and work

Read the parable of the Good Samaritan (Luke 10:*25—37*) and discuss the following points:

1 Jesus told this story in answer to the lawyer's question 'Who is my neighbour?' What central lesson do you think he was teaching?

2 The Samaritan was a despised half-caste. The priest and the Levite (one of the Temple officers) were strict Jews and would consider the Samaritan to be not only of mixed race but also outside the Jewish faith. Why do you think Jesus chose this kind of person to demonstrate what good neighbourliness meant?

3 At the end of the story the lawyer was instructed to 'Go and do likewise'. To be told to follow the Samaritan's example would be bitter indeed for a Jewish rabbi. Put the story into a modern setting, thinking of contemporary kinds of people to represent the priest, the Levite, the Samaritan and the lawyer.

1 The structure of the community

If you and I lived in a country village we should have a very strong sense of community. We should know most of the people there and when old Mrs Smith, who lived alone, fell and broke her leg, everyone would rally round to help. The local church or chapel, the women's institute, the pub, the school, the youth club, would all provide focal points for our communal life. But most of us live in towns or the suburbs of large cities where it is much more difficult to feel a sense of responsibility for others living nearby. Although centres for people to meet and know each other still exist, the community cannot be so close knit and it seems completely beyond our sphere of concern and our power to alter many of the circumstances we see. If we are going to be part of our neighbourhood, we need to understand first how the locality works and second what opportunities there are for involvement.

Local government
In this country local government plays a very important role as for centuries we have run many of our concerns locally rather than nationally. In 1974—5 the central government reviewed the growing demands placed upon local authorities and completely reorganized their structure. We have now two kinds of *counties*, the metropolitan and the non-metropolitan. Outside Greater London (which because of its size has always been rather different from other local authorities) there are now six metropolitan counties in the densely populated areas of Greater Manchester, Merseyside, South Yorkshire, Tyne and Wear, West Midlands and West Yorkshire. Each of these counties consists of a group of towns. There are 38 non-metropolitan counties in England and eight in Wales. Each county, whether metropolitan or non-metropolitan, is divided into districts.

All *county councils* are elected every four years. Metropolitan *district councils* elect a third of their members in each of the three years between county elections, but non-metropolitan districts can choose whether to have all their councillors elected every four years or to follow the metropolitan system. Every British subject (or citizen of the Irish Republic) who is over 18 years of age and whose name appears on the electoral register is entitled to vote. This register of residents is prepared annually and is also used for parliamentary elections.

Local authorities are responsible for public health, police, education, housing, traffic administration, highways, fire services, libraries, personal social service and other matters concerning the well-being of the citizen. The services they run are called *statutory* because they are imposed by the law of the land. It is very important that the individual resident should exercise his/her vote, after looking carefully at the various candidates up for election, and that he should take an interest in the management of his own district.

Central government
Central government departments provide some major social services for the local district. Although the National Health Service, for example, is run locally, the area organization is ultimately responsible to the central government health department. Similarly, the Department of Health and Social Security uses local offices to administer security benefits throughout England and Wales.

Voluntary organizations

When so much is provided by central and local government there might seem to be no place for voluntary organizations, but nothing could be further from the truth. Many problems can probably best be dealt with by a voluntary organization. Some exist to give personal help and advice, as we discussed in the case of the Samaritans (p. 54); others, such as Shelter (p. 66), specifically aim to rouse and influence public opinion. Being voluntary they are free to criticize official policy and to campaign for improvements in the statutory services. The thousands of voluntary organizations in this country range from the large national societies such as the National Society for the Prevention of Cruelty to Children to small local groups such as those which may be attached to a particular hospital. Most of the national organizations employ professional staff, but large numbers of people give part-time or full-time unpaid service, without which the organization could not survive. Voluntary organizations and individual volunteers complement the statutory services, especially when governments are cutting down on public spending.

In England the *National Council for Social Service* co-ordinates the various voluntary services and helps them to work with the statutory services. Similar co-ordinating bodies exist in Wales, Scotland and Northern Ireland.

Discussion and work

1 Do you know the name of your county and district areas and the names of the county and district councillors who represent your locality?

2 In what voluntary work is your school or church involved? How does this help out the service already provided by the local council or health department?

3 In many universities and colleges a full-time student co-ordinates voluntary services. Invite him/her to come and talk to your group about the various activities in the neighbourhood.

4 How many voluntary service bodies can you name which are at work in your locality? What steps would you take if you wished to become involved with one of them?

2 People in need

We have certain fundamental requirements for survival—food, warmth, shelter, uncontaminated drinking water and a relatively hygienic environment. These necessary things cost money to provide and so either the individual, the family, or an independent body must pay for them. In addition to these basic needs, we all like to feel necessary to another human being—being significant to someone else gives point and purpose to life. However, there are many amongst us who are short of the physical necessities and even more they lack the simple human contacts which are so important. Amongst the very old or the very young, the frail and ill, the mentally or physically handicapped, we find those people who simply have no sense at all of their importance as members of the human family.

When looking at the different categories of people in need, we have to remember three things. First, these people are in the minority in our society, therefore it is easy to forget them or even to ignore their existence. What is more, many of us may actually be ignorant of their plight. We must therefore be prepared to find out what is happening in our neighbourhood, perhaps through our local church or youth group, our school or place of work.

Second, although being informed and aware is very important, it is not an end in itself. Christians believe that everyone is of significance to God and Jesus taught that God's love was so great that even the hairs on our heads were numbered (Luke 12:*6—7*). Throughout his ministry he demonstrated the power of unselfish love and cared for the needy of his day; his love went out to the outcast, such as the lepers (Mark 1:*40—42*), the poor and defenceless such as widows (Luke 7:*11—15*) and those who were considered totally unimportant, such as children (Mark 10:*13—15*). If we want to follow his example we must be prepared to give of our time and energy to help others and it is a fact that a little help from a lot of people goes a long way. For example, some schools organize a rota of students to visit the elderly in their houses or in old people's homes on a regular basis, giving a lot of pleasure as well as practical help with shopping, writing letters or other chores.

Third, even if we can't rise to the heights of unselfish love at all times, we are bound to recognize that no one can live a life entirely free from illness, sorrow and eventual death. 'Do as you would be done by' said Jesus. On a straightforward practical level, we must be prepared to give help while we are able to do so, knowing that we ourselves will need to receive help at a later stage.

Because the area of need is so wide, I have tried to condense matters into three categories for discussion, namely the elderly, the disabled and the deprived. In the available space it has not been possible to attempt to talk about all existing organizations. Instead, for each category I have chosen one society and have given a brief outline of its work. This selection in no way implies that these particular societies are better than any other. Each one simply serves to illustrate the kind of voluntary work which individuals do so generously to help those in need. The index at the back of the book lists the names and addresses of many societies working in all the various fields. From this list you will perhaps be able to pick out those organizations which interest you and do some personal research into their work.

(a) The elderly

Officially the term 'elderly' applies to women who are 60 years or over and men who are 65 years or over and who are therefore entitled to receive the State retirement pension. In this country they represent around 17% of the present population and will probably remain about the same level up to the end of the century. Of course thousands in this age group are fit and well. They do a job of work, help run all kinds of organizations and themselves look after the very old and sick. Their contribution to society is incalculable.

There are, however, many thousands of sick and disabled and very old people who need care. To begin with, this help may be given to old and infirm people in their own homes; naturally people want to stay in their own homes for as long as possible. All kinds of home services are provided by regular visiting and personal contacts. Perhaps there is shopping to do or some gardening. The house may need some decorating or the old person may need domestic help, transport to hospital or even a night sitter-in. When old people cannot manage in their own homes any longer, they can perhaps be found accommodation in 'sheltered' housing, where there is a warden in charge of a block of flats, or a day centre nearby which will provide a main mid-day meal and recreation facilities. At a later stage the old person may need to go into a residential home or hospital which caters for the very sick and disabled or a hospice for the dying.

Unfortunately old people sometimes try to manage on their own when they are not fit to do so. This is where good neighbourliness comes in. Who are the old people in our neighbourhood who want a little looking after? Do their relatives live far away? Are they perhaps alone in the world? Many organizations offer a wide range of services for old people both on a voluntary and statutory basis. Through their meals-on-wheels the Women's Royal Voluntary Service, 'the women in green' or WRVS, serve over 17 million meals a year! They also run luncheon clubs, encouraging elderly people to get out of the house for a meal and meet their friends. If they are sufficiently able, the old people themselves often help to serve the meals at the day centres and wash up afterwards. Besides this the WRVS organize clubs with library facilities and training in various handicrafts—the well-known Darby and Joan clubs were initially sponsored by them.

(b) The disabled

This group includes not only those who are mentally or physically retarded but those who are handicapped by blindness, or deafness, or who are suffering from some chronic and crippling disease such as muscular dystrophy or multiple sclerosis.

It is hard for those of us who are fit and healthy to identify with those who, through no fault of their own, have been born with a disability or who have been stricken by illness which makes them unable to live a normal life. The 1981 Year of the Disabled highlighted the importance of integrating disabled people into the ordinary community by taking practical steps to make their lives easier—see Appendix 5.

Leonard Cheshire and his wife, Sue Ryder, are two people who have devoted their lives and energies to the relief of suffering. Leonard Cheshire, a famous RAF pilot officer in World War II, was chosen to be one of two official British observers when the Americans dropped the second atomic bomb on Nagasaki, forcing the Japanese to surrender. This unforgettable experience changed Leonard Cheshire's life. In 1948 he set up the first home for the incurably sick or permanently disabled, realizing that there were some people for whom there was no room in busy hospitals. His aim is to create places where there is affection and some family life. The residents are encouraged to take as much part as they can in running the homes, each of which is financed by a local committee, dependent on voluntary subscription.

(c) The deprived

Despite the provisions of various acts of parliament designed to help those most in need, thousands of people in this country today still live below the officially recognized 'poverty line'. These very poor people may be elderly and alone, they may be one-parent families struggling to make ends meet or they may be young couples with several children. Furthermore a percentage of our work force earns very low wages, while millions are now actually out of work. Although Supplementary Benefits and Family Income supplements do give help to families living on low incomes, such items as keeping children in warm clothing and shoes can be a great problem. In fact, the living standards of Britain's poorest families have deteriorated; their stocks of bedclothes are limited, furniture is scarce and the cost of heating may be beyond their means.

Inadequate housing dominates the lives of the poor. About 80% of the general population live in their own houses or in those rented by the local authority. A small proportion of households, another 5%, live in housing provided through their jobs or through housing associations. The remaining 15% of the population live in privately rented furnished or unfurnished accommodation. It is in this private sector that we find the greatest concentration of dwellings classified as 'unfit for human habitation' and according to the General Household Survey of 1972 this is the area in which very poor families tend to live. These dwellings contain mouldering walls and fungus; they are cold and draughty. Sometimes they lack all indoor sanitation. Often they are infested with rats, mice and cockroaches. In these properties live the very poor who cannot find anywhere else to go. Overcrowding is another serious problem. A family of two adults and three children may be sharing a two-room basement flat. Such closeness leads to tensions, family strife and ill-health. The children of these families are underprivileged, finding their amusements on the street instead of at home and having no chance of keeping up with school homework.

The National Campaign for the Homeless, better known as Shelter, is one organization trying to do something for families in desperate need. It officially came into existence in 1966, but arose originally out of Des Wilson's research into the housing situation affecting people in overcrowded parts of our large cities. Shelter aims to provide a rescue operation for those people who are living in intolerable conditions. It also raises money and distributes it to local housing associations, who then buy properties and convert them into decent homes, letting them at a reasonable rent to those in need. One of Shelter's further aims is to arouse and inform public opinion; when people are really aware of the appalling conditions which still exist they will do everything possible to persuade central and local government to remedy the situation.

Discussion and work

1 Choose a particular group of people and a particular organization which interests you. Complete a personal project, relating the national organization to your own neighbourhood. There may for example be a local Shelter group, or a local society for mentally handicapped children and adults.

2 Find out how your local church, school, youth group or other body actively helps people in need. Use the Appendix for details of booklets listing volunteer groups at work. If you do not already know something about these movements, find out more

about them and how you can become involved.

3 Discuss the arguments both for and against the proposition that people nowadays are living too long. Would you agree that a civilization can be judged by the way in which it looks after its old people? Discuss the various reasons why elderly relatives are not necessarily cared for by their families, as they were in previous generations.

4 The Nazi regime in Germany attempted to 'purge' the nation of the physically and mentally handicapped, so as to breed a 'pure' 'Aryan' race. Both from a humanitarian and Christian point of view, discuss why such a policy is morally obnoxious.

5 What can the old give the young, the weak give the strong, the disabled give the physically fit, the deprived give the privileged?

6 Some critics say that in spite of our Welfare State there is still a great deal of inequality in Britain and that people can be trapped in the cycle of underprivilege. In other words, those who are born into very poor families have less chance of good health and proper education and therefore they are unable to find adequate jobs (cf Child Poverty Action Group). Try to find out more about this issue and discuss the problems raised.

3 People at risk

Looked at superficially, it may seem unnecessary to have a separate section for people at risk; after all, if you are at risk you may also be in great need. However, I have made this distinction for the sake of clarity and to help summarize the various difficult situations which exist in our society. I have divided this section into three categories: first, those at risk because of negligence and cruelty; second, those at risk because of violence; third, those at risk because of prejudice.

As before, we have to remember that we are dealing with minority groups of people, but whereas those in need will easily call forth our compassion, it is quite possible and even probable that the plight of those at risk will demand from us an honest examination of our own ideas. This honesty may at times be painful.

When we take time to look within our own hearts and minds, we can see there the selfishness which might one day lead to negligence of and cruelty to those who are unable to fight back. We will also recognize the frustrations and anger which could spill over into violence if not seen and dealt with in the very early stages. Furthermore, we must attempt to understand the roots of discrimination. The basic cause of prejudice is often found in lack of information and lack of imagination about minority groups within our society. How easy it is to typecast people is shown by the vast number of jokes about an Englishman, an Irishman, a Scotsman and a Welshman. It is also historically true that when a nation is in difficulties, unscrupulous leaders direct attention on to a scapegoat who can be blamed for all that has gone wrong. This is what Hitler did. He managed to persuade a great many of the German people that Germany's ills were due to the conspiracy of international Jewry. As a result of his 'Final Solution', 6 million Jews were killed in Europe.

As the field of study is comprehensive, I have taken one example to illustrate each area of concern. At the back of the book you will find listed the names and addresses of various organizations which you can consult for your own private study.

(a) From neglect and cruelty

In 1979 the International Year of the Child highlighted the needs of children around the world. (See Appendix 4 for the United Nations' Charter on the Rights of the Child.) Some 600 voluntary organizations took part in the campaign in this country. From the impetus received, it was hoped that work for and amongst children would proceed by leaps and bounds. But although the situation today is immeasurably better than it was during the last century, the appalling fact remains that every year thousands of children are subjected to physical and/or mental cruelty and neglect, resulting in the annual toll of some 100 deaths.

The causes of neglect are many. Sometimes parents of very low intelligence fail to give their children proper food and attention without even realizing that something is wrong; or perhaps a woman overwhelmed by poverty and the demands of a large family finds herself quite unable to cope. Either or both parents may fall ill or be out of work; the accommodation then available may prove harmful to a child's well-being. Other parents may be subject to mental or psychological disturbances, or there may be deep friction between the parents in consequence of which the children are beaten.

Parliament has passed much legislation to protect the child. Every local authority has its Children's Officer and Child Care Service but it has been the voluntary organizations which have pioneered active concern for children and which still do considerable and much needed work. The National Society for the Prevention of Cruelty to Children is one such group. It began in 1885 as the Liverpool Society for the Prevention of Cruelty to Children. Six years later several societies combined to form the

NSPCC under the directorship of Rev. Benjamin Waugh, a Congregational minister. The NSPCC copes with about 40,000 cases of cruelty each year, some reported by ordinary people, some by the police and school officials. Sometimes a child or young person is brought before the Juvenile Courts as the 'victim of non-accidental injury' and is found to be in need of care and protection. If the authorities conclude that a child should not live with his parents, he may be placed in a children's home run by the local authority or a voluntary organization. Alternatively, he may be boarded out with carefully selected foster parents or even placed for adoption.

In many cases the parents themselves, aware of their own inadequacy, come to the society for advice. Perhaps the father has been sent to prison, the mother cannot pay the rent and is worried about the children. Perhaps one parent has deserted the other and the remaining parent has taken up with another partner who resents the child of the first relationship.

A great deal of research has been done by the NSPCC and similar organizations into the causes of cruelty and neglect and they now emphasize preventive measures, such as education for parenthood, family care units, play schemes and organized nurseries.

The vast majority of us are moved by the needs of children. For the Christian, Jesus' treatment of children is especially significant. Many believe that his teaching about the value of a child as a person in its own right (Mark 9:35—37) had considerable influence in shaping society's future evaluation of childhood. It is clear from the gospels that he loved children and when he blessed those who had been brought to him, he said that the child instinctively possessed a quality which an adult needs if he is to belong to the Kingdom (Mark 10:13—16). Although we cannot know precisely what he had in mind, we may surmise that he was probably referring to the child's receptiveness. When rightly loved, a child is dependent, trustful and loving in return. Jesus may have been saying that the Kingdom, or the caring community, cannot operate if people are proud and self-centred in their relationships with others.

(b) From violence

Criminal statistics for England and Wales are published every year. From these we can tell that crimes of violence are on the increase in our society. The statistics only cite those indictable crimes which are known to the police, but there are thousands of others which do not come up before the courts. An indictable offence means one which may be tried by a jury and includes such serious crimes as murder, manslaughter, wounding and robbery

69

with violence, as well as breaking and entering.

There are many causes for violent behaviour. Where there is rising unemployment people may become frustrated, angry and bitter about their inability to find work or to bring about any effective change in their circumstances. Some people think that vandalism is a despairing form of social action. They suggest that people who are deeply disillusioned with their lives feel tempted to rebel by smashing up whatever objects in the locality can be broken or destroyed. But such action does not cure anything and there are a thousand and one things we can actually do to create a more just society.

The suffering of women with violent husbands or partners is far from new. However, the plight of battered women has only come before the public eye comparatively recently as a result of changes in our legal system and the work of various women's movements. Major laws affording equal opportunities and equal pay for women came into force in 1975. Women now have equal rights in marriage and can make the same claims for divorce as their husbands. Nevertheless, hundreds of women are still subjected to brutal treatment from ignorant, drunken and, in some cases, psychologically disturbed men. These women sometimes attempt to get help from doctors, social workers or the police, but can also benefit from the various Women's Aid refuges run by voluntary help in accordance with the aims of the National Women's Aid Federation.

Battered women need protection, accommodation, support and advice. When they arrive at a centre, most have lost their self-confidence and even their self-respect. Realizing that others have suffered in the same way removes their terrible sense of isolation. They can then learn to take responsibility for the day-to-day running of the home and for sorting out their problems. Most homes have an 'open-door' policy, meaning that no woman is ever turned away even if this leads to overcrowding. Some women come to the refuge simply to get help and advice, some stay a few days and then go back to their own homes; others bring their children and some stay for a longer period. The centre may be run by a core of full-time members while undergraduates and young married women organize a rota of part-time help. Social workers and health visitors visit the homes to see particular women and give specific advice about social security payments, housing, the care and education of children and, if necessary, how to proceed with legal action against their husbands.

For a man of his time, Jesus was extraordinarily compassionate in his treatment of women. He harshly condemned the scribes for exploiting widows (Mark 12:*40*), he placed men and women on a basis of sexual equality in their personal relations with each other

70

(Mark 10:*10—12*), he publicly reinstated a repentant prostitute (Luke 7:*36—49*) and accepted her lavish gift of love. He also refused to condemn a woman caught in the act of adultery (John 8:*1—11*). As Jesus always pointed to the importance of inner motivation (Matthew 5:*21—24*) a Christian is specifically encouraged to look within himself for the seeds of violence such as anger, bitterness and resentment. In his own life Jesus himself demonstrated the way of non-violent protest. On one exceptional occasion he was furiously indignant to see genuine worshippers, both Jewish and Gentile, being unjustly treated through dishonest dealings in the Temple. Even then he did not physically harm any human being, although he certainly disrupted the processes of dishonourable trading (Mark 11:*15—19*).

(c) From prejudice

This country has long respected individual freedom and the rights of its citizens. In 1948 the United Nations issued a Universal Declaration of Human Rights (see Appendix 2) including the claim

> that all human beings are born free and equal in dignity and rights . . . endowed with reason and conscience and should act towards one another in a spirit of brotherhood; that everyone is entitled to all the rights and freedoms set forth in this Declaration without distinctions of any kind . . .; that everyone has the right to life, liberty and security of person.

So in a just society the kind of prejudice which leads to discrimination against minority groups simply should not exist. The fact that it does is a challenge to Christians not only in this country but throughout the world. There has been social discrimination by the rich against the poor, sexual discrimination by men against women, religious discrimination by the state church against the non-conforming minority of Christian sects as well as against people of other faiths, particularly the Jews, and racial discrimination against those whose skin is of a different colour.

The question of colour discrimination has been one of the most important issues in Britain in the latter half of the 20th century. Since the 1950s Britain has become a multi-racial society, with the influx of New Commonwealth immigrants (i.e. people born in all countries of the commonwealth except Australia, Canada and New Zealand) and people of Pakistani ethnic origin. What has made Britain different from other Western countries is that those who came to work here had the status of 'immigrant' and not 'migrant' as in Germany and France. In other words they had rights to permanent residence and citizenship. From the very

71

beginning it was therefore reasonable to expect that immigrants were here to stay.

It is important for us to remember that the first inflow of coloured immigrants came into this country by the specific invitation of both Labour and Conservative governments. After the Second World War, extensive advertising by British governments encouraged workers from India and the West Indies to come to Britain to help overcome the chronic manpower shortage. On the whole these immigrants were recruited to fill the low-paid jobs, such as public transport and domestic work in hospitals as well as engineering. In effect they formed social and economic groups at the bottom rung of the country's economy. Of course not all immigrants fell into this category; some were professional people, others worked in the clothing trade, catering and other service industries.

When the post-war boom ended in the early 1960s the government began to control the flow of immigrants by introducing new laws. There is now almost no new black immigration into Britain. In fact since 1974 more people have been leaving the country than have been arriving here to settle.

According to official Home Office publications, the stated aim of the government is that 'all people in Britain regardless of race, should be able to live and work together in an atmosphere of mutual trust and tolerance'. To this end the Race Relations Act of 1976 was passed, making it unlawful to treat one person less favourably than another on grounds of colour, race, nationality or ethnic or national origins. This applies to education, employment, the provision of housing, goods, facilities and services. The Commission for Racial Equality was set up to enforce the law and to promote equal opportunities and good relations. It also supports and co-ordinates work undertaken locally by over 100 Community Relations Councils.

Despite these steps and the strenuous work of many organizations, especially those sponsored by the various Christian churches, prejudice and discrimination do exist. They are nowhere more forcibly expressed than in the activities of the National Front and like-minded movements. The National Front believes in the repatriation of coloured immigrants, or the creation of an apartheid Britain; the prohibition of inter-racial marriages; the tightening up of law and order; severe restriction of Welfare State benefits; and an all-white Commonwealth. Being Fascist in origin, the National Front is male-dominated. Fascism is not simply a political creed. It involves belief in dictatorship and is against the universal human rights which are basic to a democratic form of government. As we have seen in Hitler's Nazism, it glorifies

violence and belittles tenderness, having no time for compassion. The causes of prejudice are many. It can stem from a sense of insecurity and inadequacy, both on a personal and social level. For example, in a serious economic recession it is easy to blame 'them' (whoever the group may be) for all the mess and to believe that simple solutions can be found to solve what are in fact complex problems. The National Front demonstrates its inconsistent attitude by both blaming the black immigrant for draining our society through unemployment benefits while attacking him at the same time for stealing all the white men's jobs.

Many people today consider that the issue of race in Britain is really a class rather than a colour problem. Immigrant communities often live in very poor conditions within the depressed inner city. These are areas of high unemployment and few amenities. Mob violence such as that of the 1979 Bristol riots or the 1981 Brixton, Liverpool and other riots is not necessarily racist as it involves both black and white people. Some commentators see such disorder as a protest against social deprivation.

The Christian must dedicate himself to work for the ending of prejudice and discrimination, not only in his own personal life but also in his community and nation. We must be committed to the policies of love rather than those of hate, fear and despair. We must aim to dispel ignorance and lack of imagination. It is high time that the myth of any kind of racial superiority was exploded. There is no real basis for thinking that the different groups of mankind differ in their innate capacity for intellectual and emotional development. As many writers have pointed out, all civilized people have been a mixture of racial strains. In fact where a human community remains isolated and segregated, it tends to stagnate and die. Human society is at its most creative where there is a free mingling of the old and new and the interchange of different cultures and races.

Paul had a vision of a new kind of humanity where the old barriers no longer existed. He wrote of a unity in Christ between man and woman, Jew and Gentile, slave and free man (Galatians 3:28). The same idea runs through a passage in his letter to the people of Colossus (Colossians 3:9—13). Jesus himself healed the daughter of a non-Jewish woman (Mark 7:24—30) and the servant of a Roman centurion (Luke 7:1—10). On both occasions he praised these people for their faith. These incidents are important in the context of Jewish exclusiveness. He also clearly stated that all those who did the will of God were part of his family, a remark which cut right across the conventional Jewish idea that blood relationships came first.

Discussion and work

  1 Discuss some of the possible reasons why a parent or parents might neglect their children or even treat them cruelly. Would you consider that education in parenthood is a vitally important issue? How can people be educated to become parents?

  2 How could a young mother with too much to do and no chance of a break from her family be helped by good neighbourliness? By discussing particular cases, show quite clearly that 'prevention is better than cure'.

  3 Many Christian thinkers consider our society unjust because it puts profit before human beings. Life is so organized that people expect to get back in return as much or more than they give out. Why do you think mothers and children are likely to be the prime sufferers from such an attitude?

  4 An expert on child development, Dr Mia Kellmer Pringle, has listed four basic human needs: love and security, new experiences, praise and recognition, and responsibility. She believes that any individual who is starved of these needs will either fight back or run away from life, will either attack or withdraw. Discuss these ideas in relation to violence and vandalism.

  5 There is some evidence from animal studies that both overcrowding and noise lead to violent behaviour. How much can we deduce from this in relation to human beings?

  6 Contrast and comment upon the following statements:

    'Since this does not affect us personally we can probably ignore it.'

    'Our generation will suffer less from the doings of evil men than from the silence of good men.' (Martin Luther King in a speech to the United States Churches.)

  7 Discuss the following:

    'From time to time a movement emerges whose aims are so inimical (i.e. the enemy of) to everything for which the Gospel stands that Christians must unite in opposition to it. This I believe is such a time and the National Front is such an organization.' (Colin Morris, President Methodist Conference, 1977.)

    Referring to the West Indians, an Anglican parish priest working in Bristol said: '. . . we are being invaded by one of the most loving, enriching and human peoples on the face of the earth . . . that's why British society is so frightened because it has become so uncaring, so materialistic and so competitive over the last 40 or 50 years . . .'. (Keith Kimber on BBC 'Heart of the Matter'.)

  8 What do you think about racial intermarriage? How does your age group's outlook on mixed marriages differ from that of the older generation? What are the difficulties which two people of different racial, cultural and even religious backgrounds must face if they are thinking of getting married?

9 How far do you think people accept the fact that Britain is a multi-racial society?

10 Do you think it is true that class division between rich and poor or middle- and lower-class people is the real cause of difficulty in our society rather than any question of colour?

4 The misuse of alcohol and drugs

In discussing those in need and at risk, we have so far seen that these people are usually the victims of circumstances outside their personal control. But now we must look at individuals who put themselves in danger through their own actions.

(a) Alcohol

Old and New Testament references

The practice of fermenting certain fruits (and in some cases vegetables) to produce alcoholic drinks goes back into the pre-history of mankind. The story of Noah contains the first *Old Testament* record of such an experiment. Noah planted a vineyard, drank the wine and became drunk in the process (Genesis 9:21). There were (and still are) many excellent vineyards in Israel and wine was in common use, especially as water could often be scarce in the dry season and was likely to be contaminated. The plentiful supply of grain and wine stood for material prosperity and ease (Genesis 27:28) especially in conditions where life was harsh and work unrewarding. Like certain herbs, wine could be used for relieving pain, and it was highly valued for bringing consolation and cheer (Judges 9:13). Nevertheless, Old Testament writers realized that excess wine was bad for man (Proverbs 23:20). The Law stated that at certain times it should be given up altogether; for example priests were forbidden to take wine during their period of service in the tabernacle (Leviticus 10:9). And as a sign of his dedication to God, any man who took the Nazarite vow forswore wine and strong drink; he even refused to eat fresh or dried grapes (Numbers 6:3). John the Baptist was probably a Nazarite (Luke 7:33).

The gospels show that wine was widely used in *New Testament* times. Jesus is said to have changed the water into wine at a wedding party to save the bridegroom from being embarrassed because he had not provided enough (John 2:3–10). Of course it is more important to understand the symbolism of this story than to try to judge whether it records accurately what actually took place, as Jesus is portrayed throughout the gospel of John as the giver of eternal life. The other gospels endorse this view. At his last meal before his death, Jesus took the wine, blessed it and gave it to his friends, using words which showed that the cup stood for the total offering of himself.

Today's society—some facts and figures

Excessive drinking is not new. Drunkenness has always been a problem in any culture where alcohol has been freely available. Nevertheless, although we have a wide variety of alternative drinks (including fresh water from the tap) which previous cultures could not obtain so readily, we are faced with a number of serious difficulties directly caused by alcohol abuse.

(i) **Drink and driving.** The cost of road accidents due to drink had already reached £100 million by 1976 (see report by the Blennerhassett Committee). Because even moderate amounts of alcohol reduce concentration and impair judgment, people should never drink and drive. The weekly magazine *Motor*, putting forward the case for stiffer drinking laws, reported:

> On a typical Saturday night three out of four drivers killed in road accidents have excess alcohol in their blood; at any time of the day or night, and on any day of the week, nearly half the drivers in their teens and twenties, killed in road accidents are over the limit (*Motor*, August 1980).

Drunken driving kills about 1200 people a year in this country.

(ii) **Drink and crime.** Chief police officers and the Parole Board say that alcohol is directly responsible for many violent crimes; about one third of murders follow episodes of drinking and two thirds of rapes are associated with alcohol. A leading psychiatrist claims that an alarming number of people aged between 16 and 20 are committing crimes under the influence of drink. He further reports that of the 5000 youths serving sentences, at least 25% are alcoholics or have a serious drink problem (*Observer*, January 1981). Drink is also involved in the offences of about 60% of the petty recidivists (those who habitually return to crime) who are a major part of the prison population.

(iii) **Drink and sport.** Excessive consumption of alcohol is seriously disrupting sport and transport. In 1980 Birmingham magistrates refused to issue an occasional drink licence for the Aston Villa football club because of increasing violence on the terraces, and British Rail have decided to ban drinks on sports specials because of the damage caused by vandalism.

(iv) **Drink and work.** It is estimated that up to £350 million per year is lost through drink problems, including absenteeism related to drink (National Association of Councils for Alcoholism Working Party Report: 'Alcohol and Work'). Furthermore, roughly three times as many accidents occur to those with drinking problems as to those without.

(v) **Drink and violence.** A study by the Royal College of Psychiatrists (1978) showed that there were drink problems associated with 50% of wife-battering cases. And the Council on Europe estimated that 60% of child cruelty came from a background of alcoholism.

(vi) **Drink and drugs.** There is danger in mixing drink with drugs, for example, by taking sleeping pills or anti-depressant tablets with an alcoholic drink. Coroners' inquests show that many people who seem to have had no intention of ending their lives, died as a result of taking barbiturates with alcohol.

(vii) **Drink and the family.** Fifty years ago most drinking took place in a public house setting and most of the drinkers were fully adult, but it is estimated that half the alcohol now sold is drunk in the home. There is a growing tendency to purchase alcohol at the local supermarket together with household food and to keep a stock of drink in the house. Alcohol can thus become easily available to children, who are forbidden by law to enter a public house and consume it.

If parents do not establish firm rules with regard to drinking some youngsters may begin a bad habit without properly realizing its harmful effects on their health and their future prospects. There is strong evidence to suggest that 18-year-old alcoholics are people who started to drink when they were 14 or under.

(viii) **Drink and health.** Medical research shows that too much alcohol can seriously damage a person's health, however we define the category 'too much'. For example, alcohol can cause stomach ulcers, kidney damage, serious and often fatal disease of the liver and in some cases deterioration of the brain cells. Heavy drinking can also lead to depression, anxiety, tremors and neurological disorders.

The Health Council's pamphlet 'Mother and Baby' specifically warns mothers that drinking is dangerous during pregnancy because alcohol may cause incalculable defects in the unborn child.

(ix) **Drink and money.** The drink trade is a very profitable business. In 1979 consumers spent about £10,200 million on alcohol. The trade itself laid out £50 million on advertising, and government revenue from duty on alcohol amounted to £2,500 million.

Definition and causes of alcohol abuse
It is known that the effect of alcohol on the body chemistry varies

widely with individuals. Some people are physically unable to drink anything intoxicating without feeling immediate consequences, while others can absorb a certain amount without harmful effects. So it is possible that a very small minority (perhaps 2%) should never take liquor at all because they are particularly susceptible to addiction.

We now recognize that there is a difference between the heavy drinker and the alcoholic, although one may lead to the other. The term alcoholic really applies to the person who is totally dependent on a supply of alcohol. The alcoholic has lost the power to choose whether to drink or not and is possessed by a constant craving for liquor. While there are degrees of alcoholism it is estimated that in 1980 there were some 740,000 people in the United Kingdom with a serious drinking problem.

Some experts compare alcoholism to a disease, others to a kind of allergy. The addiction can also be a symptom of an underlying mental illness. Whatever its cause, alcoholism results in impaired mental and physical health as well as interfering, often with tragic consequences, in personal relationships, in family life and employment prospects. Once an individual becomes an alcoholic, there is no way out of the situation other than by giving up drink altogether. There can be no return to occasional or moderate drinking, as the addict who takes one drink restarts the chain reaction of craving and total dependence.

Like all other personal and social problems, the question of drink misuse is complex. We cannot specify one cause for the greatly increased consumption of alcohol but should rather discuss the several factors which contribute to irresponsible drinking.

(i) There are those who seek solace in drink because of personal and psychological problems. Sometimes loneliness, anxiety, or a feeling of inadequacy may drive a person to escape into a state of intoxication—a temporary way of easing his difficulties. But drink does not offer any permanent solution. Alcohol is basically a depressant and may leave the drinker in a far worse state of mind than before, although initially it produces a feeling of exhilaration.

(ii) People may be led into heavy drinking because of social pressures. A group may meet primarily in order to drink, rather than to eat or talk. When this happens young people can fall into the habit of taking far too much alcohol because they want to be one of the crowd and are afraid of seeming odd.

(iii) Adverse social factors can drive the individual to drink. When people are bored, frustrated and out of work, alcohol may be seen as one of the few pleasures left in life.

(iv) Some experts blame the recent rise in consumption on the drink trade's massive advertising campaigns. The inexperienced and impressionable are especially at risk, but inevitably we are all affected by the prevailing climate of opinion. In our restless and fast changing way of life, people readily accept that a drink makes it easier to relax and be merry.

Christian attitudes

Obviously anything which disrupts family life, destroys personal relationships, job prospects and the individual's own sense of dignity is deeply distressing to Christians. They will therefore be found working to eradicate the causes of drink dependence and amongst those who are helping the addict overcome his addiction.

Christians disagree, however, about the best methods of tackling our present difficulties. In view of the enormous suffering it causes, some Christians feel that they should totally abstain from alcoholic drink. They believe there should be more control over the total amount of alcohol that is available in the community. And they consider that the government is not doing enough to help cut down consumption by raising the price of alcohol. The great 19th-century Temperance movements showed how deeply both Protestant and Catholic social reformers felt about the evils of drink. The same kind of feeling is being expressed today as the size of the present alcohol problem becomes apparent.

Other Christians maintain that moderate and responsible drinking is the best approach to this question. They do not believe that a drink in a pub with friends or a glass of wine taken at home over a meal with guests and family is harmful, but quite the reverse. Some nutritionists have argued that quality wine and other drinks such as milk stout are a valuable supplementary source of minerals and food and that taken sensibly they are an aid to good health. Christians who accept this argument think that, while the vulnerable should be protected and everybody should be educated about the possible risks involved in taking alcohol, the only workable way forward in an adult community is to advocate and demonstrate the responsible use of alcohol.

All Christians will agree, however, that consideration for others is of primary importance. Thus the total abstainer (teetotaller) will take into account the view that a negative attitude is not enough, whilst the moderate or occasional drinker will weigh the possibility that his own moderation could be misunderstood and lead another to excess.

Discussion and work

1 What do you think is the difference between addiction and indulgence?

2 Discuss, with examples, the variety of causes which may lead

someone to start drinking too much. What is your personal definition of 'too much' alcohol? What system of values would you apply when analysing the effect a drink of alcohol has upon an individual?

3 Some people describe getting drunk as having a 'good time'. What leads them to such an opinion? In what sense could being drunk be described as having a 'bad time'?

4 Discuss the propositions that teenagers start drinking to impress their contemporaries; to show that they are grown up; to appear tough; to be socially acceptable; or because drinking makes them feel good. Are the young people you know well informed about the long-term effects of too much alcohol?

5 How would you define responsible drinking, bearing in mind that the National Youth Temperance Council claims that 1 in 12 social drinkers will end up addicted?

6 What is your personal opinion about total abstention or moderate and occasional drinking as the best Christian approach? Give reasons for your acceptance of one and rejection of the other.

7 The social cost of excess drinking is very high. It makes industry and commerce less efficient and takes up time and space in hospitals, health and social services, to say nothing of the danger it creates on the road. How much control do you think there should be on the sale of alcoholic drinks? Before answering, bear in mind the fact that total prohibition in the USA did not prove very effective and caused considerable illegal traffic in alcohol.

8 Do you think drunks should be sent to prison? How else should we deal with men and women who habitually drink too much? If you knew someone with a drink problem how would you set about helping that person?

9 Alcoholics Anonymous is one of several voluntary societies doing valuable work among alcoholics. Find out all you can about the way this group of people work. What do you know about other voluntary agencies in this field?

10 It is comparatively easy to condemn excessive drinking, but should we not also consider very critically those who make money out of other people's weakness? The drink trade spends millions of pounds a year on advertising, and although the British Code of Advertising Practice has recently revised the wording of the Alcohol Appendix in recognition of their social responsibility towards consumers, some experts feel government departments should have more control over alcohol advertising. Do you agree?

(b) Drugs

From time immemorial, mankind's need of pain killers, soothing potions and ways of escape from harsh, barren reality, has led people to use certain kinds of plant drugs. Traditionally these have been of three basic types: opiates (i.e. sedatives, or calming substances) named after the opium poppy which grows in the hot dry countries of Asia; stimulants, such as cocaine, the product of the South American coca shrub; and hallucinogens (or 'mind benders'), the best known of which is marihuana, hashish or cannabis, a product of the Indian hemp plant. The term 'drug' used to be restricted to plant substances producing one of these effects; in modern usage, however, any chemical substance which alters the functioning of the body or mind can be termed a drug.

Medical use of drugs

Narcotics (i.e. painkilling drugs so named because they can produce drowsiness) are used every day in hospitals to relieve suffering. Besides this, doctors regularly prescribe barbiturates (chemical sedatives) and tranquilizers to patients with sleeping problems, nervous tension and other allied difficulties. There are more than 60 different kinds of drugs whose main effect is to stimulate the system, the most widely used being the amphetamines or 'pep pills'. In certain cases of mental depression and anxiety, the hallucinogens drugs are given under strict medical supervision.

Misuse arises when any drug is taken without proper medical direction or supervision, often in ignorance of the long-term highly detrimental consequences to the drug-taker's physical and mental well-being.

The law

Although there was some misuse of the pain-killing drugs in the 18th and 19th centuries, it was not until 1920 that the first dangerous drugs legislation was passed. There followed a series of restrictions on the import, export and manufacture, sale, distribution, supply and possession of such drugs as opium and its derivatives (morphine and heroin), coca leaves, cocaine and cannabis.

Despite the 1920 law, continuing drug abuse created widespread concern. People recognized that drug misusers could become addicts and, in particular, society became aware of the great harm being done to young people. All this finally resulted in the 1971 Misuse of Drugs Act and the creation of an Advisory Council to deal with the various related problems.

The 1971 Act names three categories of drugs which it is illegal to supply or possess without medical supervision. These are listed in order of their power to harm misusers.

Class A includes opium, morphine, heroin, methadone and other opiate drugs placed under the strictest control by the United Nations Single Convention on Narcotic Drugs, 1961. It also includes mescalin (a hallucinogen derived from the Mexican peyote cactus), injectable amphetamines and other hallucinogens such as LSD (Lysergic Acid Diethylamide). The World Health Organization regards LSD as particularly dangerous in its effects on the brain.

Class B covers opiate drugs, including codeine, which are less strictly controlled by the Single Convention; certain stimulant drugs of the amphetamine group; cannabis and cannabis resin.

Class C contains other drugs which, judged on present experience, are thought to be less dangerous than those already mentioned, although no drug is completely free from side effects.

The Act distinguishes very clearly between the offence of 'trafficking' drugs and the offence of possessing them. The former carries much more severe penalties. The maximum penalty for illegally supplying drugs in categories A and B is 14 years imprisonment. This is double the maximum sentence for possessing the same drugs.

Treatment

Arising out of the report of the Rolleston Committee in 1926, drug addicts in this country were regarded as patients in need of treatment—including the continuing prescription of heroin where appropriate—rather than as criminals. At that time only a tiny group of people were involved in drug addiction.

The 1960s saw a great increase in drug misuse. The Brain Committee which was set up to review the situation and which reported in 1961 and 1965, recommended that known heroin and cocaine addicts should be registered and that treatment of addiction be restricted to a limited number of doctors, most of whom would be working in specialized clinics. These recommendations were accepted and today several National Health Service hospitals contain special treatment centres under the clinical direction of a consultant psychiatrist.

The law recognizes that if we absolutely refuse to supply addicts, we encourage the black market. In fact, of course, imported heroin and a growing range of drugs do come into the country through illegal channels despite the activities of the drug squad.

The complete cutting off of all drugs at once is called 'cold turkey'. Serious withdrawal symptoms are experienced, especially by heroin and cocaine addicts. The addict will experience severe muscular cramps, bad pain in arms and legs, violent and frequent sickness and diarrhoea. Intense itching, hysteria and periods of great mental unbalance can also occur. Humane considerations demand that addicts should not be subjected to this kind of suffering so the treatment actually given is of two kinds. First, there is a 'maintenance therapy' for those addicts unwilling to undergo withdrawal treatment. The aim is to stabilize the addict by providing a small and non-progressive amount of the drug in order to help him function reasonably normally in the community until he comes to feel he may be able to accept withdrawal treatment. When a new patient presents himself at an out-patient clinic for this kind of maintenance therapy, the centre tries to satisfy itself that the patient is genuinely addicted and that he is not already obtaining drugs from another centre.

Second, the purpose of the in-patient centre is to provide treatment for those patients willing to be withdrawn from their dependence. After the detoxification process, rehabilitation help is essential as the former addict now has to learn to live a meaningful life without the false prop of the drug.

If an addict is sent to prison for being unlawfully in possession of a drug, he will then be given compulsory withdrawal treatment under medical supervision.

By the end of 1977 registered heroin and cocaine addicts numbered 2023, but according to a report by the Standing Conference on Drug Abuse (*Observer* January 1981) there are known to be double that number now and at least another 10,000 unregistered addicts.

Prevention

If society is to prevent the spread of drug abuse, it is very important to increase knowledge about its potential dangers. Heroin, for example, poisons the liver and kidneys, leads to malnutrition, infections, tuberculosis and death, frequently within three to five years, or suddenly from too large a dose. Those addicts who inject intravenously suffer from skin infections and abscesses, septicaemia and infective hepatitis (disease of the liver). LSD or 'Acid' is obtained from ergot (or diseased) fungus on rye. The Greek word 'lysis' means dissolution or breaking down and in medical terms it is used to denote the breakdown of a cell or other structure. This drug is potent and can produce definite mental disorders, which in some cases are incurable. Excessive doses of barbiturates, especially if taken with alcohol, can lead to death. Severe drug abuse almost always leads to personality changes, often to a ruined career and a broken family. The drug abuser is also prone to periods of crisis and deep depression when suicide seems the only answer. By becoming an addict, a person can place himself in the category of suicide risk.

Another aspect to consider is the availability of drugs. The law quite rightly exercises strict control on the supply of harmful drugs; nevertheless, an extremely profitable black market exists. The powerful and unscrupulous people who control illegal drug syndicates do not take drugs themselves, but use addicts as 'pushers', relying on the fact that these pushers need the money to buy their own supply of drugs. Customs officials have the responsibility of preventing illegal material coming into the country, but the police deal with drugs once they are here. All the 43 police forces in England and Wales have full-time specialist drug officers and drug squads, although some experts in drug addiction feel that these specialist branches are undermanned.

The medical profession has now recognized that over-prescribing legally accepted drugs can cause considerable harm. Realizing that patients may become very dependent on their pills, a group of doctors has actually launched a campaign to restrict the use of barbiturates (CURB). Another group in America, disillusioned by the side effects of drugs, is promoting 'holistic medicine'—aimed at health for the whole person.

Christian attitudes

All the evidence suggests that drugs, taken without proper precautions and knowledge, diminish a person's capabilities, render him unable to lead a truly creative life and often ruin his relationships with other people. A Christian approach should always be compassionate and this means we must try to understand what leads a person to drug dependence and experimentation.

The causes are many. A person living in extremely stressful circumstances may take refuge in drugs. Boredom, frustration or unemployment may lead an individual to try something new, especially if he is introduced to drugs by a friend. He may be made to feel foolish, unsophisticated, old-fashioned, or even cowardly if he refuses to try drugs; so he gives way in order to be one of the group. To smoke heroin casually with a group of friends may prove an exciting first experience but after a few weeks of regular smoking other interests fade into the background and eventually the reality of addiction begins to bite. Even an experiment with a relatively harmless drug may lead on to other kinds of drug with definite addictive qualities.

The addict may have deep emotional problems which are unresolved; under the stimulation of drugs the mind thinks itself capable of dealing with these difficulties but the relief is false. When the drug wears off, the problem is still there and nothing has been changed for the better.

The Christian is also concerned to distinguish between a genuine religious experience and that which a drug may provide. Some drug users have claimed that through drugs they have almost reached God; all their senses were heightened and the world was filled with glory. There are important differences between a true mystical apprehension of reality and the kind of consciousness reached through drugs. In the first place, the mystic has practised long to achieve that peak experience. Second, where religious illumination is given, the mystic recognizes it as a gift from God and does not hanker to repeat the insight over and over again. The moment marks a step in his constant journey along the road that always leads to a closer union with the divine. By contrast, the drug-induced experience is a short cut and the drug taker is inevitably spiritually unprepared. Therefore when it is over he longs for a repetition which he may never have, for drugs can more often transport the individual into a kind of hell than heaven. The drug experience does not enable the user to make any spiritual progress because it is artificially induced. It does not strengthen faith or enable the person to live a better life afterwards. It is completely unrelated to moral insight or behaviour, another hallmark of the true mystical experience.

Christians are especially involved with the after-care and rehabilitation of drug addicts. When a person has received hospital treatment he needs encouragement to leave the drug sub-culture group to which he formerly belonged and to develop new social contacts. Without this, treatment of the addiction cannot be successful. A great deal of social and family case-work needs to be done in which friends, employers and voluntary agencies are involved. There are special hostels, but not enough of them, for addicts who have completed hospital treatment and many of these hostels are run by religious organizations using various rehabilitation methods. But they are all very short of money. Christians, in common with all those professional and voluntary workers who come into very close contact with drug abuse, view the present rise in addiction with deep distress. They further urge the government to look again more closely into present policies and to make more resources available to those who are already heavily engaged in dealing with this tragic situation.

Discussion and work

1 Discuss these two propositions, both in general terms and in relation to drugs:

(a) my personality is my own and I may do whatever I like with it;

(b) no man is an island unto himself.

2 Do you think the stresses and conditions of modern life encourage dependence on drugs?

3 Should drug offenders be put in prison? Distinguish carefully between those who are the victims of drug abuse and those who market drugs for the sake of making a great deal of money.

4 What is the difference between drug taking and drug addiction?

5 Before you read this chapter, how much information had you been given in school about the known effects of drug taking? What information have your friends in other schools been given? Do you think there is sufficient education about this area of experience?

6 Many people believe 'there is a pill for every ill'. Do you agree? Or do you think that our society depends too much upon pills to solve all our problems?

7 In 1965 Britain was one of 38 countries or states which signed the United Nations Agreement not to legalize cannabis (pot, weed, grass), but pressure is being put upon the government to change its policy. Much controversy surrounds the subject of cannabis because, although it is not in itself addictive, many experts believe that it leads the way to dependence on hard drugs. Discuss some of the arguments both for and against legalizing cannabis. If cannabis were legalized, what age limit would be desirable?

8 Discuss the statement 'drug misusers are people with social, psychological and sometimes health problems, who must be helped accordingly'. Is enough being done to deal with these problems?

9 Look up the work of one of the voluntary agencies involved in after-care work with drug offenders.

10 Discuss the reasons which might lead a person to experiment in drugs. What solutions other than drugs might be found to some of the problems listed as causes of drug experimentation and addiction?

11 Addicts admit that they feel a great need to talk to and associate with other drug addicts, hence they inevitably form a drug sub-culture. How much influence do you think this sub-culture exerts on young people, especially those who want to be part of something unconventional? What is the relationship between the pop scene and drug culture?

12 Can religion help the drug taker? What should the Christian do to tackle the causes of drug taking?

5 Law and order

One of the most significant characteristics of human beings is that they are capable of making independent moral choices. This capacity has led to the formation of moral codes and laws which are the foundation of all cultures whether primitive or advanced. Generally speaking, most people in any given society obey the laws of the land, thus making community life possible. For many different reasons, however, there is always a minority which does not conform; consequently they suffer various degrees of social isolation, depending on the nature of their non-conformity and the threat which it poses to the well-being of the majority. In a sophisticated culture like our own, none of these issues is simple. For the sake of clarity, we shall first look at the biblical background, then the present structure of criminal justice in Britain, next the dilemmas we face today, and finally modern Christian attitudes.

Biblical background

The Jewish people based their whole religion on three articles of faith: the Lord God was Creator of the Universe; he was the Lord of history; and he had made his will known to his chosen people by giving them the Law. According to the Exodus story, Moses received the Ten Commandments on Mount Sinai. These commandments may be regarded as the core of the matter, although the law books of the Old Testament contain many other ritual and ethical regulations upon which both the nation's and the individual's life should be based. In the centuries following Moses, prophetic voices added fresh insights and further understanding of God's will and purpose. A considerable oral tradition grew up alongside the sacred scriptures. Based on constant study of the law it related legal principles to the changing circumstances of the nation's life. The community was responsible for punishing law breakers; blasphemers, for instance, were stoned to death. In later times a court of elders gave judgment and officials executed the penalties. The Jewish people also believed that God punished the evil doer, either directly by sending misfortune or illness, or indirectly through God's appointed rulers.

In Jesus' day there was much discussion as to whether ritual and moral laws were of the same importance. When Jesus was asked which he thought had priority, he summed up the whole duty of man in words taken from Leviticus and Deuteronomy:

The first is, 'Hear, O Israel: The Lord our God,
the Lord is one; and you shall love the Lord
your God with all your heart and with all your

soul, and with all your mind, and with all your strength.' The second is this, 'You shall love your neighbour as yourself.' There is no other commandment greater than these (Mark 12:*29—31*).

The basis of Jewish ethical law is the recognition that man owes his highest allegiance to God and therefore must deal justly with his fellow human beings. The striking element in Jesus' teaching, however, is his emphasis on compassion and forgiveness and the importance of inner motivation (Matthew 5:*21—22*; *38—48*).

The present structure of criminal law in Britain

The stated purpose of British criminal justice is to protect the community both from disorder and anti-social behaviour. It also aims to ensure that those who break the law are detected and dealt with according to well-defined legal principles. There are four stages in this process: first, laws are passed defining crime, i.e. action against the common good, and courts are set up to deal with offenders; second, steps are taken, usually by the police, to prevent crime and enforce the law; third, a court of law decides the guilt or innocence of a suspected offender and selects the appropriate sentence for those found guilty; fourth, the convicted offenders are punished.

Responsibility for administering the entire system rests with the Lord Chancellor, the Home Secretary and the Secretaries of State for Scotland and Northern Ireland.

Crown courts are presided over by a High Court judge, a full-time circuit judge or a part-time recorder. Technically judges are appointed by the Crown, i.e. the Prime Minister recommends them to the Queen, but they are completely independent of the government. No minister has any control over them, nor do they take part in politics. Another important factor in the Crown court is the presence of a jury. Ordinary men and women on the electoral register can be called upon to form an independent panel who decide the guilt or innocence of people accused of the most serious crimes.

Magistrates' courts deal with about 98% of criminal cases in England and Wales and carry out preliminary investigations into the more serious offences which are later heard in a Crown court. There are 300 courts throughout the country served by 23,500 lay (i.e. without professional training) magistrates or justices of the peace. Three magistrates usually sit together on the Bench to hear cases and they are advised on points of the law by legally qualified justices' clerks.

A *Coroner's court* holds an inquest on, i.e. investigates, violent, unnatural or sudden death where the cause is unknown.

The criminal law of this country *presumes that a person is inno-cent* until he has been proved guilty beyond 'reasonable doubt'. Every accused person has the right to employ a legal adviser for his defence and if he cannot afford to pay his legal costs he may be granted legal aid from public funds. If found guilty, more often than not he has the right of appeal to a higher court and finally to the Crown.

Except where children or state security may be involved, pro-ceedings are usually held in public and are normally reported in the press. The most common punishment is a fine. A young offender, however, may be put under the supervision of a social worker or probation officer or even required to undertake some community service work. He can also be sent to a borstal or detention centre. Adults who have been sentenced to custodial treatment (i.e. prison) will find themselves in one of several categories of prison. This will depend on the seriousness of their crime and whether their escape might be a public danger.

The whole question of enforcing the law of the land depends upon the co-operation and consent of the majority of citizens. In this country the police force is relatively small, officers do not nor-mally carry firearms and their powers are strictly limited. There are 43 police forces in England and Wales and women form part of the force.

The Probation and After-care services aim to provide a wel-fare service in prison and to help rehabilitate offenders when they have been released either on parole or when their sentence has run its course. Many voluntary organizations, especially ones with a Christian basis, work with the statutory authorities, taking a par-ticular interest in resettlement after prison.

Our present dilemmas
The harsh reality which faces our society is this; despite the dedi-cation and hard work of legislators, the legal profession, magis-trates, police, probation officers and the prison service, crime continues to increase at an alarming rate. Between 1967 and 1977 the number of indictable offences nearly doubled. Although most crimes were property offences, recorded crimes of violence against the person have also increased.

Two further points must also be made. As a result of the troubles in Northern Ireland and several acts of terrorism in this country, Parliament found it necessary to bring in the Prevention of Ter-rorism (Temporary Provision) Act in 1976. Society needs to review this act constantly and to note its effects on civil liberties.

Second, because of the increase in crime, our prisons are very overcrowded. Many were built over 100 years ago and are not satisfactory by modern standards. The high and increasing cost of maintaining prisons is also a matter of concern.

These present questions affect every citizen both young and old. All kinds of organizations within the legal profession and independent groups such as the Howard League for Penal Reform and the National Council for Civil Liberties, as well as private individuals, publish articles, pamphlets and books suggesting further measures and reforms. The government also regularly consults these different bodies and from time to time institutes a Royal Commission such as the one on Criminal Procedure which published its report in January 1981.

Broadly speaking there are two main lines of approach. First, there are those who might be called traditionalists. They believe that the only way to cope with rising crime rates is by stricter controls and harsher punishments. They believe the police force must be strengthened and prisoners subjected to greater discipline. Within this group there are some who want to bring back corporal punishment, i.e. the birch for young offenders, and capital punishment, i.e. the death sentence for convicted murderers, more especially if a policeman has been killed in the course of his duty. Many think that the sole purpose of the criminal system is to punish the offender thus protecting society as a whole by deterring the criminal.

The other section of opinion might be called reformers. They believe that fear of punishment does not really deter a person from a criminal act. In the main, people break laws because they think they can get away with it and, of course, very many crimes do go undetected. The lawbreaker views criminal justice like the heavy smoker, who thinks lung cancer will always catch other people, or the reckless driver, who is convinced he will not have an accident. The reformers want investigation into the causes of crime. They believe anti-social behaviour can stem from all kinds of industrial and economic problems such as unemployment and poverty. They doubt whether the present prison system can justifiably claim to rehabilitate a criminal and they believe that harsher police and prison procedures can harm those who have to enforce them, as well as the criminals themselves.

Of course the views of many individuals do not fit neatly into either the traditionalist or the reforming category but are a mixture of the two. What matters is that we all find out as much as we can about the way our legal system works and consider the issues of law and order instead of simply leaving it all to the experts.

Christian attitudes

Christians disagree about these matters, as they do about other important topics. Some base their ideas mainly on Old Testament teaching; they see punishment as a means of teaching morality and fully accept the state's right to impose penalties on those who break the law. But as Christians they commit themselves to soften the harsher effects of the penal code and to prevent its possible misuse. Some may even believe that the legal system is an instrument of the will of God. Other Christians have a more radical approach. They believe that the fierce and competitive search for material wealth creates a society that encourages crime. In their view the Christian ideal should not be a community of fearful conformists but of truly adult people who take responsibility for their own actions. They do not expect people to change their ways through fear, control or compulsion, but by recognizing and therefore admitting to the effects of their own actions upon others, especially those who matter to them. They argue that Jesus showed we must always treat people with love and compassion. This is the hard option not the soft option, because it means we must all change our attitude towards the person who has opted out of society and ceased to identify with the well-being of the community. The criminal may break the law because he is sick in mind or greatly deprived or incompetent or bitterly resentful, but whatever his reason he needs help, just as his victim needs compensation and society protection.

Discussion and work

1 Discuss the propositions:
  (a) society gets the criminals it deserves;
  (b) violence breeds violence;
  (c) you can't be both merciful and just.

2 The main concerns of the police force are crime prevention, crime investigation, preservation of the peace and bringing offenders to trial. Do you think all these aims can be carried out by the same force? Are we asking too much of the police if we expect them both to prevent crime and also bring to trial those who commit it?

3 What image do you think the police force has today in your age group? In your neighbourhood? In other age groups? In other areas of your community? In rural areas? In the inner city?

4 How successful do you think prison is in reforming criminals? Find out current statistics of the proportion who return to prison for a second term. What criticism can be made of our present prisons? In what ways are some of them out-of-date?

What is meant by an open prison? A closed prison? A maximum security prison?

5 Try and find out about the work of some of the great Christian prison reformers of the past such as Elizabeth Fry. Look into the work of one of the Christian organizations today which concentrate on the aftercare and rehabilitation of ex-prisoners, helping them to find employment and accommodation.

6 To what extent do you think punishment prevents people from committing crime?

7 Do you think that rule by fear of consequences is the effective way of running a school community? Can we compare the working of a school community with the community at large?

8 Do you think that any of this country's laws are unjust? Discuss examples.

9 Should offences such as drunkenness be punished by some other method than prison? Does this apply to any other offences currently carrying prison sentences?

10 Draw up and discuss the arguments both for and against capital punishment. You will find that murder statistics since the abolition of capital punishment in 1969 do not much help the case for either side.

11 Discuss the proposition 'True justice is achieved when everyone's needs are equally met'.

12 Which is more important, compensation for the victim of a crime or punishment of the criminal? Or is it a mistake to make such comparisons?

13 Find out what you can about voluntary organizations which concentrate on helping the victims of crime.

14 Discuss the following statement: 'The subject matters intensely to every one of us, to you and to me, to every citizen, for it concerns our liberty and our rights; the way a free civilized society ought to treat people in the area of criminal justice.' Sir Cyril Philips, chairman of the Royal Commission on Criminal Procedure in his introduction to the Commission's report.

6 Mass communication

(a) The media

We shall limit our discussion of the media to the press, radio and television.

(i) **The press.** Before the invention of printing, the means of communication in a society were limited to the spoken word or hand written instructions. Books and pamphlets were relatively scarce. With the coming of the printing presses everything changed, including the degree of literacy (i.e. the ability to read and write) amongst ordinary people. In this country the first *newspapers* were published in the 17th century and, despite the state's early attempts to exercise direct or indirect control over their contents through taxation and restrictive laws, they have always been independent. The money needed to found and produce a newspaper has come from private sources.

Earlier in this century many national presses were owned by wealthy individuals such as Lord Beaverbrook, founder of the *Daily Express*. Nowadays, mainly owing to immense production costs, more national newspapers are the property of trusts or big commercial groups, although individual 'press barons' do still exist. What goes into the paper, however, and how the news is presented, depends largely on the editorial staff and the journalists, although the owners have some control over the general policy. Of course once an individual paper has built up a certain reputation, it cannot easily abandon this outlook as readers expect this emphasis and buy the paper because of it.

A newspaper depends not only upon sales but also upon advertising for its survival, but in the end it stands or falls by the number and preference of its readers, since they can choose which paper to buy and can withdraw their custom at any time. Britain possesses relatively few national morning papers and what there are may be divided into two categories—popular and quality. There are many daily evening papers and hundreds of different kinds of weekly publications ranging from the national Sunday press to local journals and specialized papers covering such interests as music, religion, sport and many hobbies.

A free press is a vital ingredient in any democratic society. People must be kept informed of what is going on and they must be able to make independent judgments, as far as possible, about important issues. The force of public opinion is a major factor in our democratic way of life. In the USSR by contrast the press is an agent of government control and does not publish the views of those who criticize the régime. But where criticisms can be voiced and heard, the way is open for creative change. Public outcry over some gross mismanagement or injustice can alter the course of events. Newspapers have always believed they had the right to criticize government policies, although in times of national emergency they have been guided by considerations of security. They have also believed they should uncover or expose scandalous conduct or dishonest dealings. Although in practice journalism may at times be guilty of seriously distorting facts, its lofty aim is to find out the truth, and its job is primarily to inform and only secondly to entertain the general public. Behind the ideal of a free press lies the conviction that if people are truly informed, democracy has a healthy chance of working.

(ii) **Radio and television.** The position of radio and television can be compared with that of the press, although the state itself owns the British Broadcasting Corporation with its two television channels, four national radio networks and 20 local radio stations. Its charter from the government is renewed at 10-year intervals, but the BBC depends on licence fees for its income. Because the state owns the Corporation and all its equipment, the BBC has to fulfil certain obligations, such as giving an impartial day-by-day account, prepared by professional reporters, of the proceedings of both Houses of Parliament. The BBC, however, is in no way an instrument of government and its staff make their own decisions about programmes and presentation. This independence sometimes results in bad relations between the BBC and the political party in power at the time.

The Independent Broadcasting Authority Act of 1973 established the rights of Independent television (two channels in 1982) and local radio networks. At present there are 19 independent local radio stations run on the same lines as independent television. The Independent Broadcasting Authority (IBA) is entirely financed by advertising. Legislation lays down, however, that advertisements must be clearly distinguishable from regular programmes and prohibits advertisers from sponsoring particular programmes. The programme companies sell time for advertising and advertisements may only be inserted at the beginning or end of programmes or during the 'natural breaks'. All advertising must comply with the IBA Code of Advertising Standards and Practice.

At present 95% of British homes have television but the radio is still very popular.

Problems
The benefits of broadcasting are obvious. It is a major source of information and entertainment. Further, its educational potential is enormous. Since the foundation of the Open University in 1971, degree courses have been taught by radio and television, while there are many excellent programmes for schools. Nonetheless, some people see grave dangers in television's all-pervading influence, especially as it enters the privacy of the home and its daily showings are readily available to the very young, the immature, the impressionable and the emotionally or mentally unstable person.

The three main areas of concern are as follows: first, the degree

94

and frequency of violence shown on the screen and its particular influence on young people; second, the possibility that social and moral values may be undermined by controversial plays and documentaries; third, the corrupting effect of continual advertising, which encourages people to equate happiness with possessions thus fostering greed and envy.

Both the government and the television companies themselves are aware of their responsibilities to the general viewer. In 1963 the government appointed the Television Research Committee to examine the part television plays in influencing attitudes. In brief, the Committee's conclusions were that the amount of influence depends on the particular individual's response. The IBA also gave a large sum of money to help set up the Centre for Mass Communications Research at Leicester University. Research must continue, however, as there is considerable support (especially from work done in the USA where programmes are much more violent than in Britain) for the view that television violence does affect some children, making them more aggressive than they would otherwise have been.

With regard to censorship and advertising, see below.

Christian attitudes

Christian attitudes towards the means of mass communication are as varied as their views about other issues. The particular problems we face are shaped by the industrialization of our society and man's technological skill. In going back to the insights of Jesus, the Christian will aim to clear his thinking on matters of principle rather than detailed procedure. We may perhaps summarize three basic strands of commitment.

First, the Christian is committed to safeguarding the dignity and integrity of the individual. He endorses the view that a free press is an essential part of democracy while believing that freedom must always go hand in hand with responsibility. There should be no infringement of people's right to privacy, especially in matters of grief. The Christian believes that man should free himself from overwhelming self-regard, so that he is free to give himself to others. He will therefore criticize the media when they pursue their right to know only in order to sell more of their product, especially if this is done by exposing people to further suffering.

Second, the Christian is committed to protecting and helping the weaker members of society, whether these are vulnerable children or those young people and adults who, for various reasons, are easily influenced and even unbalanced. He therefore supports honest research into the effects of television and the general reporting of violence, cruelty and crime. As television is a comparatively recent institution, parents must be helped to take a responsible attitude towards viewing—to recognize that it can become compulsive or addictive and to regulate their own and their families' lives accordingly.

Third, the Christian will want to encourage all that is positive and creative in the media as a means of enriching and ennobling life. To this end Christians should be encouraged to work in the media. They should be amongst those who plan the programmes, or write the articles, plays, documentaries and reports which flood into our homes every day.

Discussion and work
1 What do you look for in a newspaper—the gossip column, the horoscopes, the leader article, the photographs, the foreign news, the sports page? In what way does the newspaper your parents take reflect your own interests and tastes? Do you ever write to the local paper about an issue on which you feel strongly?
2 Give examples of recent stories in which you consider that a journalist may have acted irresponsibly. Discuss with the group examples of good resulting from a newspaper's disclosures. You might consider the case of the *Sunday Times* which in October 1971 published evidence that the interrogation methods used in the treatment of internees in Northern Ireland could be a threat to their sanity.
3 How much television viewing do you do? Of what kind? Do you find it interferes with your homework pattern or the possibility of entertaining your friends?
4 Do you think there is too much violence shown on the screen? The BBC seems to think that late night viewing begins at 9 pm by which time most children will be in bed. Their most controversial items occur after this time. Do you think this is a realistic assessment for people of your age-group? Should people in your age-group be protected viewers? If not, why not?
5 Both networks pay a great deal of attention to market research. Have you thought of writing to either the BBC or ITV expressing your views of broadcasting?
6 Discuss and compare these two views:
   (a) Since television came into people's homes in 1951, the number of crimes with violence has multiplied more than 10 times. This must be a case of cause and effect. Violence on the screen has created a more violent society.
   (b) Television's main function is to reflect the attitudes of society rather than mould them. As we live in a violent

society it is inevitable that violence should be portrayed on the screen.

7 Do you think people can become addicted to television? Is it true that too much television viewing makes people passive and less personally creative, so that they wait to be entertained instead of finding their own amusements?

(b) Advertising

The practice of advertising goods both for buying and selling is long established. The use of mass circulation magazines, newspapers and broadcasting, however, has made advertising a major industry rather than a matter of local handbills. And more recently government and interested groups have realized that advertising is a useful means of relaying information to the general public. It is interesting to note that the government is the largest advertiser in Britain, spending millions of pounds each year.

As an industry, advertising has its own professional organizations and code of practice, while the customer is also protected by legislation. The Trades Description Act prohibits false or misleading statements about goods, prices and services, while the Fair Trading Act (1973) established the office of Director-General of Fair Trading whose job is to keep a close watch over the consumers' interests.

The pros and cons of advertising

Obviously in a free society people should be able to choose the kind of goods and services they want, and monopolies in particular items of supply should be avoided. But Christians may question the whole ethic which underlies our consumer society. As we live in a world of finite resources and gross inequalities, many Christians believe that we need a complete and radical change of direction. People should not be continually persuaded by expert techniques to buy things they do not really want and certainly do not need. Some of the country's best brains are used to sell fringe commodities and an immense amount of money is spent in market research to find out what will appeal to us. Particular products are associated with attractive qualities such as masculinity, or femininity, or social status, even though there may not be enough real difference between, for instance, one brand of cigarettes or petrol or toothpaste and another, to justify the rival claims of the competing companies.

Christians feel particular concern at the commercialization of sex. Many products are advertised in a sexual context so that their appeal is quite falsely linked to sexual attraction. Often, too, man's less generous instincts, such as greed and rivalry are exploited by advertising.

When commercial television first appeared, critics were afraid that because the advertiser wanted to reach the widest possible audience, the programme would be trivial and on the lowest level of entertainment. Although there may be some justice in these criticisms, ITV has produced excellent informative and educational material. Nevertheless, to be entirely dependent upon advertising revenue can put undue pressure on the programme directors.

Advertising and the Third World
Most advertisers reply to their critics that the general public's robust common sense guards it against advertising excesses; but although a sophisticated people may be able to cope with the subtle half-truths which are often the stock in trade of the advertiser, it is completely unethical to apply those same methods to a different culture. For example, breast milk substitutes are quite unsuitable in countries where water is contaminated, poverty is rampant and illiteracy is high. Even a malnourished mother can produce the safest milk for her baby herself and any extra food should be taken by her. The sale of baby milk formulae in developing countries is not a form of aid, but it is commercially profitable. Oxfam and War on Want have been drawing public attention to this issue which was on the agenda for the 1981 World Health Assembly. It has been estimated that 10 million babies are ill and dying from man-made disease.

The World Health Organization is also very concerned with the dramatic increase in smoking in the developing countries. In a review of their 1980 campaign 'Smoking or Health—the Choice is Yours', WHO say that this sharp rise is due to the 'imitation of life-styles practised in industrial countries, deliberately promoted by tobacco companies'. Inevitably smoking-related diseases are increasing too. It appears that advertisers are successfully persuading people in developing countries that affluent people smoke, although in fact non-smokers now outnumber smokers in Britain, America, Sweden and other Western democracies. Furthermore, while most Western countries have strict controls over tobacco advertising, the same is not true of many Third World countries.

Discussion and work
1 How much do you think you are influenced by the advertisements you read and see on television? Does having a wide range of products help you to make a sensible choice or fill you with

resentment if you have not got the money to buy the best on the market?

2 Discuss several examples of government advertising. How influential and useful do you consider them to be?

3 The voluntary Code of Advertising Practice accepted by industry placed cigarette advertising in a category subject to special rules. This is why manufacturers print government health warnings on cigarette packets and ban cigarette advertisements on television. Do you think these restrictions on potentially harmful products are sufficient, or is this a case in which there should be no advertising at all?

4 How many advertisements can you think of which use sex, either directly or indirectly, as a means of persuading the consumer to buy goods? What proportion of advertisements aimed at your age-group and at adults fall into this category? What do you consider to be the general effect of this kind of advertising?

(c) Censorship

Members of a free society often dispute whether there should be any censorship at all, but censorship within a democracy is quite different in kind from that found in either a right-wing military dictatorship or a left-wing communist country. Under both extreme left- and extreme right-wing government, dissident opinion against the policies of the state may be strictly forbidden. Whereas political opinion in our country is free provided it does not incite to violence.

Our own censorship laws are mainly related to obscenity (although an ancient blasphemy law has been once invoked in recent years). The Obscene Publications Act of 1959 classified certain kinds of material as obscene if they were considered able to deprave and corrupt those whose minds were open to such immoral influences. The Act did acknowledge, however, that a publication which some people considered offensive might, in the opinion of the experts, prove to be 'in the interests of science, literature, art or learning'.

We need to bear in mind two related points. First, social conventions and public taste do alter so that changing generations will have different ideas about what is acceptable. On the other hand, there are outer limits of tolerance beyond which it is wrong to go. Hard-core pornography for example is essentially dehumanizing in its approach. It seeks to depersonalize men and women and to turn them into mechanisms which automatically respond to lust and cruelty.

Christian attitudes to censorship vary. Some believe that the protection of the innocent is all-important and they deeply deplore the exploitation of sex for commercial purposes. They would like to ban material which they consider to be undermining the moral and religious basis of our society. Others believe that censorship can produce uniformity and that we must be prepared to explore areas previously covered up, always provided that people are treated with respect and are not exploited for monetary gain. Many Christians are convinced that open debate is essential in a free society.

Discussion and work

1 The broadcasting authorities decide for themselves what shall be seen and heard, although the Television Act of 1954 required that nothing in a programme should offend against good taste or decency or incite crime or disorder. Discuss any controversial plays which might be thought harmful as well as distasteful. Consider the argument that there is nothing to prevent people from simply switching off the television if they find the programme disturbing.

2 An X certificate film grading indicates that no child under the age of 16 should be present when the film is shown. What films, if any, have you seen within this category? To what kind of reactions and emotions are the makers of these films appealing? Do you think a person of 16 is mature enough to cope with scenes of sexual violence or even sadistic brutality? Should people of any age be subjected to such influences?

3 How would you define hard-core pornography?

4 Do you think you can make people morally good by acts of parliament?

Conclusions

In considering the community we have glanced at the work of local government and at the great variety of statutory and voluntary organizations which help people who are in need and at risk both from the actions of others and themselves. We have also briefly discussed some of the great issues concerning law and order and the related topics of crime and punishment. We have attempted to understand some aspects of the media. In this particular section we have said nothing about industry or politics, partly because space is limited and also because you can find Christians in all kinds of jobs and political persuasions.

The Christian trade unionist may find it difficult sometimes to reconcile his faith and the demands of his union to take strike action in support of a pay claim. He may feel that his pay is already quite adequate and he should not withhold his labour, especially if other people may suffer as a result. Questions of conscience may arise if he is asked to adopt a 'work to rule' policy in support of a pay claim. He may find that he disagrees with certain trade union practices such as a closed shop. On the other hand, he knows how much the unions have fought to establish better conditions of work and fairer pay.

Equally, a Christian capitalist may have difficulties in squaring his conscience with certain market techniques. He may see the accumulation of wealth as a basic contradiction of the gospel teaching and dream that one day he may establish a more equal basis of power-sharing between management and men in his company. The ethics of the market place may turn out to be incompatible with the ethics which govern his personal relationships, and yet he may be caught in circumstances beyond his control.

Each individual Christian has got to work out his own commitment to his faith according to his own understanding of the demands it makes upon him. But the hall-mark of a true Christian is his sense of responsibility for his own conduct and the respect, concern and compassion which he shows to others.

Religion and politics are of course inevitably intertwined. The 8th-century Hebrew prophets were social reformers in their time and modern Christians engage in just as many important issues. They have not attempted to form a Christian political party in this country, for diversity is the breath of life in a democracy and Christians are amongst the foremost in claiming the right to be different or at variance to each other in many matters. The important thing is to attempt to live a life of integrity and to be open to the challenge of new ideas and new commitments.

Section C — The World

Introduction

When we think about being citizens of the world, our hearts may sink a little at the many problems which exist and their enormous scale. All the things which we have discussed in relation to the community are magnified innumerable times throughout the world, where the people in need and at risk run into millions. Daunting as these facts are, we must consider our worldwide citizenship because today as never before, human civilizations are linked together by a vast network of communication systems, trade patterns, travel facilities and multi-national organizations. On our television screens we can see live coverage of the World Cup soccer final, wherever the match is being played. We can share in the suffering of people hit by the latest natural disaster and can observe the world's political leaders as they carry out their various jobs. If we have the money, we can pick up a telephone and speak to a friend in another continent. The contact is immediate though our clocks are registering a different time. We can even view man's exploration of outer space. And if we have the resources, we ourselves can fly to the four corners of the earth. The technological skills of the 20th century have allowed us to see our marvellous spherical planet from outer space for the first time in man's history; we can now indeed appreciate that we are living in a global village. Whether we realize it or not, we are bound together by intricate and often invisible bonds of our common humanity, of industrial and commercial interests, of recognizable rivalries and bitter conflicts. We must accept our responsibilities and grasp at the opportunities which are open to us.

In the following sections, we will look first at the major concerns of the peoples of the world and the organizations which exist to cope with some of the world's basic problems. In order to reduce this vast canvas to human proportions, we will also consider the life and work of several individuals to illustrate how people with courage, determination and inspiration can succeed in tackling difficulties and can resolve them. Second, we will face up to the consequences of the arms race and the questions of war, peace and disarmament. Third, we will discuss various forms of social protest and terrorism. Lastly, we will come back to the earth, its limitations, its exploitation by man and the need for conservation.

1 Major world concerns

(a) World population, hunger, poverty, health and literacy: the plight of women

Historical and archaeological research estimates that the *world population* at the time of Jesus was about 200 million. This figure did not greatly increase until the 18th century when the Industrial Revolution, which had begun in Britain, spread to Europe and America. From that century onwards, due to great advances in medical care and social services, improved public and personal hygiene and a general raising of living standards, the number of children surviving after birth became greater than the overall death rate. The same pattern, that of survival overtaking the death rate, is now emerging in the developing countries (i.e. the Third World). In 1975 the world population was assessed at 4000 million (i.e. 4 billion), increasing annually by 2% to reach the 6 to 7 billion mark by the turn of the century. Furthermore, children under the age of 15 now account for 36% of the world's population. Although some countries have achieved or are approaching a stable population—these include Britain, USA, Sweden, Switzerland, West and East Germany—others are experiencing high growth rates. In India, for example, the population had doubled in the last 50 years to reach 650 million.

The 'population explosion', as it has been called, affects almost every major social problem. Already in the developing countries about half the population is undernourished and perhaps a quarter are on the verge of starvation. Some estimates say that there are between 500 and 600 million people suffering from malnutrition. UNICEF (see below) reckoned that in 1978 alone more than 12 million children under the age of five died of *hunger*. In the poorest countries one out of every four children dies before the age of five, but a third of these deaths arise not from malnutrition but from polluted water.

Growth of towns and cities
Since the 18th century, and especially in the last 50 years, towns and cities have grown rapidly. In 1975 191 cities had more than a million inhabitants. It is estimated that in this century city dwellers will rise from one-sixth to over one-half of the world's population. The global impact of this dramatic shift from rural to urban

life was the subject of the UN HABITAT conference in 1976. In the major capitals of the less developed countries over 30% of the population are slum dwellers or squatters. Where homes are made of insubstantial material and there is no proper sanitation or unpolluted drinking water, serious health problems arise.

High unemployment

Many hundreds of millions of people in the poorer countries cannot find enough work to provide for their daily needs. In some countries job seekers outnumber jobs by two to one and where work is available the pay is very low and the conditions barely tolerable. In these countries there are no public systems of social security or unemployment benefits. And when natural disasters such as floods, drought or an epidemic of some disease strike a community, there is very little hope of compensation. In this country we find it hard to imagine the kind of poverty which exists in the Third World, where the average expectation of life for the great majority is 50 years or under.

Europe had coped with its own population explosion between 1850 and 1930 by sending 50 million Europeans overseas to find work. Then in more recent years, many developing countries were able to use emigration to North-west Europe as an escape valve for high unemployment. But now that the wealthy and highly industrialized nations are experiencing high unemployment themselves (10% of the labour force in Britain was out of work in February 1981) they are encouraging 'guest workers' to go home.

Education

According to the 1977 UNESCO report, one in three adults cannot read or write. Of these 800 million illiterates, two-thirds are women. Although the developing countries have made considerable progress in establishing primary school education, people living in the poorest areas need their children to work on farms or earn some sort of income. As for women in these districts, it is not considered necessary or appropriate for girls to receive any education.

The special hardships of *women* in the developing world were highlighted by the UN Conference held in Mexico for the International Women's Year in 1975. The UN Decade for Women (1976–85) stresses the need for equality, development and peace. In many developing countries women's present status not only bars them from receiving education, but prevents just recognition for the work they do. It is, for example, the women who largely produce the food, carry water (often over long distances), besides also bearing and rearing the children; yet despite all this they have

104

very little say in influencing the size of their family. The United Nations Voluntary Fund for Women is an attempt to sponsor a programme which will begin to tackle these problems.

Discussion and work
1 Discuss and contrast the following propositions.
  (a) The only way to deal with the population explosion is by *compulsory* birth control.
  (b) There is a basic need to educate women in the Third World, so that they will regulate the size of their own families. Research in Latin America has shown that even when women receive only a primary school education, they tend to have fewer children than those women who have had no schooling at all. Education also delays the age of marriage and therefore reduces the number of child-bearing years.
  (c) You cannot expect the desperately poor families in the Third World to limit the size of their families when many children die while under the age of five and the family needs able-bodied children to support it by working. The real problem is not population but poverty and the unequal distribution of wealth. This is the thing which must first be tackled.
  (d) What we need is far more primary health care. The World Health Organization has estimated that 3 dollars per head would be sufficient to immunize every new born child in the developing world against the six most common childhood diseases. If parents could feel reasonably sure that their children would survive and would grow up healthy, they would not feel the need for so many children. The present situation in the developing world is exactly what this country experienced in earlier days when a large family was necessary so that one or two strong children might survive into adulthood. With greater health care, that has changed.
2 It is possible to control population by many methods: artificial contraceptives, sterilization, abortion, infanticide, euthanasia, government legislation. Which of these proposals do you find morally and religiously unacceptable? Give your reasons why and also consider which solutions, if any, you would consider acceptable.

(b) The United Nations

Its purpose and structure
In the face of the problems we have just discussed, it is easy to lose faith in the future, but that is because we have only seen one side of the picture. For the first time in human history, science and

technology have made it possible to extend the *benefits* of civilization to the whole human race. The fact that benefits are not equally shared among all mankind shows that our moral and spiritual development has not kept pace with our intellectual achievements. Yet, if world peace is to be attained, these technological advances must ultimately be directed by our spiritual/moral insights. The setting up of world organizations is the first basis of hope.

The United Nations was established on 24th October 1945. The nations who had fought against the totalitarian regimes of Germany and Italy and the militarism of Japan, determined that such a war must never happen again. They met in San Francisco to work out a plan for peace. The Charter of the United Nations (see Appendix 1) was originally signed by 50 nations, but the number has now grown to include 151 countries, comprising practically every nation in the world. The broad aims of the UN are to preserve world peace and security, to encourage economic and social progress and to support human rights and freedom.

All member states are represented in the *General Assembly*. Each nation has one vote regardless of its size, wealth or influence. It controls the UN budget and member states legally bind themselves to fulfil their monetary obligations. In other matters, the Assembly decisions, reached by majority vote, are not legally binding on its members. The Assembly holds one regular annual session of three months' duration, but a special session can be called if peace is threatened.

The *Security Council* is primarily responsible for keeping the peace. Five of its 15 members are permanent and it is these which have a special voting right called a 'veto', meaning that a 'no' vote by any one of them bars a proposed action. These five members are France, Britain, China, Russia and the United States. The other 10 members are elected to two-year terms by the General Assembly.

The *Secretariat* is the international civil service of the UN, employing about 9000 people. Its chief figure is the Secretary-General, nominated by the Security Council and appointed by the General Assembly. The present holder of this post (1982) is Perez de Cuellar of Peru.

The *Economic and Social Council* is the first international organization concerned with improving the way people live and with human rights. It works mostly through its special agencies and in co-operation with more than 100 other organizations as, for example, the Red Cross.

The *International Court of Justice* has 15 judges, each appointed for nine years. It deals with matters relating to international law and treaties.

Specialized Agencies

These are self-governing international organizations related to the UN. The most important are:

(i) FAO—the Food and Agricultural Organization: it aims to raise the level of nutrition throughout the world and prevent world hunger.

(ii) WHO—the World Health Organization: this works to promote the highest possible level of health throughout the world. It succeeded in almost eliminating smallpox over a period of 10 years.

(iii) UNESCO—the United Nations Educational, Scientific and Cultural Organization: this promotes education, science and the arts throughout the world. Through international co-operation it is trying to establish compulsory primary education in most of the developing world.

(iv) UNICEF—the United Nations International Children's Emergency Fund: working with WHO, this helps governments to improve mother and child care, aiming to help children in need, especially the poorest children.

(v) ILO—the International Labour Organization: this aims to improve working conditions throughout the world. It has set up an International Labour Code on many aspects of working conditions, such as the employment of children, young persons and women.

(vi) UNHCR—the first United Nations High Commissioner for Refugees was appointed in 1950 (see Appendix 6).

UN and other agencies at work

Working alongside the UN agencies there are also many international voluntary organizations. Oxfam, Christian Aid, Save the Children Fund and War on Want are some of the best known. These groups bring relief to millions of people suffering from the latest natural disaster or the effects of malnutrition and terrible poverty. The human rights organization, Amnesty International, was awarded the Nobel Peace Prize in 1977 for its efforts to publicize the plight of victims of political discrimination; Amnesty supports only those who have neither used nor advocated violence.

The *World Bank* and two other financial organizations work to encourage both small and large development schemes. Other international organizations are concerned with Maritime Consultation, Civil Aviation, Telecommunications, Postal Unions and Meteorological forecasting, while the Monetary Fund helps adjust differences between money systems so that countries can trade with each other.

UNCTAD—The UN dedicated the years between 1961 and 1980

as Development Decades. It held a Conference on Trade and Development (UNCTAD) in 1964 and set up a board which became a permanent organ of the General Assembly.

It is not possible to judge adequately the achievements and failures of world organizations which have only existed for comparatively few years. One of their main difficulties has been a desperate shortage of money (some nations have not paid their dues); another has been the mutual distrust and fear between the superpowers of America and Russia. In the period up to September 1975, for example, the USSR and the USA were actually responsible for 120 out of 141 uses of the Security Council veto (109 by USSR, 11 by USA). These vetoes effectively prevented any action on the major issues involved. Nevertheless, since 1945 the UN has acted as a third party in over 100 disputes in an endeavour to keep the peace. It has sent out fact-finding missions to problem areas, supplied military observers to patrol ceasefire lines between countries and has provided a peace-keeping force. Both economic and military embargoes have been imposed on countries who have attacked or acted against the interest of another country or group of people.

On 10 December 1948, the UN General Assembly adopted the Universal Declaration of Human Rights (see Appendix 2), while in 1976 it published Covenants on Human Rights which are now legally binding on the 50 nations (including Britain) which signed them. Although many UN countries have not agreed to sign as yet, recognition of basic human rights has begun and must continue.

Discussion and work
1 Undertake and complete a project on one of the major agencies of the United Nations, such as FAO, WHO, UNESCO, UNICEF or UNHCR.
2 Find out all you can about one of the major voluntary organizations such as Christian Aid, Oxfam, Save the Children Fund, or War on Want.
3 The problem of refugees is very acute in the 1980s, especially in Africa and Asia. Make a study of one of the areas most affected and the task of one of the voluntary relief organizations working there.
[For a project on human rights, see the Section 'Social and Political Protest', p. 122.]
4 Your school may have a society which is linked in some way to the United Nations Association. There will certainly be a local branch in your town. Ask a member to come and speak to you about the work of the UN.

(c) The Christian response

In the past the Christian church has pioneered the relief of suffering, the care of the aged and the education of the young. Now its role in the world is perhaps somewhat different. It might be summarized under three headings:

(i)   education in awareness;
(ii) acceptance of responsibility;
(iii) commitment to work for change and the resolution of problems.

As a concrete example of these three aspects of the Christian response we will look at the lives of three 20th-century Christians.

Barbara Ward

As an active Christian (she was a member of the Roman Catholic church), Barbara Ward (Baroness Barbara Ward Jackson) devoted her life to bringing home to people the facts, figures and problems of the developing countries, as well as the immense environmental, economic and community dilemmas which face the whole human family.

Graduating in politics, philosophy and economics at Oxford, Barbara Ward served for a time on the staff of the magazine *The Economist*. In 1957 she became a lecturer at Harvard University and from there went on in 1969 to become the Schweitzer Professor of International Economic Development at Columbia University. From 1973 she was President of the International Institute for Environment and Development until illness forced her to give up that position. She was given many honorary degrees and was twice publicly honoured in this country, being made a Life Peer in 1976. Her books include *Spaceship Earth* (1966), *The Lopsided World* (1968), *Only One Earth* (1972, with René Dubos), *The Home of Man* (1976), and *Progress for a Small Planet* (1979). She was a member of the Pontifical Commission for Justice and Peace, which considered how the Roman Catholic church could help developing countries. In 1968 she addressed the World Council of Churches Assembly and she used all her skill and knowledge as an economist to work for a more just distribution of wealth and resources. She died in 1981.

Although it was not an official report, her best selling book *Only One Earth* set the scene for the UN Conference on the Human Environment in 1972. *The Home of Man* was actually written for the UN Conference on Human Settlements—HABITAT—held in 1976. Her most recent book drew together the themes of her previous writing, dealing with the basic problems of pollution and the environment, the desperate needs of the world's poor and how the inequalities between rich and poor nations can be lessened to the benefit of both. She had a prophetic sense of a 'planetary society struggling to be born', believing that we cannot live in isolation. We are all interdependent, needing one another. The rich, developed countries of the North have largely achieved their status by exploiting the poor, developing countries of the South for their own benefit. We need now a balanced and conserving planet to save humanity itself.

Mother Teresa of Calcutta (Agnes Gonxha Bojaxhiu)

Born of Albanian parents in Skopje, Yugoslavia, Agnes knew as a schoolgirl that she wanted to help the poor. In 1928 she joined the Roman Catholic teaching order of Loreto nuns and after being trained she went to India. For 20 years she taught geography at St Mary's High School, Calcutta, then in 1946 she felt God was calling her to give up her teaching at the convent so that she could work more directly with the very poor people in the city. She received permission from the Pope to become an unenclosed nun. Quite alone she began to care for destitute and abandoned children, but gradually she was joined by some of her former pupils and eventually the new Congregation of Sisters was formed. She and her nuns then turned to help the dying in the streets of Calcutta, for these were people whom others ignored. In 1952 her first Home for the Dying was opened, where people could spend their last days in an atmosphere of love and peace. Help came from other volunteers who gave what they could, even if they did not join her Order. In 1957 Mother Teresa extended her work to the many lepers in the city. The Congregation grew in strength and spread to other towns in India and to other countries. In 1971 she was awarded the Pope John XXIII Peace Prize.

Mother Teresa has visited England on several occasions and has appeared on television. During one of these broadcasts she said 'We chose the poor for love of God. In the service of the poorest of the poor, we are feeding the hungry Christ, clothing the naked Christ and giving shelter to the homeless Christ.' Her deep faith has led her to take responsibility for those whom others had abandoned. She and her sisters have brought love, peace, comfort, hope and renewed purpose to tens of thousands of people.

Malcolm Muggeridge has written of her: 'in a dark time she is a burning and shining light; in a cruel time a living embodiment of Christ's gospel of love' (*Something Beautiful for God*).

E.F. Schumacher

German-born Fritz Schumacher first came to England in the 1930s as a Rhodes Scholar to study economics at New College,

Oxford. Realizing that he could not possibly accept living and working under the Nazis, he later emigrated permanently to this country. During a very varied career, he taught economics at Columbia University, New York, worked on *The Observer*'s editorial team and was Economic Adviser with the British Control Commission in Germany from 1946 to 1950. For the next 20 years he was Economic Adviser to the National Coal Board and in 1974 he was awarded the CBE. His first book *Small is Beautiful* looked at the economic structure of the Western world in a new and radical way. The subtitle gives the essence of his thought—'A study of economics as if people mattered'. His emphasis was on the person, not the product, and he wanted to create a world where man used capital for his greater good instead of being enslaved by it. He founded a system of Intermediate Technology based on smaller working units, communal ownership and regional workplaces using local labour and resources.

The catchphrase 'Small is beautiful' has passed into our language and although his ideas have aroused fierce controversy, no one can doubt the depth of his religious conviction that the individual is important or the originality of his mind. Two other books *A Guide for the Perplexed* and *Good Work* (the latter published after his death in 1977) offer his readers a philosophical basis for life and answer the fundamental question 'What is the purpose of our work?'. Britain has given official support to the Intermediate Technology Development Group which Schumacher founded in 1965. The American government has also set up a fund for research into alternative technologies and several Third World nations have welcomed the practical idea of simpler technologies which they can better afford than the expensive and more sophisticated products used in the industrialized countries.

The World Council of Churches
Remarkable individuals such as Barbara Ward, Mother Teresa and E.F. Schumacher invariably work with and through other people. All of them acknowledge that they depend upon colleagues and are indebted to them, so it is perhaps right to end this section with the corporate efforts of Christians, exemplified in the World Council of Churches and its associates.

The WCC was set up in Amsterdam in 1948 by 147 churches, although the inspiration for this ecumenical movement goes back to 1910. Today Anglicans, Orthodox, Baptists, Reformed, Lutherans, Methodists, Pentecostalists and many other groups representing some 400 million Christians throughout the world, are joined together in Christian fellowship. The Roman Catholic church is not yet a member but in recent years it has shared in several co-operative ventures. SODEPAX, for instance, is the joint WCC/RC Committee working for world justice, development and peace. Delegates from the representative churches join in Assembly every seven years, but detailed decisions are taken by an elected Central Committee of 134 members which meets yearly. Dr Philip Potter of Dominica is the General Secretary to the small executive committee and is in charge of the permanent staff based in Geneva.

The WCC is engaged in three major programmes of study, consultation and action: Faith and Witness; Justice and Service; Education and Renewal. The Justice and Service unit is perhaps the most well-known and controversial as it includes Inter-Church Aid, Refugees and World Service, a Medical Commission, the Programme to Combat Racism and the church's participation in development and international affairs.

The growing desire for Christian unity is reflected in the Yearly Week of Prayer as well as in all kinds of communal efforts at local, national and international level.

Discussion and work

1 In Matthew 6:23 Jesus emphasized how a wrong perspective, especially about money, could be likened to eye disease. Look up the passage. In what senses do you think this saying is applicable to us today?

2 'The North, including Eastern Europe, has a quarter of the world's population and four-fifths of its income. The South, including China, has 3 billion people, three-quarters of the world's people, but is living on one-fifth of the world's income. . . . Over 90% of the world's manufacturing industry is in the North. Most patents and new technology are the property of multi-national corporations of the North, which conduct a large share of world investment and world trade in raw materials and manufactures' (The Brandt Report 1979). The report further claims that recession in the North and grinding poverty in the South can only be overcome if both areas work together. That process will only begin to come about when people in every country are educated in these ideas and facts. Have you heard of 'North—South: A programme for survival'? What do you know about it? Willy Brandt was the Chairman of the report; who represented Britain? Do you know how Britain responded to the report? Collect any newspaper reports or facts that you can find about the summit meeting on the Brandt Report in Mexico in 1981.

3 Choose one of the three people mentioned in this section and find out as much about her/him as you can; concentrate on the kind of work this individual has done and his/her contribution to promoting and suggesting remedies for world problems.

4 Find out about your local Council of Churches: who belongs to it? What kind of things do they do in the neighbourhood? Ask someone to come and speak about its work to your group at school.

2 War and Peace

(a) Traditional views

The vision of justice and peace is inherent in the Old Testament. The 8th-century prophet Amos condemned the cruelty and horror of war (1:*3,6,9*) and the prophets Isaiah and Micah spoke of a day when men would beat their swords into ploughshares and their spears into pruning-hooks; war should be no more (Isaiah 2:*3—4*; Micah 4:*2—3*). They believed that injustice was the root of war and that peace would come when men were truly governed by God's moral law. Nevertheless, in the ancient song of Moses (Exodus 15:*3*), God himself was depicted as a man of war, and the Israelites believed he fought with and for them in the conquest of Canaan (Joshua 6:*13—15*, Judges 5:*23*). There was such a thing, therefore, as a just war. War in the form of invasion and oppression could also be seen as an instrument of God's judgment upon a sinful nation (Judges 13:*1*).

The New Testament clearly shows that Jesus was heir to the highest level of prophetic teaching, but he also added a new dimension to the whole subject of conflict and violence. He specifically said that peace-making was a godlike activity; 'Blessed are the peacemakers, for they shall be called the sons of God' (Matthew 5:*9*). He forbade his disciples to fight for him in the Garden of Gethsemane: 'Put your sword back into its place; for all who take the sword will perish by the sword' (Matthew 26:*52*). And when he was dying on the cross, he asked God to forgive those responsible for his crucifixion (Luke 23:*34*). Paul echoed this example and teaching of Jesus when he wrote to his friends in Rome: 'If possible, so far as it depends upon you, live peaceably with all. . . . Do not be overcome by evil, but overcome evil with good' (Romans 12:*18—21*). All Christians must work to establish a time of peace when men may live in harmony with each other. But they have disagreed in the past about the best way to bring about a new era and about how society should deal with those who commit evil and who wrong others.

The case for pacifism

A minority of Christians believe that we can only establish peace by a definite refusal to engage in war. They use all their energies to understand the causes of war and thus to help prevent it. They seek to bring conflicting sides together by throwing fresh light on areas of disagreement. Nonetheless, many pacifists consider that it is necessary to have an international armed force, rather like a police force, to restrain nations from making war with each other, until the time comes when their dispute can be settled by rational and peaceful means. Christian pacifists point out that Jesus condemned violence as a way of overcoming evil. They argue that if you use evil means (i.e. all the horror, suffering and death that making war involves) you will yourselves become contaminated by the evil you have released, even though you think you are serving a noble end. Jesus himself did not use violence. He overcame his enemies' personal hostility and hate by refusing to become a part of it, even though his way of love led to his own death. His disciples must follow his example, on every level from the personal to the international. Only when they do so will true peace be established.

Christian pacifists further argue that making war is not only morally wrong but bad sense as well; war never justifies the terrific expenditure of lives and resources which it entails and it never really solves any problem. Sometimes the victor is exhausted by the struggle and the defeated, filled with resentment and bitterness, may harbour plans for revenge. Thus war sows the seeds of further conflict. This is the plain lesson to be learnt from the past.

The case for non-pacifism

Other Christians have maintained that there is such a thing as a just war. A very famous medieval theologian, Thomas Aquinas, laid down four principles for this. His argument included these words: 'A just war is . . . one that avenges wrongs, when a nation or state has to be punished, for refusing to make amends for the wrongs inflicted by its subjects, or to restore what it has seized unjustly.' He also insisted that a just war should be waged in a just manner; this meant, among other things, that certain categories of people should be left untouched and certain standards of behaviour observed by soldiers. Modern Christians who believe in a just war say that if one nation deliberately and unjustifiably attacks another, it is right to come to the aid of the attacked nation. As an example they cite Germany's unprovoked attack on Poland in 1939, an act of aggression which sparked off the Second World War. Non-pacifists argue that it is loving and therefore Christian to give your life for the sake of others, even when this leads you to take aggressive action against the oppressor—how else can his aggression be contained and halted? In their view we are usually faced with a choice between two evils; either we resist tyranny by using force, or we allow the nation to suffer evil oppression.

Although some of these Christians deeply respect the pacifist witness for peace, they consider it to be a personal vocation only. They believe that pacifism as a national policy for dealing with an evil aggressor will not work in a sinful world.

(b) Our present dilemma

Whatever the arguments about the limited wars of previous centuries and those put forward to justify the 1939 World War against the evil of Nazism, we are faced today with an entirely different situation. This has been brought about by nuclear weapons and the total involvement of civilian populations in the holocaust of modern warfare. In previous centuries wars were mainly fought by small numbers of professionals. In this century civilians have become increasingly bound up with the war machine, as these statistics show:

First World War deaths:	8,418,000 military;	1,300,000 civilian;
Second World War deaths:	16,933,000 military;	34,305,000 civilian.

A third world war, using nuclear weapons, would destroy civilization as we know it. It could also bring about the ultimate destruction of human life on this planet. Because the issues are so complex, I will summarize the various strands under four headings:

(i) **United Nations resolutions.** Almost the first resolution adopted by the United Nations General Assembly on 24 January 1946 called for 'the elimination from national armaments of atomic weapons and of all other major weapons adaptable to mass destruction'.

The 1952 Assembly created a Disarmament Commission and in 1959 the item 'General and Complete Disarmament' was placed on the agenda of the General Assembly: '*Considering* that the question of general and complete disarmament is the most important one facing the world today, *Calls upon* Governments to make every effort to achieve a constructive solution to this problem.'

In the following years the Assembly passed resolution after resolution expressing the same fundamental belief in the urgent necessity for disarmament. As time went on 'general and complete disarmament' became a more distant goal, the immediate aim being 'the elimination of the danger of nuclear war and the implementation of measures to halt and reverse the arms race and clear the path towards lasting peace' (Paragraphs 19 and 8 of the Final Document of the UN Special Session on Disarmament 1978).

The UN's continuing and tireless endeavours led to the 1978 Special Session on Disarmament. This historic occasion of great significance and importance was attended by representatives from every nation, including China, which had been excluded from the UN for many years. This session produced a final document and decided to create a new UN Disarmament Commission to work on a Comprehensive Programme for Disarmament. As follow-up, members agreed to hold another Special Session in 1982.

For the first time, non-governmental organizations were given an opportunity to address the Special Session; for example, the Rev. Philip Potter, General Secretary of the World Council of Churches, spoke on behalf of the Commission of the Churches on International Affairs.

Unfortunately, talk was not matched by action, in the sense that no concrete decisions were taken about reducing the arms build up. The Final Document did, however, contain a programme of action outlining measures needed to achieve nuclear and conventional disarmament.

(ii) Disarmament — the various approaches. Although peoples everywhere long to live creatively and in peace, opinion is divided about the best way to achieve disarmament. Some believe in total unilateral disarmament. This means that individual nations should lay down their own arms of all types in the hope that others will follow. Others campaign solely for nuclear disarmament. They argue that if Britain disarmed, other nations in Europe would do the same. Europe could then become a nuclear weapon-free zone. A third group think it safer to work for arms control, leading to the eventual abolition of the arms trade. They argue that peace can only be achieved by multilateral disarmament, i.e. disarmament by treaty and agreement between the powerful nations.

The multilateralists point out that during the last 20 years there have been 18 bilateral or multilateral agreements on disarmament or arms control. These included The Antarctic Treaty 1958; The Partial Test Ban Treaty 1963 (signed by Britain, USA, USSR but not France or China) which basically stopped air pollution; The Peaceful Uses of Outer Space Treaty, 1967, and The Sea Bed Treaty, 1971, banned nuclear weapons from environments which did not belong to any one state and which were not inhabited. Another important treaty, that of Tlatelolco, 1967, prohibited

116

the use of nuclear weapons in Latin America. This was the first and so far the only successful attempt to create a nuclear weapon-free zone in a populated region of the world, although Argentina and Brazil have not yet signed the treaty. The Non-Proliferation Treaty of 1968 has been ratified by more than 100 countries which have undertaken not to receive, manufacture or otherwise acquire nuclear weapons. Some countries with nuclear potential have not, however, signed the treaty. Lastly, there was a Convention on Biological and Toxin Weapons, 1972, which prohibited biological means of warfare; chemical weapons are still the subject of disarmament negotiations.

Critics of these treaties say that they banned things nobody wanted to do anyway and were merely 'cosmetic'; they did not actually bring real disarmament any nearer.

(iii) **Opponents of disarmament.** Broadly speaking, there are two main arguments against pursuing a policy of disarmament. First, the arms trade is an important part of our national economy. Britain is reported to be the fifth largest exporter of arms in the world, coming behind the USA, USSR, France and Italy. To disarm would throw thousands of people out of work. The second objection is that disarmament would seriously affect our national security, i.e. without arms we would not be able to protect ourselves and all the values we cherish most, against an aggressive or oppressive nation or state. This was the argument originally used in favour of a nuclear deterrent and modern armaments aimed at achieving a balance of power. In support of their objections to disarmament, people point to Russia's aggressive policy in putting down an East German rising in 1953, the Hungarian rising in 1956, in sealing the borders between East and West Berlin in 1961, and in invading both Czechoslovakia in 1968 and Afghanistan in 1979. It is argued that if Northern Europe, Britain and America had not possessed nuclear weapons, there might well have been another major war.

It must also be admitted that the armaments business is financially very profitable and that many men have made their names as experts in the theory and practice of war. Furthermore, some of the country's best brains have exercised their skills to perfect new and more sophisticated weaponry. For a variety of personal reasons therefore, both conscious and unconscious, opposition to disarmament finds expression in our society.

Although these arguments may appear strong, there is much to say on the other side. First, industry could after all be converted to other purposes than armaments. One practical example is the Lucas Aerospace Combined Shop Stewards' Committee and the North East London Polytechnic effort to set up a Centre for Alternative

Industrial and Technological Systems (CAITS) in 1978.

Second, in answer to the claims of military necessity, the late Earl Mountbatten stated:

> As a military man who has given half a century of active service, I say in all sincerity that the nuclear arms race has no military purpose. Wars cannot be fought with nuclear weapons. Their existence only adds to our perils because of the illusions they have generated.
>
> (Speech to the Stockholm International Peace Research Institute, May 1979.)

Lord Mountbatten considered the world to be standing on the brink of the final abyss.

In 1979 Lord Zuckerman, former Chief Scientific Adviser to HM Government, said that although he could see why the arms race first started, he found it difficult to understand the logic of the continuation of the technical race between the super-powers. He considered the nuclear arms race to be irrelevant to the issue of national security.

While Dr Henry Kissinger was American Secretary of State in the early 1970s, he declared that no meaning could any longer be attached to the concept of nuclear superiority, as the threshold of nuclear armaments for both Western and Eastern blocs was already well above what was needed to assure a state of mutual deterrence.

The paradox is that if we seek for security by acquiring more and more weapons we defeat our purpose, for the possession of arms by all states results in far greater international tension and threat of war.

(iv) **Military expenditure and world development.** According to the 1978 UN report, the world has been spending annually about 450 billion dollars on military purposes. This means that altogether more than one twentieth of the world's total production of goods and services is devoted to military ends. Current stocks of nuclear weapons are already sufficient to destroy the world population more than 40 times over. But the arms race between the major powers continues unabated. They compete not only in quantity but also in quality. Sophisticated new technologies are affecting attitudes to nuclear war; instead of considering such a war unthinkable, some people now think in terms of surviving a nuclear attack and therefore want to train people in civil defence. Recent developments in conventional weapons have also been far reaching.

Although all this change and development originates in a few powerful countries (the USA, USSR, China, France, Britain, Italy and the Federal Republic of Germany) the effects of the new technology have spread rapidly throughout the world. Developing countries are now spending more and more upon weaponry and have started producing their own arms. In fact the world's military spending is about 20 times the total official development aid given by developed countries to the Third World. Large military expenditure leads to a reduction in world trade; it helps to increase both inflation and the gap between rich and poor countries. The waste of humanity's own potential is even more serious. More than half of the world's research and development physicists and engineers work full-time on military projects.

Here are some examples of relative costs cited in the Brandt report:

The World Health Organization spent approximately 83 million dollars over a period of 10 years to eradicate smallpox from the world. That amount of money would not be enough to buy a single modern strategic bomber. Although the WHO has plans prepared to eradicate malaria and other endemic diseases, it cannot put them into effect for lack of money. Yet the world's military expenditure for only half a day would be sufficient to finance the whole malaria programme. A modern tank costs about 1 million dollars. This amount could improve storage facilities for about 100,000 tons of rice and thus save 4000 tons or more annually: one person can live on just over a pound of rice a day. For the price of one jet fighter (20 million dollars), about 40,000 village pharmacies could be set up. These examples could be multiplied 10 times over in all the areas of education, nutrition, health and manpower. It needs little imagination to see how resources at present being used in the development of chemical and biological warfare could be diverted to research into producing high-yielding protein food.

It is interesting that Japan's 'economic miracle' has happened since she decided upon unilateral disarmament, after experiencing at first hand the effects of a nuclear bomb. Japan has had vast sums of money available for development, money which in other countries would have been spent on defence.

(c) The Christian commitment to peace

At the Special Assembly of the United Nations, all governments pledged themselves to co-operate in seeking disarmament, but the Final Document stressed: 'It is essential that not only governments but also the peoples of the world recognize and understand the dangers of the present situation'. Disarmament will only come about when millions of ordinary people demand it.

The threat of nuclear war has caused many non-pacifist Christians to reconsider their views and to decide that the new crisis demands a courageous commitment to peace. This view is reflected in the 1980 Autumn Assembly of the British Council of Churches which unanimously carried a five-point motion on Nuclear Weapons and Disarmament (for details see Appendix 7). The last paragraph of this motion called on all Christians to support the World Disarmament Campaign as one way of advocating the multilateral or unilateral approach to disarmament.

The World Disarmament Campaign was initiated by Lords Noel-Baker and Fenner Brockway in April 1980. Its sponsors include many church and religious leaders, politicians, trades unionists, members of peace organizations, universities, the arts, the professions, women and student bodies (for details see Appendix 8). Its special aim is to help put into practice the UN Special Assembly Resolutions, in view of the Geneva Committee Meeting 1981 and the Special Assembly 1982. The Executive Committee of the United Nations Association of Great Britain and Northern Ireland has agreed that UNA should become an Associate of the World Disarmament Campaign and, through its regions and branches, it is working to achieve the Campaign's Ten Point Programme of Action.

Pope John Paul II has pinpointed the immoral aspects of the arms trade on several occasions. In his 1979 encyclical he said: 'Instead of being offered bread and cultural aid, the new states are being offered, sometimes in abundance, modern weapons and the means of destruction'. Speaking to diplomats in 1981, he described the international arms race as ruinous for all humanity, while in his 1981 New Year address he declared that money spent on arms would be better used for medical research to aid the world's 400 million handicapped people.

Many Christians therefore believe that the threat of nuclear war is totally discredited as a means of attempting to settle any dispute. Man must use his ingenuity and creativity to find other ways of resolving conflict and tension and to restrain aggression. Christians must work ceaselessly to bring into being a just and peaceful society where the rule of law and order prevails over violence and oppression. The money at present spent on armaments must be used constructively to bridge the gulf between riches and poverty in the world.

Discussion and work

1 Discuss the following proposition. 'The former categories of Christian pacifist and non-pacifist no longer apply. Under the threat of nuclear war a Christian now has no alternative but to work for disarmament in whatever way he can.'

2 The phrase 'I would rather be dead than red' was coined a few years ago. What did it mean? Do you agree that there are no other alternatives available?

3 Examine the following statements:

'People need work. If we do not export armaments, other nations will take our trade. It is not our responsibility how and when these weapons might be used.'

'The only purpose of armaments is to kill and so the country that exports arms exports death. To take part in such a trade is fundamentally opposed to the life-giving principles of Christianity.'

4 Discuss the notion that an unarmed nation is safer than one with arms. Costa Rica is one of the few nations in the world which has deliberately refused to maintain an army. It came to this decision after the horrors of a bloody civil war. Find out facts and information about life in Costa Rica.

5 Discuss the following statements:

'Experience tells us that we are unable to reach any disarmament unless the public demand it' Stockholm International Peace Research Committee.

'It is clearly dangerous nonsense in these small islands, to have both civil defence and nuclear weapons' Campaign for Nuclear Disarmament.

'Passive defence embracing all aspects of civil defence is just as important for the protection of our society as active military defence.' An Air Vice-Marshal.

6 What did President Eisenhower mean when he said, 'War in our time is an anachronism'?

Compare this view with that expressed by Lord Zuckerman: 'There is no technical road to victory in the nuclear arms race. Both sides are bound to lose such a race, a race in which there is no finishing post. Defeat is indivisible in a war of nuclear weapons.'

7 Lord Noel-Baker, who has spent his life in working for peace, states that in his opinion by far the most dangerous opponents of disarmament are the editors of the press. For example, the press treated the UN Special Session on Disarmament as a non-event, which resulted in three out of four citizens being unaware that the Special Session took place at all.

Would you agree that your daily newspapers report more about war and the threat of war than about people's positive efforts at peace-making? Do you consider Lord Noel-Baker was fair in his assessment?

8 Many people argue that 'as there is no means in the USSR by which a general population initiative for peace can be mobilized,

it is unrealistic to expect that official Soviet policy will be changed as a result of open debate and of pressure from below.' What do you think?

9 'Nothing can defeat an idea whose time has come' Victor Hugo. Would you agree with Lord Noel-Baker's declaration of faith that: 'The time has come for the transformation of world society from the slavery of militarism and desperate human need to the liberty, equality and fraternity of a world at peace, to a social order based on human happiness and the rule of law. The time has come at long, long last, after our century of blood and sorrow, for civilization to begin.' In what sense can civilization 'begin' here and now and what can we do to further its real progress?

3 Social and political protest

Although it marked a great step forward, the Universal Declaration of Human Rights was not a legally binding agreement. In 1966, after many years of detailed preparation, the General Assembly adopted two international covenants which would transform the Declaration into International Law. The Covenants came into force in 1976 and are now legally binding on the 45 nations which signed them, including Britain. A substantial majority of UN members have still not signed and major violations of human rights continue under both left- and right-wing governments such as the USSR, South Africa and some South American countries.

As no government can be absolutely blameless in the matter of citizens' rights, all kinds of social and political protest arise, depending on the circumstances within the particular country.

(a) In a democracy

Under a democratic government such as our own, every adult citizen has the right to vote in free elections. Laws are passed by majority vote in the parliament thus elected. There is freedom of speech and assembly, religious toleration, social and industrial welfare. In these circumstances non-violent forms of social protest are readily available to all citizens; they may, for example, march or hold demonstrations and petition in protest against whatever government policy they think unjust or unreasonable. During an industrial dispute there are accepted channels for negotiation between management and the relevant trades unions. There can therefore be no justification for violence, whether from those who

122

are protesting or striking or picketing strike-bound premises, or from the police, whose job it is to maintain lawful access and orderly behaviour.

Within such a democratic society important changes can be brought about legally and criticism of existing structures is allowed. All kinds of independent organizations exist, such as the National Council for Civil Liberties, and the Minority Rights Group, which are concerned with safeguarding rights. We are also free to join the radical alternative groups which are working to alter social and economic structures in the country. In a democratic society the process of development and change may be slow and sometimes delayed, but non-violent means must always be used if the society is to maintain its essential freedom and character. There is no moral justification for planting bombs in postal packets or in public places, thus maiming or murdering innocent people in order to draw attention to some political cause. However urgent that cause may appear to the organization responsible, such behaviour is totally unethical and can be classed as *terrorist* activity.

The democratic countries of Western Europe are particularly vulnerable to terrorist activity because of the freedom which their citizens enjoy. Thus, terrorist groups working in West Germany and Italy have carried out a series of kidnappings and murder, have taken hostages, hi-jacked aeroplanes and organized bomb attacks in order to further their aims. The Basque Separatist organization in Spain has used these tactics in an attempt to gain a measure of independence for the Basque region. Holland, France and Britain have all been subjected to this kind of violent pressure.

The case of Northern Ireland is very difficult to analyse and exceedingly tragic. The Provisional IRA would say they were fighting to free their country from occupying British troops and to unite Northern Ireland with Eire. They regard themselves as being 'at war' with the authorities. On the other hand, the Protestant para-military organizations which also commit murder and violent outrage, claim they are using suitable means to protect their country from a take-over by Eire and the Roman Catholic minority. It is not possible to discuss here all the issues involved, but church leaders of all denominations have condemned bombings and murder, pleading with all groups to scale down their terrorist activity and to attempt to resolve the problems by the peaceful means which must be available in a democratic society.

(b) In a non-democratic country

Elsewhere, whether the government is the right-wing or left-wing, the situation is complex and difficult. Attempts to change the pattern of government in Eastern Europe to gain greater freedom of expression and political rights have been harshly suppressed by the military power of Russia. In the USSR itself *dissidents*, i.e. those who disagree with official policy, are deprived of their jobs, exiled to remote areas and sometimes sent to hospitals for 'psychiatric' treatment. They are regarded as mentally ill and forced to submit to drug therapy, shock treatment and other coercive methods of mind-changing. All kinds of protest are suppressed, including that of the groups who set out to monitor Russia's response to the Helsinki Agreement (see Appendix 3). It remains to be seen how successfully Poland can be changed by social and economic unrest. This protest has so far taken a non-violent form.

In *Latin America* the struggle for civil liberties is very intense. Its root cause lies in the great inequalities which exist between the small elite of rich and powerful ruling classes or ruling families and the vast majority of people who are desperately poor. Many countries are ruled by military juntas. The USA and, to a lesser extent, Japan and Germany have invested large sums of money in industrial development from which they derive great profit. For example in a recent 12-year period the USA put 6·9 billion dollars into Latin America and took 11·9 billion dollars out—mainly in interest on loans and dividends (UN Economic Commission on Latin America). US aid for the same period amounted to 3·3 billion dollars but interest had to be paid on this entire sum. Big business wants stable conditions in which to operate, so the USA has also taken steps to keep military regimes in power through consignments of military equipment and military training schemes. But as education spreads, ordinary people become restive and begin to demand a greater share in their country's facilities and wealth. Thus civil trouble arises.

The movement for change in Latin America is being led by three groups of people: student organizations, workers' leagues (which will contain Marxists among others) and radical Christians. Their goal is to establish a more fair and just society, but the Christian often faces a crisis of conscience over the question of what methods he should use. He has to decide whether the end justifies the means.

(c) Other forms of violent and non-violent protest

To illustrate how different Christians have reacted to the pressures within their own countries we will look at the lives of four men.

Father Camilo Torres of Colombia

Born into a rich and aristocratic family, Camilo became a priest and then a professor of sociology and student chaplain at the University of Bogota. In a country where a few powerful families control about 65% of the agricultural land and where the plight of the landless peasant is indeed terrible, Camilo saw the necessity for drastic change. He became involved in political activity. After a period in charge of the Institute of Social Administration, he came to believe that welfare was no answer to poverty and injustice. He toured the country to speak to workers and peasants, sharing with them his vision of a Christian revolution.

My analysis of the Colombian society made me realize that revolution is necessary to free the hungry, give drink to the thirsty, clothe the naked, and procure a life of well-being for the needy majority of our people. I believe that the revolutionary struggle is appropriate for the Christian and the priest. Only by revolution, by changing the concrete conditions of our country, can we enable men to practise love for each other.

Revolutionary Priest: The Complete Writings and Messages of Camilo Torres.

Ordered by the Cardinal to choose either his cause or the priesthood, he left the ministry and founded the United Front of the Colombian People, but he continued to regard himself as a priest and was known wherever he went as Padre Camilo. In the end he came to believe that the ruling classes would put up violent resistance against any peaceful attempt to give the people a share in the balance of power. He lived in constant threat of assassination. Feeling there was no other choice open to him, he joined a group of guerillas in the mountains and was killed in a skirmish in 1966 when he was 36 years old.

Camilo's personal influence amongst the ordinary people was so great that the authorities buried him secretly to prevent his grave from becoming a revolutionary shrine. Two years after his death, 48 priests and a bishop signed a manifesto in Golconda calling for multiple forms of revolutionary action against imperialism and pledging themselves to create a socialist state that would begin to solve the acute problems of their people. They were inspired by Jesus' words recorded in Luke 4:*18,19*: 'He has sent me to bring good news to the poor, to proclaim liberty to the captives and to set free the oppressed.'

Ernesto Cardinale

In Nicaragua, acute civil strife erupted into war in which the corrupt regime of the dictator Somoza was eventually destroyed.

Many priests and nuns actively supported the people's cause, among them Ernesto Cardinale, poet, priest and champion of the poor. Ernesto Cardinale has stated his belief that the unlawful arrests, the mass killings, the torture and suppression which then existed in Nicaragua added up to a state of war. He felt Christians had no option but to fight back with arms. His inspiration came both from the life and work of Camilo Torres and also from Che Guevara, the Argentinian guerilla leader who played such an important part in the Cuban Revolution. Che Guevara's challenge to Christianity was: once Christians dare to join the Latin American revolution, it will be invincible. During the Somoza regime, Cardinale managed to survive several attempts on his life. Despite these threats he remained identified with the people's movement and now holds a government post in the new administration. His brother, also a priest, is a minister in the revolutionary government.

Dom Helder Camara

Archbishop of Recife and Olinda in North-east Brazil, Camara has worked unendingly for the poor in his own country. He was founder and for 12 years Secretary-General of the Brazilian National Conference of Bishops and helped to create the Latin America Council of Bishops. It was his aim to make the church open its eyes to the wretched conditions under which millions of Latin Americans lived. Having seen the truth, the church should then strive to alter the situation.

Helder Camara is dedicated to the way of non-violence and is a great admirer of the American negro leader, Martin Luther King, also an apostle of non-violence. When King was murdered, Dom Camara made this pledge: 'I hereby make the donation of my person, physical and spiritual, to non-violent action'. The methods of protest which he has advocated are those of boycott, strike and fasting; the values of his movement are Action, Justice and Peace.

Since 1964 Brazil has been controlled by a military government which insists that national security is all important. The military have promised that when the economy is flourishing then justice and rights will also abound, but until then order comes first. According to their definition order means conformity. Any group which might resist or protest against the government's unscrupulous actions is soon reduced to silence by arrest, dispersal and even liquidation. Although its government signed the UN Declaration, it is the church which is the real champion of human rights in Brazil. Helder Camara believes that the Third World is being oppressed in two ways: the outdated colonial attitudes of its leaders oppress countries internally, and the unjust policies of international commerce put pressure on them from outside. Within Brazil, Camara himself is opposed by the vested interests of powerful industrialists and landowners who accuse him of communism and subversive activities. Dom Camara replies: 'Pope Paul VI has well said "The earth was given to all, not merely to the rich". Surely this is not the voice of communism. It is the voice of the Pope.'

Dom Camara's secretary and several of his aides have been murdered, while his collaborators have been imprisoned without trial and tortured. His own house has been bombed several times and his life is constantly threatened. For some years now he has been, to use his own words, condemned to civil death. This means that, although an Archbishop and public figure, he is not allowed to use the media except for a regular weekly radio programme on a local station. No journalist may mention his name. His books have been banned. The Archbishop actually lives in three furnished rooms which form some of the out-buildings of a parish church. Despite his clerical rank he has neither servants nor a car, but he lives alone and opens his door to rich and poor alike who call on him throughout the day and late into the night. Outside his own country he has travelled widely on behalf of the world's poor and has three times been nominated for the Nobel Peace Prize. The young people of Scandinavia created 'The People's Peace Prize' for him in 1974. Camara invested the money in agriculture in the province where he lives, and that land now belongs to workers who run farms as co-operatives. 'To take non-violent action', says Dom Helder, 'is to believe more firmly in truth, justice and love than in the power of falsehood, injustice and hatred.' *Non-Violent Action in Latin America*, April 1968.

Steve Biko

Of South Africa's 29 million citizens, $4\frac{1}{2}$ million are of white European origin, 21 million are native African ('Bantu') and 1 million are Asian. The remaining $2\frac{1}{2}$ million, known as 'coloureds' are of mixed parentage. Apartheid means that these different groups of people are kept separate by law in almost every part of their daily life. There is separation in transport, education, hospitals, cemeteries; marriage and sexual relationships between black and white are illegal. Pass laws restrict blacks from white areas. Outside the nine 'homelands' or Bantustans the African has no political rights, yet very many have to seek employment in white areas and one in three black workers are therefore classed as migrants. Although non-white trade unions were legalised in 1978, their leaders suffer governmental harrassment and the average black worker earns four times less than the average white.

127

The majority of African or coloured people oppose apartheid and many church leaders have spoken out strongly against the system and suffered accordingly, either by detention or deportation. Many Africans have been imprisoned and have died as a result of violent or peaceful protest.

Steve Biko was one such courageous man. Although not conventionally religious he had broad religious sympathies. He was founder of several important black organizations, including the Black Consciousness movement, which protest against South Africa's apartheid policy. An important figure in his people's politics, Biko was well-known internationally. In 1973 Steve Biko was 'banned' by the South African government. This means that he was not allowed to continue his medical studies at Natal University but was forced to return to his place of birth, King Williamstown. He was not allowed to travel further than 10 miles from home without special permission, could not speak to more than one person at a time, could not be quoted and could not enter any publishing or educational premises. (In fact some of the restrictions are similar to those imposed on Helder Camara in Brazil.)

When he was only 30 years old, in September 1977, Biko was imprisoned for breaking the banning order. Eight days later he was dead, having been interrogated and beaten. The post-mortem on Biko showed that he died as a result of head injuries leading to extensive brain damage. He had also sustained at least a dozen other wounds and injuries which had been inflicted over a period of time from eight days to 12 hours before his death. He was the twentieth detainee to die in South African police custody in less than two years. Although the enquiry into his death stated that there was no evidence to suggest that the police or prison authorities were in any way responsible for Steve Biko's death, reaction abroad was different. The United States, Dutch and West German governments recalled their ambassadors from South Africa for consultations and the United Nations imposed a mandatory arms embargo on South Africa.

Donald Woods, exiled former editor of the South African paper the East London *Daily Despatch*, wrote of his friend:

Steve Biko represented, in my opinion, the last hope for a peaceful accommodation to resolve the growing South African race crisis. . . In killing Steve Biko, and in condoning his killing, they (the Nationalists) have forced black resistance to apartheid into dark and violent channels.

Discussion and work
1 Choose one of the men we have discussed in this section and

write a project about him, discovering all you can about his country, its problems and his philosophy of life. If you wish you may work instead on Martin Luther King and his non-violent resistance to the problems of racial segregation in America.

2 Discuss with examples the important distinctions between a terrorist and a freedom fighter or guerilla. Does the term used depend upon which side you support?

3 Look up the Declaration of Human Rights in Appendix 2. Write an essay on one of the rights involved, illustrating how this principle operates in the United Kingdom or how you think our own society could be improved in this respect.

4 Some national newspapers include a regular 'Prisoner of Conscience' series, highlighting the fate of individuals suffering for their beliefs under various regimes. Christian periodicals do similar work under the caption 'Pray for this man'. Collect a series of these and note which countries are plainly not keeping to the freedoms supported by the UN Declaration. What good do you think such notices do?

5 Discuss the pros and cons of violent or non-violent protest given a situation where oppression and injustice prevail.

6 The British Nationality Bill published in January 1981 has aroused strong opposition from the British churches as well as from minority rights groups. The bill proposes that there should be three new but unequal types of nationality and would lead to all kinds of distinctions between citizens. One of the most serious results would be that some children born here could find themselves stateless. Christians argue that Britain is now a multi-racial, multi-cultural society and that anything which suggests racial discrimination is totally unacceptable.

Find out what you can about this bill and discuss the various measures which have aroused such strenuous protest from all branches of the Christian church.

4 The earth's resources

(a) The earth's limitations

Scientists and geographers have calculated that the surface of the earth is about 200 million square miles. Seventy per cent of this area is sea, while about two-fifths of the land mass consists of desert or ice. In other words humanity has to live and support itself on the remaining 18% of the earth's surface. This means of course that we have limited space and limited resources. At present about 11% of the earth's total land surface is being cultivated.

This amount should be enough to provide food for everyone in the world because one acre of good soil can provide adequate food for one person. However, millions of acres of fertile land are being lost every year throughout the world due to the demands of transport, housing and industrial development, not to mention soil erosion. In the USA for example, half a million acres of farmland disappear annually; Britain loses well over 40,000 acres of good agricultural land each year for the sake of transport and industrial or town developments. We can begin to appreciate what a serious matter this enormous loss is when we realize that it may take 1000 years of natural evolution to produce good top soil that is only two inches deep.

We now know that Nature is made up of biological communities of interdependent plants and animals. This is called the eco-system. Man is part of this ecosystem and he deceives himself if he thinks he can go on indefinitely exploiting it for his own purposes without suffering the consequences. We do not yet fully under-stand the delicate balance of the ecosystem nor have we grasped the environmental side effects of many branches of modern tech-nology; we are coming to realize, however, that all life on this planet may be threatened by some of man's actions. The problems of pollution and the need for conservation are rapidly becoming in practical terms a matter of man's own survival.

In the Genesis parable of creation man is given dominion over the natural order. He is told to go forth, multiply, 'fill the earth', and 'subdue it' (Genesis 1:26–31). But the earth is still the Lord's and man must undertake his task of responsible government only as God's representative. In the Old Testament times man's relationship with the animal kingdom and to nature itself was one of mutual dependence and partnership. The Israelites were well aware that their very survival and prosperity depended finally upon God. Indeed later prophets, such as Joel, called upon the people to repent in view of the devastation which would otherwise come upon their land: 'the seed shrivels under the clods, the store-houses are desolate; the granaries are ruined because the grain has failed. How the beasts groan . . . because there is no pasture for them' (Joel 1:17–18).

The great religions of the East declare that life should be lived in unity with all creation. Man must not engage in any activity that is harmful to others or to the cosmos itself. In Islam nature is regarded as man's partner not his slave. Man's mark upon the landscape must be gentle because he is only a traveller through the world.

In the past man's bad husbandry, ignorance and selfish use of his environment have not necessarily had a major impact upon the earth, but events in this century has changed the whole picture. Technological man, forgetful of the wisdom contained in the great religions of the world, has tried to gain such complete mastery over nature that unless he exercises this power with restraint and humility, not only his own species is endangered but much else besides.

(b) Pollution

Although the subject of pollution is controversial, the term itself simply means the physical fouling of any feature of the environment. Controversy arises because people disagree about the extent of the contamination and how important is its effect. Some say that man is by nature a polluting animal, so we must accept the fact without fuss. Others point to the grave dangers which inevitably occur when man releases into the world substances or forms of energy which the environment cannot break down or render harmless to life itself.

Some experts consider that over-population is the root cause of pollution on this planet. As our numbers multiply, so we need to draw more heavily on the earth's resources and our waste products continue to spill out more filth and garbage. At one time the sewage from homes, workshops and towns could be dealt with and recycled by nature itself. The volume of sewage has now so increased that the rivers, the sea, the winds, the air and the soil remain contaminated by toxic waste products.

A different group of environmentalists argues that, although the rise in population has created a major problem, it is even more important for mankind to adopt a complete change of attitude to the world on which it depends. This is especially true of the industrialized nations of the world. We in the rich countries are extravagant, wasteful, selfish, heedlessly reckless in using resources. As an example, these experts cite the continuous pollution of the seas. We all become aware of this for a short time when the latest oil slick washes up on our beaches; but we do not realize oil pollution is happening all the time. By the mid 1970s, between 10 and 12 million tons of oil were being added to the world's waters every year, either through accident or carelessness or sheer irresponsibility. In addition, millions of factories throughout the world dump untreated waste products into the sea. The damage is so far-reaching that even in the Antarctic, miles away from any industry, penguins have man-made chemicals and insecticides in their tissues. We cannot as yet calculate the accumulated damage to living organisms all over the world, but we should be asking questions about relative costs. Crude oil for example is being transported across the world at great expense. Rigs are built and maintained, again at enormous cost, but how is this oil being used? Is it being conserved for necessary operations, or is it being wasted and inefficiently converted into trivial goods which only expert advertising makes us want to buy?

To illustrate these points, let us consider the facts which Barbara Ward gives (*Progress for a Small Planet*) about the Mediterranean Sea. Its coastal population is already 100 million and could double in the next 20 years. In addition some 100 million tourists visit the area every year and their numbers may well increase. Already there are 120 coastal cities emptying their almost untreated sewage into the water. More tourists will mean more hotels, thus increasing the pollution unless present practices change dramatically. On the northern side of the Mediterranean, thousands of new factories have sprung up and these empty their waste products into the sea. Oil tankers which pass through from Suez to the major northern ports give off about 300,000 tons of oil pollution a year. Already in some areas the small bacteria which decompose filth and put it back into the food chain are threatened by lack of oxygen and could become extinct. At the southern end of the Mediterranean, there are comparatively few coastal cities and industries, but if these were to increase, the problem of pollution could become acute.

The United Nations Energy Programme called a conference of all Mediterranean coastal nations to decide upon a common policy of conservation and development. But although some progress has been made, agreement to limit land-based pollution has not so far been reached. This failure is at least partly caused by the affluent countries who will not accept a major share in the cost of cleaning up pollution which they themselves have largely created. Understandably the poorer southern states do not see why they should be expected to contribute large sums to solve a problem for which they are not really responsible. The UNEP estimates the total cost of cleaning the Mediterranean at 10 billion dollars, which is little more than a week's expenditure on world armaments. If something is not done within the next few years, the deterioration in the Mediterranean will have gone beyond recall. It could become a dead sea where no fish live and whose beaches are littered with rubbish that will not dissolve. Its oil and chemical waste would then constitute a serious health risk to the inhabitants and would successfully frighten away any tourist industry whatsoever.

(c) Conservation

To some people conservation merely means saving an endangered species of wildlife or preserving a particularly beautiful piece of countryside, but to many more the word embodies a new approach to our finite earth. It represents a belief in ecological world management upon which the future of life as we know it could ultimately depend.

Up to 50 years ago, most economic theories seemed to depend on unlimited growth; at that time many believed that man could always find answers and provide substitutes for dwindling reserves of non-renewable resources. They believed that conservation as such was unnecessary. Although attitudes are gradually changing today, some conservationists believe that the human race is involved in a very difficult race against time if we are to halt the environmental deterioration before it has gone too far.

We are learning by trial and error that living things are interdependent. For example, we have given the name photosynthesis to the process whereby green plants use the sun's energy for producing oxygen and organizing material from water, carbon dioxide and simple mineral salts; but we do not yet know how much we depend upon the world's great forests for the recycling of oxygen and minerals. Many of these forests are being cleared for agricultural land or quick-growing trees which produce good financial returns. In the past man has created deserts by deforestation, over-grazing and over-cultivation of the soil. While earlier generations acted in ignorance and could not foresee the consequences, we now realize that man-made deserts on our planet cover an area equal to that of China (UNEP, 1977). This process of creating deserts should clearly be stopped before the casual, ignorant or misguided programme becomes too costly to the environment.

In *Earth in Danger* Michael Crawford quotes an experiment in Tanzania as an example. One large area of rain forest consisted of mahogany, fig and olive. These trees are deep-rooted and can thus find underground springs of water. But they were cut down and the timber was used for housebuilding and firewood. For four years the local people were allowed to grow corn in the deforested area, after which quick-growing pine trees were planted. They were seen as profitable cash crops. But pine trees are shallow rooted. They are also resinous and inflammable and they therefore belong to the north, temperate zones. When the Tanzanian pine trees were fully grown and many of their cones lay scattered on the ground, they succumbed one day to the hot African sun and went up in a blaze of fire, causing severe damage to the surrounding rain forest as well as the total destruction of the plantation itself.

It is common knowledge that conservationists recognize the importance of preserving a rare species of plant or the many kinds of wild-life which are threatened with extinction. We must become aware that they are also deeply concerned at any deterioration in the natural habitat which houses both plant and animal. We are slowly awakening to the fact that, thanks to man's greed, the whale, the African elephant and Indian tiger are all in danger of extermination during this century. Many conservationists, however, believe that all wildlife, not just a few species, is at serious risk from man. They deplore the fact that the world's wildlife and its natural habitat are being constantly diminished, as their value and significance could be basic to man's future needs. The preservation of the whale and many species of fish, for example, is sound economic sense, apart from any other reason.

Problems and solutions

Man's increasing population makes the search for food, water, land and energy an ever-deepening problem. Migration can no longer be used to solve these difficulties. At first sight, modern agricultural methods seem to open up vistas of untold plenty. Vast amounts of chemical fertilizers stimulate growth and pesticides control disease, insects and weeds. But although these agricultural methods proved successful in the short term in Northern Europe, they have been found singularly unproductive in other parts of the world where water is scarce. Even in Europe the cost of fertilizer is enormous and insecticides destroy harmless creatures whose death may affect the whole food cycle, even up to man himself.

Industrial man fouls his rivers and pollutes his atmosphere. He is also extremely wasteful of fresh water. And yet in many parts of the world prolonged drought leads to famine and encourages deserts to creep over the edges of once fertile lands.

The world's consumption of energy doubled between 1970 and 1980. Many factors were responsible, the change from manpower to machinery in agriculture being only one. Increased travel facilities are another. A Boeing 707 flying from New York to San Francisco uses up more energy than it would take to feed thousands of people for a day.

One method of solving the energy crisis is to develop nuclear power from nuclear fission. In theory this was supposed to provide the world with cheap and clean power, but it has so far been extraordinarily costly to produce. Furthermore, many experts are seriously concerned about the risks involved. It is essential to prevent nuclear raw material and fuel from escaping during processing and transit. When this is achieved, the vexed question of radioactive waste disposal still remains. As yet no completely safe container for nuclear materials has been designed and the radioactive life of

134

nuclear waste products is estimated in thousands of years. Some scientists have pinned their hopes on nuclear fusion—the process of fusing nuclear material together at very high temperatures. But this again is a very costly process and no one knows precisely what risks are involved.

Many leading Christians (amongst them Hugh Montefiore, Bishop of Birmingham, and John Taylor, Bishop of Winchester) have stressed that we must get our priorities right. Man is a part of creation. He must work *with* nature, not attempt to change it or over-ride it. Man has been dependent on the environment for his evolution. He will not survive if he despoils his planet. He needs to study the ecosystem more comprehensively and to learn from nature. Industrial and technological man needs to develop life-styles which are not spendthrift and extravagant.

Conservation does not necessarily mean cutting back, although it does involve cutting down on futile and unnecessary expenditure of vital resources. It also has the positive goal of cleansing the seas, purifying the waters and the air, and reclaiming the deserts. It can include the concepts of organic farming, i.e. using natural processes; of research into less costly and dangerous ways of harnessing the sun's power, and that from wind, waves and the natural heat of the earth (geothermal energy). It has been pointed out that if a tiny fraction of the money consumed by nuclear development had been earmarked for research into renewable sources of energy, many of our problems might have been already solved. Some conservationists campaign against the cruelties of factory farming, seeing such practices as fundamentally opposed to humanitarian and Christian concepts of justice. Others may equally oppose intensive monoculture (i.e. single crop farming) in developing countries, considering it very irresponsible to make a vulnerable economy entirely dependent on one product.

There are hopeful signs of a global strategy for world conservation. In the early 1980s the International Union for Conservation of Nature and Natural Resources, the United Nations Environment Programme, and the World Wild Life Fund, published the World Conservation Strategy whose aim is 'to help advance the achievement of sustainable development through the conservation of living resources'. Before this document was published more than 450 government agencies and conservation organizations in over 100 countries were asked their views on conservation priorities and the final draft was also submitted to the FAO and UNESCO. All the organizations involved will work closely together to put the strategy into action. They will also need the support of the ordinary person if nations are to achieve anything.

Discussion and work

1 The Women's World Day of Prayer for 1981 took as its theme 'The Earth is the Lord's (Psalm 24:1). The service was prepared by Christian American Indian women representing Indian tribes throughout the United States. This interdenominational service showed the Indians' special reverence for nature and their feeling of kinship with all creatures of the earth, sky and water. Find out what you can about the religion of the North American Indian, as opposed to what you may have seen on Western films. In what ways do you think their attitudes to nature are different from our own?

2 Look up Luke 6:38. In what way do his words apply to our present situation in the Western world? In what sense should we be prepared to share what we have with others?

3 Complete a project on any one aspect of pollution or conservation that interests you, whether it is to do with the earth's seas or inland waters or air or soil or wildlife.

4 If possible, ask someone involved in conservation to come and talk to your group. See the list at the back of this book for possible societies and addresses or consult your local library.

5 You have probably studied some of the topics touched on here in geography or in the humanities. Do you think more teaching about the environment is essential in order that ordinary people may understand what is involved and can influence decisions made by industrialists and governments?

Section D — Some Relevant Biblical Ideas

Introduction

What we call the Bible (from *biblos*—Greek for papyrus bark), is really a library of books divided into two sections. The Old Testament is the sacred literature of the Jewish faith, to which has been added the New Testament. This records the life, teaching and impact of Jesus of Nazareth, himself a Jew, but regarded by Christians as the founder of their faith. We may well ask how it is that writings dating from thousands of years ago could be at all helpful to us as a guide for our changing and disturbing century, but there are several reasons why this should be so.

First, both the Jewish and Christian religions believe in the one true God, who is a moral being and who makes moral demands upon his people. Thus the moral codes derived from Jewish/Christian sources have been the basis of our own moral inheritance and, together with the Graeco-Roman civilization, have been formative influences in Western culture. Second, within this collection of books there are inspired accounts of how men and women interpreted the events of their own personal lives and the history of their nation according to their religious convictions. Although it is possible to trace a development of thought and understanding in these ancient texts, the fact that human nature has not changed in essentials makes the truths of human experience still relevant in any age. Third, in the person and teaching of Jesus, whom Christians believe to be the greatest and most profound religious and ethical teacher of all time, we can discover the radical ideas that are not only appropriate to our own age but for countless ages still to come.

1 God

In Genesis 1—12
Men and women have always wondered about the beginnings of their world. Ancient man made up stories about the origins of life based upon his observations and experiences, just as modern man puts forward scientific theories which are either proved or found to

be inadequate in the light of subsequent reasoning and experiment. The beliefs of the Hebrew people about the creation of the world are found in the first 11 chapters of Genesis. At one time these accounts were regarded as actual historical events. We know now that they belong to a type of literature called myth; that is to say, they were probably originally the spoken part of religious ritual. Today we may call these stories parables. We do not know precisely how the Hebrews arrived at their conclusions about their God and his world but we treat their ideas with respect, recognizing in them insights which later generations of men and women have found to be immensely helpful in furthering their own understanding of and relationship with God.

According to Genesis 1 and 2, God is the Creator of the Universe. In the first chapter creation takes place through God's spoken word; in the second, through God's breath man becomes a living soul. God is depicted as resting on the seventh day, as seeing his creation as 'good' and at the last as 'very good'. He fashions man out of clay like a potter; he walks in the garden in the cool of the evening and has direct conversation with his creatures. The ancient priestly writers of Genesis 1 thought of the sun, moon and stars as the great cosmic clock which God had set in the heavens. Therefore they regarded him as the Lord of Time. In this chapter, man is described as being made in God's image. We can speculate about the meaning of this phrase but one thing is crystal clear; no other idol or image of God was ever allowed in the Hebrew faith. Man could see the product of God's work in the Universe around him, but only in his fellow human beings could he truly catch a glimpse of a godlike nature.

In Genesis 12−50
The stories of Abraham, Isaac, Jacob and Joseph are known as the patriarchal sagas. A saga is different from a myth in that it need have no religious significance. It is first and foremost a story about a clan or tribal hero, or the adventures of such family groups. It has been passed down by word of mouth through the generations in order to preserve it in times when written documents were very scarce. Sagas are greatly valued by the historian even if they are not history in the modern sense of the word. The patriarchs were the fathers or great ancestors of the Hebrew people and the nation treasured their memories, but it is hard to know precisely from these stories the exact relationship between the patriarchs and God. Probably God was regarded as their tribal chief, although God's promise given to Abraham (Genesis 12:1−3) had implications for all men. God's special Hebrew name has been variously interpreted, but many modern scholars now write it as 'Yahweh'.

138

At first he was seen as one god among many, although in later Hebrew thought he was worshipped as the one, true and only God. The term monotheism (*monos*—Greek for alone or single; *theos*—Greek for god) is used to describe a religion which believes in one supreme divine being. In the Genesis sagas, God is represented as a kind of superhuman being; in one story he appears in human form to Abraham (Genesis 18).

In Exodus and Numbers

The real history of the Israelites or Hebrews begins with Moses. This leader was almost certainly an actual historical person. In the narratives, Moses is called by God to deliver his people from slavery in Egypt. Through the eyes of Moses, God is seen as the Lord of History, who takes decisive action both through men and women and through natural disasters to bring about his purpose. God is represented as speaking to Moses face to face—a privilege granted to no other man. The many conversations Moses had with God show us what kind of man Moses was and how his understanding of God's nature deepened and developed. Moses believed God's chief concern was with Israel and that the Israelites had been especially chosen to be God's people. In the period of the escape from Egypt and the wanderings in the wilderness, the biblical text recognizes other gods, but the God of Israel was regarded as supreme and as demanding the total allegiance of his people (Exodus 20:*1–2*). If they will be utterly faithful to him, he will give them victory in battle, will grant them land, prosperity and will make of them a great nation. God is even depicted as a Man of War (Exodus 15:*3*) and as directing the campaign of conquest in Canaan (Joshua 5:*13–15*).

The special relationship between God and Israel was sealed by a Covenant or Agreement made at Mount Sinai. The vision of Moses was that his people were to become a 'kingdom of priests, and a holy nation' (Exodus 19:*5*), that is to say, they were to mediate or be the channel through which knowledge of God was to be brought to the rest of mankind. According to the terms of the Covenant, God expected personal faithfulness to him and also a certain code of behaviour. Moses acted not only as a deliverer on God's behalf, but also as the great law giver. The Ten Commandments (Exodus 20:*1–17*; Deuteronomy 5:*6–21*), the heart of the great Old Testament law code, are amongst the most famous of all ancient prescriptions for right living. Many other laws were later added and form the basis of the books of Leviticus and Numbers.

In Judges and the historical books

When the Israelites finally settled in Canaan they came up against all kinds of problems, especially concerning the agricultural gods of the land. The theme of the book of Judges is how unfaithfulness to Yahweh was punished by foreign invasions, but when the people repented God raised up a Judge or deliverer who saved the situation. In the succeeding history of Israel (as told in 1 and 2 Samuel, 1 and 2 Kings, 1 and 2 Chronicles) God is thought of as King. Even when human monarchs were appointed to weld the people together (and there were some who believed this to be a bad step), they were only regarded as God's Vice-Regents, governing in God's name. Their successes and failures were ultimately judged by their loyalty to the Law of God as given both through the laws themselves and in prophetic teaching. For centuries God's kingdom was defined in geographical and political terms. Israel was a theocracy (*theo*—Greek for God; *cracy*—Greek for government or state) and her material prosperity, or lack of it, was assessed in relation to her faithfulness to her role as the special possession of the Lord God. The fact that disaster so often fell upon the nation and that it became divided into northern and southern kingdoms, both of which eventually fell to foreign invaders, was seen by the great 7th- and 8th-century Hebrew prophets as just punishment by God upon his fickle and unfaithful people.

In the prophetic writings
The Old Testament prophets were not simply people who foretold the future. When they did prophesy impending doom for their people, it was because they realized the inevitable consequences of present folly. They called for repentance now before it was too late. In a very real sense they were the successors of Moses. They were the men (and occasionally the women) through whom God spoke and acted. The biblical way of describing this activity is that the Spirit of the Lord came upon his servant and thus he spoke under the inspiration of God's revelation. 'No prophecy ever came by the impulse of man, but men, moved by the Holy Spirit, spoke from God' (2 Peter 1:*21*). Each of the great prophets made his individual contribution to a further understanding of God's nature.

Elijah. In his courageous stand against the plots and terror of Queen Jezebel, Elijah found that God spoke to him not in the furies of natural events but in the still small voice within him (1 Kings 19:*12*). His rebuke of King Ahab's corrupt use of power (1 Kings *21*) illustrated Elijah's understanding of God's moral nature.

Amos. Almost a century later, Amos the Shepherd was declaring that God was weary of sacrifices. Instead 'let justice roll down like waters, and righteousness like an overflowing stream' (Amos 5:*21—24*). He condemned the rich for exploiting the poor (8:*4—7*) and for their selfish indulgence (6:*4—6*). Amos saw God as Universal, that is to say he believed God was concerned with the conduct of other nations as well as Israel. His first oracles were against Israel's neighbours for their cruelty and inhumanity (1:*3, 6, 11, 13, 2:11*). Amos' passionate concern for social justice arose out of his interpretation of the nature of God and he saw with startling clarity that Israel was heading for disaster. God would punish the nation's evildoing as surely as any natural effect follows upon its cause (3:*1—6*).

Hosea. He began to prophesy some 20 years later than Amos and has been called the prophet of love. From his own personal suffering caused by an unfaithful wife, Hosea perceived that the love of God was steadfast and forgiving, willing to ransom his people from death if only they would return to him and repent (Hosea 2:*19—20*; 11:*1—3*). He also condemned the social ills of his day (4:*1—3*) and spoke out strongly against the worship of idols and other gods (13:*2—4*). He saw a possible invasion by Assyria as God's punishment upon his sinful people (11:*5—6*), and yet realized that if he himself continued to love an unfaithful wife that God could not cease to love Israel (11:*8—9*). His book ends with a poignant message of love and compassion (14:*4—9*). However, the people of the northern kingdom paid no more attention to Hosea than they had done to Amos and in 721 BC with the fall of its capital, Samaria, to the Assyrians, the kingdom came to an end.

Micah. Probably contemporary with Hosea was Micah, the countryman who prophesied both to the people of the northern kingdom and also to Judah (the southern kingdom). Although his book is short some of his teaching had a profound effect on later generations. 'But as for me, I am filled with power by the Spirit of the Lord' he declared (Micah 3:*8*) and in that power he emphatically denied that God was interested in formal ritual. What God required of man was that he should be merciful, humble and just in all his dealings. True worship of God was dependent upon moral living (6:*7, 8*).

Isaiah. The great statesman-prophet of Jerusalem whose call came about 740 BC, is credited with the first 39 chapters of the writings which bear his name, although there may even be passages in this section which were not spoken by him. (The anonymous writers of Isaiah 40—55 and 56—66, sometimes referred to as Second and Third Isaiah for convenience, belong to different centuries.) The call to be a prophet came to Isaiah one day when he was in the Temple (Isaiah 6:*1—13*). In his vision of God he was overwhelmed by the realization of God's holiness and, by contrast, with his own unworthiness or sinfulness. In certain stages of Old Testament history, holiness signified a mysterious force or power with which it was dangerous to come into contact unless you were initiated into the right rituals and even, in some cases, wore the right clothing. But for Isaiah the holiness of God meant his moral perfection and the only worship which was acceptable to him was in right living. In a biting attack upon hypocritical forms of ceremonial worship, the prophet declared to the people that what God wanted from them was 'Cease to do evil: Learn to do good: Seek justice, correct oppression, defend the fatherless, plead for the widow' (1:*11—20*). Apparently Isaiah was successful in his ministry for a time as he helped his people through two periods of crisis, but in the end Jerusalem was overrun by the Babylonians and the nation's leadership were exiled for 70 years in the country of their conquerors. Isaiah, however, had the supreme vision of an Age of Peace and Justice, ruled over by the future King, the Lord's Anointed (9:*6*; 11:*1—9*).

Jeremiah. The great later prophets—Jeremiah, Ezekiel and Second or Deutero Isaiah—saw terrible disasters fall upon their nation. Jeremiah, who lived about 654—584 BC, would witness the two sieges of Jerusalem and its eventual destruction. He was persecuted by his contemporaries because of his unpopular view and prophecies (Jeremiah 11:*19*). He loved his people deeply and suffered so greatly that he wished he had never been born (15:*10*). But in his darkest moments of despair he found that God was with him (15:*20,21*). From this experience came the conviction that everyone could have a personal relationship with God and was individually responsible to God. Because of this profound insight, Jeremiah has been called the prophet of personal religion. Amos and Hosea had thought about God's relationship to his people as a whole rather than to any individual, and although Isaiah had conceived of a 'remnant' or faithful few, who would be saved by God because of their upright fidelity to his wishes, the individual was not really significant to him. But Jeremiah talked of a new covenant with God which would be an inner reality, written on men's hearts or consciences (31:*31—34*). In this respect he was a forerunner of Jesus. He saw that the right relationship with God depended not primarily on outward ritualistic observances but on inner motivation. God was righteous, compassionate and holy and a man's understanding of this was all important (9:*23—24*).

Ezekiel. The priestly prophet, Ezekiel, was amongst those taken into exile in Babylon at the conquest of Jerusalem. Much of his writing is difficult to understand, but he made several important additions to the Old Testament concept of God. In his earlier visions of God, he uses the conventional symbols of wind and fire (Ezekiel 1:*4*), but in a magnificent later chapter (34:*11—16*) he speaks of the Lord as the Good Shepherd in words which are very similar to those of Psalm 23. Like Jeremiah before him, he refuted the Israelite doctrine that a man may be punished by God for his father's sins. Each individual was responsible to God and would be judged by him 18:2—4, 30). During the dark days of exile, he kept alive the worship of Yahweh among his people. He gave them a message of hope for the future and prophesied the coming of the Messiah, the Anointed One, of the line of David, who would establish an Age of Peace (34:23—25; 37:24—26). When the people had been cleansed of sin, national unity would be restored in the land of Israel's origin. In a now famous passage (37:1—14), Ezekiel likened the physical and spiritual resurrection of his desolate people to a valley of dry bones restored to living men by the Spirit of the Lord. Again, like Jeremiah before him, Ezekiel looked forward to a new covenant between God and man which would be initiated by God himself (36:26,27). Man would be given a new heart and a new spirit. Ezekiel probably died many years before the exile was ended. Although in Christian eyes much of his teaching is limited and restrictive, he laid the foundations for a renewal of national life. This was especially based on a rebuilt Temple in Jerusalem and on a re-editing of the Law Codes.

Second Isaiah. Perhaps the greatest of all the prophets was the unknown author of Isaiah 40—55. He believed the exile was coming to an end and that his people would soon be restored to Judah. No other prophet before him had categorically stated that there was only one God, but Second Isaiah saw that this one God was the creator of the universe and that all things were under his control (Isaiah 44:6; 45:22; 54:5). Moreover, he was quite convinced of Israel's mission to the world (42:6—7; 43:21). Included in chapters 40—55 are four short poems about a servant of God (42:1—4; 49:1—6; 50:4—9; 52:13—53:12). The poems visualize God achieving his purpose for mankind, that of bringing them back to a right relationship with him through the faithfulness of his chosen servant. It is not clear whether the author thought of the servant as an individual, or a loyal few ('remnant'), or even the nation as a whole. The servant, though guiltless, was willing to suffer on behalf of others who were guilty. Thus he was able to save them. In the last poem God speaks to the servant saying that despite the servant's great pain and suffering, when he sees what has been achieved by his sorrow, he will know joy and satisfaction and will be raised by God to glory and honour.

Third Isaiah. When Cyrus, the Persian King, conquered Babylon, the Jews were given permission to return to Jerusalem in 537 BC and work started on the rebuilding of the Temple. The ideas of two further prophets known as Third Isaiah and Malachi must be mentioned here. The writer of Isaiah 56—66 believed that

Gentile nations would come to Jerusalem to worship the one true God (56:7). The prophecy was quoted by Jesus when he cleansed the Temple (Mark 11:17). In the difficult and depressing times of the country's restoration, Third Isaiah encouraged his people with visions of a New Age (60:1) and of a future Day of the Lord when God would reveal himself in all his glory (60:19; 65:17).

Malachi. (In Hebrew this means 'My Messenger' and was therefore probably a title rather than a proper name) also saw Yahweh as the God of all nations (Malachi 1:11).

Nehemiah and Ezra
Eventually prophecy declined. The Law became all important and through the work of Nehemiah the Reformer and Ezra the Scribe, the Jewish people became a community whose life was entirely governed by the Law of God. God seemed more remote and thus the idea of angels acting as messengers between God and men assumed a popularity and significance not known in earlier periods.

Wisdom literature
The conquests of Alexander the Great (334–323 BC) ended the centuries of Persian domination; Greek language and ideas spread throughout the new empire. We can detect some of this influence upon Jewish thought in the so-called Wisdom literature, which consists of three books in the Old Testament (Job, Proverbs and Ecclesiastes), and two (Wisdom of Solomon and Ecclesiasticus) in the Apocrypha—a collection of sacred writings excluded from the Hebrew canon, but included in the Greek and Latin Old Testaments. In these books the religious and moral teaching of the prophets was applied specifically to the individual, but the concept of Divine Wisdom was personified. She was seen as the companion and helper of God (Proverbs 8:29,30) and she inspired men to live rightly and successfully.

In the New Testament gospels of Matthew, Mark and Luke
It is against this Old Testament background that we have to look at Christian beliefs about God. The whole theme of the biblical story is that of reconciliation. Humanity has become estranged from the source of well-being and true life, which is God himself, and must be won back to that right relationship. To have knowledge of God, in biblical terms, does not imply an intellectual exercise in the sense that you would sit down and work out in your mind the answer to some mathematical problem. It implies entering into a personal relationship and gaining the kind of knowledge

which comes from the person to person encounter. In New Testament belief, it is Jesus who *knows* God as no one has ever done before because of their intimate relationship; he is God's son (Luke 10:*22*). Jesus' personal name for God was 'Abba'—a tender Aramaic form of the English 'Father' (Mark 14:*36*). He taught his disciples to pray to God as a loving Father (Matthew 6:*9*). His parables show God's care for the sinner and the outcast (especially for example in Luke 15:*1—32*). The major theme of Jesus' preaching, according to the gospels of Matthew, Luke and Mark, was the Kingdom of God. He saw his purpose as bringing mankind into the Kingdom (Mark 1:*15,38*). For Jesus the Kingdom was not a geographical or political concept at all but an inner reality. It was the rule or reign of God in men's hearts and lives (Luke 17:*21*). It was both here and now in the ministry of Jesus himself, but also a future event or expectation. He summarized the whole of man's relationship to God and to his fellow human beings in terms of love (Mark 12:*28—34*). One of his favourite topics was the need of a loving contrite heart. We must constantly be willing to forgive others, otherwise we will not be able to look for and receive God's forgiveness (Matthew 18:*21—35*).

John's Gospel
In the Fourth Gospel Jesus is described as the Word of God. The Greek 'Logos' which in English is translated as 'Word' means far more than speech. It also stands for Mind or Reason (among other things) and can be interpreted as Creative Activity. We have seen how in Hebrew thought God was considered active in the world through his Word (Psalm 33:*6,9* and Jeremiah 1:*4,9*), through his Spirit (Genesis 1:*2*; Isaiah 42:*1*; and Ezekiel 37:*14*) and through his Wisdom (Wisdom 9:*1*). Thus for John to call Jesus the Word of God is to say that Jesus is of God himself. Jesus can therefore bring men to a knowledge of God and so to eternal life. 'For God so loved the world, that he gave his only son, that whoever believes in him should not perish, but have eternal life' (John 3:*16*). In the life and death of Jesus is manifest the love of God. Paul echoes this thought in his letter to the Corinthians. 'God was in Christ reconciling the world to himself' (2 Corinthians 5:*19*).

In John's gospel, Jesus is reported as saying 'I and the Father are one' (10:*30*) and 'He who has seen me has seen the Father' (14:*9*). The basis of this unity is reflected in the prayer of Jesus before his arrest (17:*22*) and in the farewell conversation that he had with his friends: 'As the Father has loved me, have I loved you; abide in my love. If you keep my commandments, you will abide in my love, just as I have kept my Father's commandments and abide in his love' (15:*9—10*).

145

1 John
In this later New Testament letter, the writer reflects on the life
and witness of Jesus and draws the ultimate conclusion about
God. He declares that God *is* Love and that the supreme way of
knowledge of God is through love. 'God is love; and he who abides
in love abides in God, and God abides in him' (4:*16*).

Discussion and work
1 In such a short space it is of course impossible to summarize
adequately the biblical concepts of God, but look up the biblical
passages used to illustrate the points made.
2 Write a short paragraph explaining some of the ideas about God
which lie behind the following Psalms: Psalms 19, 24, 95, 103,
104, 130.
3 Note how men's understanding of the nature of God was influenced by their own experience and how there has been a progres-
sion of thought culminating in the Old Testament in Second
Isaiah and in the New Testament in the teaching of Jesus. We
shall be dealing with the implications of Jesus' teaching more
fully in later passages.
4 If God does exist, how it is that man's ideas of him have changed
throughout the centuries?
5 Humanists i.e. those who believe there is nothing higher than
man, criticize Christians by saying that the idea of God as an all-
powerful father figure, albeit loving, encourages men to go on
thinking of themselves as children. Therefore they do not take
adult responsibility for their lives. Do you think there is any
degree of justification for this view?
6 What effect do you think it has had on the status of women that
God is so often depicted in masculine terms? (Only in the Wisdom literature is the Wisdom of God sometimes personified as
'She', 7:*25,26*.)
7 What difference do you think it would make to people's lives if
they really believed in a God who was Creative Love?

2 Mankind and Jesus

Man as the crown and climax of creation
The Old Testament view of man is clearly portrayed in the parables of Genesis 1 and 2. In the first chapter man is the crown and
climax of creation, being made in the image of God. It is very difficult to know what the original priestly writers of this chapter meant
by the phrase 'the image of God'. Perhaps they actually thought
that man was physically like his creator. More probably they

recognized that something in man's make-up gave him kinship with God. Man is able to communicate with God, hence the assumption that he has a spiritual nature; he is capable of moral choice, so that he can respond in trust and obedience to God's wishes or he can withhold that response. Genesis 3 and 4 tell the story of how man broke his fellowship with God by disobedience— a matter we shall discuss in section 4.

In the second chapter man's body is moulded by God out of the dust of the earth and he becomes a living being when God breathes into him. The animals and birds are also fashioned out of the soil to become living creatures but they are not given God's breath. Man therefore shares a fundamental nature with the animal kingdom, but he is different from them in this vital respect. He is also given mastery or lordship over the rest of animate creation. According to Hebrew thought the fact that Adam names the animals means that he has authority over them. It is thus implied that he has the gift of self-conscious reason. In the first chapter man is also com-missioned to rule, but only as God's representative.

According to Genesis 1, men and women are created at the same time, so woman is not considered inferior to man. In Genesis 2, however, woman is created out of man's rib, a symbolic way of saying that she is his soul mate, complementary to him in every way. Even if Adam (a poetic personification of man) is created first, he is incomplete without woman. He is made for fellowship with others. Mankind receives from God the blessing which enables the species to reproduce itself. There is no suggestion in these first two chapters that child-bearing was punishment for sin. On the contrary, man's sexual nature belongs to the natural order which God sees is 'very good' and which is given the power of self-propagation.

Man is put to tend the garden in Eden, so work is not a curse but a blessing and all living things are given a vegetarian diet. Killing and slaughtering were not part of the original design.

This beautiful idyll pictures a perfect state when men and women were in harmony with God, with each other, with the animals and with the soil.

Man possesses an elementary law of conscience
Through disobedience, however, disaster comes upon mankind. According to the parable of the Flood (Genesis 6—9) man's wicked-ness causes God to make a fresh start with humanity, represented by Noah and his family. The covenant between God and Noah is made for all mankind (9:1—16). God promises stability of the natural order (v.8) which will be sufficient to provide for man's physical needs, but in return man must also fulfil his human

147

obligations. There is an elementary law of conscience, of right and wrong, which all men possess, so man may only kill the animals for food and must not kill another human at all. Murder is to be punished by death. Originally, it was the duty of the next of kin to avenge murder, but this later became the office of the state. In this story we find the seeds of an ordered society without which human life could not survive.

This community life is further strengthened by later Old Testament passages which deal with the provision of laws and regulations. When Moses brings the people out of Egypt to Mount Sinai, they enter into a solemn covenant or agreement with God, their deliverer. In a famous passage (Exodus 20:*1—17*) which has now become part of our inherited moral code, Moses gives God's commandments to his people. The first three commandments are about man's relationship with God; only he is to be worshipped. The fourth concerns man's day of rest—a basic need; the last six deal with man's obligations to his family and his community and they represent the *minimum* requirements on which any society could exist. (The *maximum* requirements of course are found in the teaching of Jesus where he summarizes the whole of the law in terms of love (Mark 12:*29—31*). Jesus also gives man a Golden Rule (Matthew 7:*12*): he should always treat others as he would like to be treated himself.)

Man as a responsible being
From these passages we can see that although the Bible views man as a unique individual—he is himself and no other, as his fingerprints indicate—he is also a responsible being, created for fellowship with other human beings and with God. Indeed he has a responsibility to the natural order itself. Early Hebrew thought considered the individual to be so much part of the community that he could use the first person singular when speaking in the name of the community. For example, when someone in the clan or tribe had been killed, any other member could say 'my blood has been shed'. A man's private carelessness or disregard for others was never simply his own affair. His actions for good or evil could affect the whole of his society. This thought is probably carried through to its furthest point in the Old Testament in the Suffering Servant Songs of Deutero—Isaiah.

Our modern society recognizes that dirt and disease are not simply an individual concern because they can have devastating effects upon others. The Old Testament writers looked on disobedience to God's moral commandments in the same light. The prophets were always calling upon their people to walk in the way of God, not only for their own good, but also for the sake of their

148

nation and indeed the world. Deeply stirred by man's inhumanity to man, prophets like Amos thundered against torture, slavery, war, murder of women and children and all kinds of international crime (Amos 1:*3, 6, 9, 11, 13*; 2:*1*) as well as the continual exploitation of the poor by the rich (Amos 8:*4—7*). The Hebrew proverb 'The fathers have eaten sour grapes; and the children's teeth are set on edge' illustrates the truth that in a close knit family and community we all suffer for one another's irresponsibility. But both Jeremiah and Ezekiel refuted the idea that this was God's doing (Ezekiel 18:*1—4*). Each man would be judged according to his own conduct. God did not punish the innocent for the wicked.

Man's power of reason
Humanists distinguish man from the animals by his power of reason. By reason he can attempt to understand himself and change the circumstances of his existence. He can construct a political system or form of society by which he can organize his individual and corporate life. Another aspect of his human dignity is the fact that he is capable of moral choice and therefore must be treated as a free and creative being. But a look at man's history, especially in this century, will reveal how disappointing his attempts to create a better world have proved so far. Wars, genocide, exploitation, rape and torture indicate man's irresponsibility and blinding selfishness. He may be a rational and moral being, but passion and prejudice often distort his reason, while self-deception and destructive egotism can negate his morality.

The Old Testament depicts man as a creature. He is finite and mortal:

As for man, his days are like grass;
he flourishes like a flower of the field.
For the wind passes over it, and it is gone,
and its place knows it no more   (Psalm 103:*15,16*);

although if he uses his wisdom and free will aright, he can be glorious:

What is man, that thou are mindful of him,
and the son of man, that thou dost care for him?
Yet thou has made him little less than God,
and dost crown him with glory and honour.
Thou hast given him dominion over the works of thy hands;
thou has put all things under his feet   (Psalm 8:*4—6*).

Shakespeare describes man in similar terms:

> What a piece of work is man!
> how noble in reason, how infinite in faculty!
> in form and moving, how express and admirable!
> in action, how like an angel!
> in apprehension, how like a god!
> the beauty of the world; the paragon of animals! (Hamlet II:*ii*);

but, as the play reveals, man is a complex being, capable of great heroism and great treachery. The Bible attempts to explain man's complexity by the fact that he is sinful. It is sin which distorts and negates his spiritual potential.

Man's capacity for growth and development

Man's nature is not fixed and static. He is capable of growth and development throughout the whole of his nature, in body, mind and spirit. And because the human personality has the capacity for growth and change, human society can also be progressive. Man is able to remember and treasure his past experiences. He can read, learn and document the history not only of his own life, but of his community or nation. From this vast storehouse of past experience he can plan the future or at least visualize its possibilities and disasters. He is a creature of time, but his mind and spirit can surpass the boundaries of the present moment. He can even dream of eternity. The theme of man's destiny is strong both in the Old and New Testaments. He is called to be a son of God by the exercise of his free will in loving, responsible relationships.

Jesus, the true, representative man

The New Testament shows Jesus of Nazareth to be Son of God in a special and unique way, fulfilling the promise of what a man may truly be like if he is really formed in the image of God. Christians believe that Jesus is both Son of God and son of man. He is therefore the true representative of God to man and the true representative of man to himself. 'Christ's face is the face of all men's faces', Turgenev wrote. He is also the realization of man's potential without the basic flaws which bedevil us all.

His realization of his task

If we look at the life of Jesus as shown in the gospels we see that apparently at an early age, he was aware of a special relationship with God (Luke 2:*49*). It was not until he was about 30 years old, however, that he emerged from the obscurity of his home town and identified himself with John the Baptist's work for the renewal of Israel. His own baptism by John was a decisive moment in his life when he felt filled with the spirit of God to begin his task (Mark 1:*9—11*). The Jews had long awaited a deliverer, or the Lord's Anointed; this is the meaning of the Hebrew title Messiah, which in Greek is Christ. The majority expected a rightful heir of the house of David who would restore the lost fortunes of Israel and establish God's Kingdom on earth. The national independence of Israel had been destroyed by the Roman general Pompey in 63 BC through the capture of Jerusalem. Many devout Jews saw the Roman oppression as God's punishment upon his unrighteous people, but they believed that God would visit and save his people through his Anointed.

According to the gospels of Luke and Matthew, Jesus went through a period of intense mental conflict before he decided what kind of Messiah or 'deliverer' he was to be (Luke 4:*1—13*; Matthew 4:*1—11*). He rejected both the popular and the traditional ideas of Messiahship. He refused to seduce people by abundance of material things, or to exploit and oppress them by political and military might, or to pull wool over their eyes by clever propaganda. He chose the way of sacrificial love, showing men the Kingdom of God by example and teaching, but leaving them free to respond or not, thus giving them the dignity of individual choice. He must have been aware, even at the beginning of his ministry, that this way of the Suffering Servant of God might lead to his own death at the hands of those who would oppose his ideas.

His ministry
After he had thought through the nature of his Messiahship, Jesus left the wilderness, returned to Galilee and gathered around him a group of his disciples. He was both prophet and teacher and possessed a strange power of healing not only for the body but for the mind and spirit too. The essence of his message concerned the Kingdom of God. While the Jews thought of God's Kingdom in political, geographical and economic, as well as religious terms, for Jesus the Kingdom was the reign of God in men's hearts and lives. This was the rule of absolute love working itself out in every aspect of human existence. It was a present reality in Jesus himself and was also a future expectation. In the Sermon on the Mount (Matthew 5—7), Jesus told his disciples of the quality of life they must possess if they were to become citizens of the Kingdom. He always emphasized inner motivation which was the basic cause of outward acts. True greatness in the Kingdom was service to others (Mark 10:*32—45*). It was a life of joyous loving compassion. But Jesus also believed that by their response to his ministry and his teaching, men passed judgment on themselves. His authority lay in the fact that his life was the perfect demonstration of what he

151

thought. He was the friend of outcasts and sinners. He forgave his enemies. He was sublimely consistent and never compromised his service to love.

His death and resurrection

Some three years after he began his ministry, Jesus was arrested and executed for treason against Rome—a crime he did not commit. Although his friends deserted him at his trial and crucifixion, they afterwards experienced something which was later called the Master's Resurrection from the dead. They were utterly convinced that death had no more dominion over him and that after being with them for a short period of time, he had returned to the Father from whom he had originally come. The theme of the resurrection was central to the early disciples' preaching about Jesus and was their proof that he was the Christ. They had the living experience of the Risen Christ in their midst, leading his disciples and inspiring them to further the work which he himself had begun. This vital certainty was the secret of the early Christians' astonishing achievements in the years which followed.

Through the exercise of his own free will, Jesus had fulfilled his mission; he had demonstrated the way in which a creative, loving spirit can transform the human situation.

Paul on Jesus

When writing to the Corinthians (2 Corinthians 5:*17*) Paul stated his own belief that it was only when a man identified with Jesus Christ in the deepest sense that he could find the power to overcome his sinful nature and his tendency to self-destruction. Paul thought of Jesus as the Second Adam, the new type of humanity to which we must all aspire. His first letter to the Corinthians (1 Corinthians 13) gave a picture of how a person who was governed by love would behave and in his letter to the Galatians (3:*28*) he wrote of his vision of a society from which all barriers and inequalities of sex, social distinction and race would be banished.

Discussion and work

1 Read the parables in Genesis 1 and 2 and also the Covenant with Noah in Genesis 9. Once men thought these stories were literally true. What difference does it make to our value of them and the truth they are expressing when we now recognize them as parables or symbolic stories?

2 Do you agree with the picture of human beings as given in these parables or do you think man is merely a naked ape, a product of his environment and heredity, incapable of change? Or do you think man is an extremely complicated piece of machinery that

can be manipulated by the very clever few?
3 Look carefully at the Ten Commandments. How important do you think they are today? Which do you think is the most important of the Ten? Why are they described as the minimum requirements on which society can be built and Jesus' commandment as the maximum? How easy is it to love your neighbour as yourself? What do you think would happen if everyone kept the Golden Rule? Cite some of the changes which would take place in your own community.
4 Look up in newspapers and magazines and discuss in class, examples of people's irresponsible action which has cost others a great deal. Find and discuss instances in which people's self-sacrifice and kindness have benefited others a great deal.
5 Consider the ways in which man misuses his cleverness; look at his present capacity for destroying his species and polluting his world.
6 Consider the ways in which man's reasoning power rightly used has brought benefits through advances in medicine and science.
7 What do you think is your own personal potential? Do you agree at all with the picture of man's future that George Orwell gave in his novel 1984? Orwell feared that ordinary people could be completely controlled. Are you optimistic or pessimistic about the future?
8 What do you think about Jesus? Do you think he is what man should and might one day become? Can you think of examples in other people's lives of the transforming quality of love? Read the passages from Paul's letters quoted above.
9 Yehudi Menuhin has described conscience as 'the heart tapping at the mind'. Discuss fully what he meant by this phrase and how true his description is. What would your own description be?

3 The nature of evil and suffering

Man misuses the gift of free will
The fact of evil and suffering and the idea that one man's irresponsibility could cause disaster for many others was mentioned in section 2. We see examples of evil and suffering every day of our lives, so the question arises: how does the Bible attempt to explain these realities of human existence and yet at the same time maintain that God is good and that he is almighty?
The parable of the Garden of Eden portrays man, woman and the animals in an idyllic situation. Here is the statement that God's original creation was good. There is no evil, no pain. Man and

woman are happy together. There is no bloodshed. The animals are not killed, nor do they kill each other. The man is a gardener and enjoys his work. The soil is fruitful. Then the serpent appears but is not as yet identified with Satan or the devil; it is described as 'one of God's creatures' and in the parable it represents *temptation*.

The woman falls to the temptation of disobeying God and she is credited with seducing her husband to do the same. Disobedience breaks the relationship between man and God—man hides in fear when he hears God walking in the garden in the cool of the evening. It also spoils man's relationship with woman, because he blames her for the whole affair and speaks resentfully of her to God. As punishment for disobedience, God tells the woman that she will suffer pain in child-bearing and will be subservient to man. So woman's inferior position is regarded as the direct result of her own disobedience. Man is also punished, but indirectly, through the cursing of the soil. He is told that the earth will only yield up its crops by his arduous and unceasing labour. Man and woman are then banished from the garden and the source of eternal life. The parable expresses the conviction that evil and suffering entered man's experience through his misuse of the gift of free will. When tempted to do so he disobeyed God. It offers no explanation as to why the serpent acted as it did. Although it was also punished by God, it was not cross-questioned about its actions.

Man brings suffering to those who do not deserve it
Genesis 4 gives the second illustration of how evil brings further suffering. Cain was jealous of his brother because Abel's offering was acceptable to God and his was not. Hating Abel, Cain ignored God's warning to master his resentment and murdered his brother. Abel was the innocent victim of Cain's hatred. God punished Cain by condemning him to a life of permanent wandering. Cain suffered remorse when he realized the frightening implications of his terrible future, but his fate was deserved as Abel's was not. So this story introduces a new twist to the human drama. The evil man brings suffering not only to himself but to others who do not merit it.

Another theory of the origin of evil
The Flood story of Genesis 6—9 is preceded by a strange myth; the sons of God (or angels) marry human women (6:*1—4*). Probably this very ancient material was first designed to explain the origin of the 'mighty men' or heroes of old; their extraordinary powers could be put down to their mixed ancestry. As the story now stands, the

Genesis writers are apparently attempting to show that evil cannot be completely accounted for by man's misuse of his own gifts. The angelic beings in the story also rebel against God through their infatuation with human women. God then contains the spread of evil by curtailing man's life-span to 120 years. But the fact of evil remains and here we meet the suggestion that it must have spiritual or even supernatural origins.

Like the angel marriages, the Genesis Flood story is also based on very archaic legend stemming from Sumerian and Babylonian sources, but the Hebrew writers have used it imaginatively to show God trying to wipe out evil without entirely destroying his creation. The teaching of this story is that evil brings its own terrible consequences, although 20th-century man may consider that natural disaster has nothing to do with man's wickedness. The story also plainly states the belief that evil is now an inherent part of man's nature 'every imagination of the thoughts of his heart was only evil continually' (6:5). According to Hebrew belief, the heart was the centre of man's consciousness, his essential being. Man's heart has now become naturally evil. The later prophets, as we have seen, had the profound insight that eventually man would have to be given a new heart, i.e. a new being or spirit, if God was really to remedy this defect.

God uses evil for good purposes

Readers of the first 11 chapters of Genesis may have felt gathering gloom and despair about the future of mankind. If sin and evil have become so firmly established, what hope is left? However, a sense of plan and purpose for the whole of creation emerges out of the patriarchal narratives. And in the longest saga of all, that of Joseph, God is shown to use evil creatively for good purposes. Joseph's brothers envied and hated him because he was their father's favourite. They disposed of him to traders journeying to Egypt, where he was enslaved to Potiphar, an officer in Pharaoh's army. Potiphar's wife tried to seduce this handsome young Israelite and when he refused her advances, she falsely accused him of attempted rape. Joseph was thrown into prison. He was the innocent victim of jealousy and frustrated sexual passion, but he did not waste his energies on resentment and bitterness. 'The Lord was with him', so Joseph used the present experience as an opportunity for service. In the end he rose to supreme office and saved both Israel and Egypt from the disastrous effects of years of famine. When Joseph and his brothers were eventually reconciled, he was able to say, 'As for you, you meant evil against me, but God meant it for good' (Genesis 50:20).

The problem of natural disasters

Scholars think that the stories of the Plagues of Egypt (Exodus 7—12) were originally acted at Passover time, one of the most important festivals of the Jewish year. The ancient Israelites would feel pride and satisfaction that their God was shown to be all-powerful, able to inflict plagues and disasters upon the most mighty nation of the known world in order to release his people from slavery. At the time these stories were written and preserved, people believed that God directly controlled all natural phenomena. But on reflection this idea leads to very serious moral and theological problems. When we really think about the latest natural disaster, whether it be an erupting volcano, a hurricane, earthquake, or tidal wave in which hundreds of innocent people are killed and thousands more made destitute, we cannot reasonably believe that God is responsible. The New Testament supports our modern view since Jesus explicitly stated that nature is neutral (Matthew 5:45). As he has a moral sense, man is bound to interpret the workings of the natural order morally, but nature itself is not moral. It is, however, full of potential and challenge and man as a moral being can turn it to good or bad account.

One conflicting element in these stories is that God apparently controls Pharaoh's behaviour. The king is presented as a kind of ninepin, set up to be knocked down again and knocked down to be set up. The Israelites believed the whole earth was the Lord's and his power was without limit. He could make a fool of Pharaoh if he wished. So Pharaoh's obstinate refusal to let the Israelites go even after the visitation of a plague, is attributed to God's action (Exodus 7:13). Later generations realized that evil could not come from God. Man had free will.

In fact, Pharaoh was probably a brave and resolute ruler. He did not at first believe Moses' claim that Israel's God caused the exceptionally severe disasters which hit Egypt that year during the Nile's inundation. Later the pressure of events compelled him to give in and let Israel go. If we look carefully at the plague stories, we can see that God manifested his power through the man Moses and not by the natural disasters which occurred. The genius of Moses, his courage, resolution and faith, enabled him to use the perilous time of the plagues to make Pharaoh release the Israelites. Moses had a vision of his people as God's possession and brought them out of Egypt to establish this covenant relationship. For the Christian the basic lesson of the plague narratives is that disaster and even evil itself can be turned to good account by the enlightened, God-directed man.

Was God in control of all things?

Although the Old Testament writers sought to explain evil as the misuse of free will or the revolt of angelic beings, there was a further dimension to the subject. Men experienced evil as a spiritual power, i.e. they experienced the temptation to do that which they instinctively knew to be against God's will. They knew it was wrong to lie, to cheat, to steal, to murder, to ravage and exploit, yet they felt impelled to do these things. Ancient man recognized the conflict within his own complex nature and came to the conclusion that the tendency to do evil and cause suffering, whether deserved or not, was part of his inheritance. How could man account for the presence of evil while firmly believing that God was ultimately in control of all things? To begin with, evil was considered another aspect of God's power. 'I form light and create darkness. I make weal and create woe. I am the Lord, who do all things' (Isaiah 45:7). God inflicted evil upon his people (and in Amos' view upon other nations also) as a punishment for sin. 20th-century man recognizes a law of cause and effect in the scientific universe, but Amos saw this natural law as operating in the moral sphere.

Does a snare spring up from the ground,
   when it has taken nothing?
Is a trumpet blown in a city   [a sign of approaching danger]
   and the people are not afraid?
Does evil befall a city
   unless the Lord has done it?   (3:5—8)

Even failure in battle could be attributed to the Lord, if Israel had been unfaithful to his Law (Judges 2:15).

Eventually, the concept of an evil spiritual being developed; Satan, like God, also had his dominion.

Satan or the Devil

The word Satan means Adversary. Satan first appears in the Old Testament as a member of the heavenly court (Job 1 and 2). His office was like that of a Public Prosecutor who had to question and sift the evidence to establish whether or not a man was speaking the truth when he said he loved God. Thus he came to be regarded as an adversary or opponent of man, even though still a servant of God. Later writers saw his role differently; he was a rival power, who was himself the Evil One. This development of thought was natural. If God is good, holy and righteous, evil cannot come from him at all. Man must detach evil from the person of God and attribute it to another cause. Eventually, Satan came to be identified with the serpent in Genesis 3 (cf Wisdom 2:24): 'it was the devil's envy which brought death into the world'.

157

Beelzebub, the prince of devils and demon possession, figures prominently in the New Testament, where Satan is finally described as a fallen angel who had rebelled against God— Revelation 12:7—9:

> And now war broke out in heaven, when Michael with his angels attacked the dragon. The dragon fought back with his angels, but they were defeated and driven out of heaven. The great dragon, the primeval serpent, known as the devil or Satan, who had deceived all the world, was hurled down to earth and his angels were hurled down with him. (*Jerusalem Bible*)

The devil, or Satan, thus became the symbolic personification of the force or power of evil which men experienced in their lives.

A definition of evil

From a biblical point of view, evil can be defined as the negation of that which is good. It is a negative motivation, a misuse of man's potential goodness. It diminishes man's essential being by despoiling truth, beauty, unity, wholeness, harmony and radiance, and it destroys man's physical, moral, mental and spiritual life. Just as compassion and tenderness are the opposites of indifference and cruelty, so goodness is the opposite of evil. Goodness is essentially creative. Evil is totally destructive. Countless people of different cultures have dreamed that one day evil and suffering would be no more. This was the vision of both Old Testament and New Testament writers—that at some future date evil and suffering would be finally overcome.

The problem of innocent suffering

Meanwhile how was man to cope with evil and with the further pressing problem of innocent suffering? Right through the Old Testament there runs the persistent idea that if a man sins, he will be punished by poverty, sickness or untimely death. If he is good, he will prosper and live to a ripe old age with many children and grandchildren to honour him. But in fact righteous, good people often experience undeserved suffering, either through another's deliberate carelessness or malice or through something totally outside anyone's control. The book of Job attempts to come to grips with this problem. The central character is a good and saintly man whose sons and daughters unpredictably die and who loses all his wealth and possessions. The poem is an account of a conversation between Job and his friends and Job and God. Job, covered with boils, is sitting on a refuse dump outside the city when his friends come to see him. They take the conventional view that Job must have sinned deeply to be so punished by disaster. But Job

158

passionately protests that he has not deserved his intense suffering. He also points out that the wicked prosper. They get away with their downright disregard of God's moral law. Furthermore, many good men suffer. In his own case, even if he had sinned as all men do, this terrible punishment was in no way a fair judgment on his life.

The poem hints at the mystery of evil. It offers no complete solution to the problem of innocent suffering, but it establishes the important view that suffering does not prove sin and that therefore the sufferer can find fellowship with God in his pain. Job's suffering in fact brought him to a deeper knowledge of God: 'I had heard of thee by the hearing of the ear, but now my eye sees thee, therefore I despise myself and repent in dust and ashes' (Job 42:5). The poem is not saying that we suffer in order that we may find God, nor is it saying that suffering comes from God for this purpose, although the later addition of a Prologue and an Epilogue rather give this impression. It is saying that evil is something which is impossible to understand. Yet if a man can keep hold of his faith in God, he will go through the experience of even the most terrible disaster with his courage and faith enriched and deepened. It will not have been a totally destructive happening.

Suffering voluntarily for the sake of others

The question of innocent suffering is taken a stage further in Second Isaiah's Suffering Servant songs. These songs reflect the most profound Old Testament thought on the mystery and purpose of suffering because the servant of the Lord, whose mission is not only to Israel but also to the Gentiles (i.e. all non-Jews) realizes that he must accomplish his task through his suffering and death. The sufferings of this man of God are not deserved. They are endured for the sake of others, so when in the end he is vindicated by God, those who had previously despised and rejected him, now recognize that he suffered in order to save them.

Jesus

Many people have seen Jesus of Nazareth, who lived five centuries later, as the fulfilment of Isaiah's prophecy. What he hoped to accomplish by his suffering and death we shall discuss in the next section. His whole philosophy, however, was that evil could be overcome by good through the transforming power of love (Matthew 5:44). His disciples endeavoured to follow his example: 'But when you have behaved well and suffer for it, your fortitude is a fine thing in the sight of God. To that you were called, because Christ suffered on your behalf, and thereby left you an example; it is for you to follow in his steps' (1 Peter 2:*21*). 'Do not let evil conquer you, but use good to defeat evil' (Romans 12:*21*).

Discussion and work
1 'And God saw that it was good'. How far does this description of our world agree with what we see about us?
2 Write an essay on how the early Old Testament writers tried to explain how the good world became corrupted.
3 Can we always find a neat, tidy solution to the problem of evil as Joseph did when he said: 'As for you, you meant evil against me, but God turned it to good'?
4 Find out what you can about Anne Frank and discuss what her story illustrates about the nature of evil.
5 Find out what happened in Aberfan in 1966. Can we possibly fit this terrible tragedy into Joseph's category?
6 What examples can you think of where apparent tragedy was turned into triumph?
7 What moral and logical problems arise if you think that God is in charge of the weather? How appropriate is it to pray for rain in a dry season?
8 Think of and discuss examples to show that the misuse of something potentially good and creative brings about suffering and disaster.
9 Who believes in the devil nowadays? Do you?
10 What do you know about the practice of black magic?
11 Why do you think belief in the devil was more common in the Middle Ages than it is in the 20th century?
12 How would you define evil?
13 Discuss modern examples of innocent suffering. What does the case of the Thalidomide babies illustrate about this problem?
14 Can you think of a modern Joseph and a modern Job?
15 What is meant by a law of cause and effect in the moral sphere? Do you see any evidence of its existence?

4 Sin and salvation

In some ways this section overlaps with the last because biblical writers consider that sin, suffering and salvation are all interwoven; certainly these concepts are inseparable when we look at the Christian appraisal of the life and purpose of Jesus.

Sin is disobedience to God's will
The fact of sin appears in the biblical story from the very beginning. Various terms for sin are used in the Old Testament, but

160

basic to them all is the belief that to sin is to disobey the will of God. As man has been given the ability to choose whether to respond to God or not, he can decide to reject God's commandments. In the story of Paradise, Eve deliberately elected to eat the fruit from the tree of Knowledge of Good and Evil. She was tempted to eat it for various reasons, but chief among them was that she wanted the knowledge which it would give and which the serpent said would make her like God. It is not relevant to discuss here what kind of knowledge the parable means us to infer that Adam and Eve obtained from eating the fruit; what matters is that after his act of disobedience Adam hid himself from the face of God. So we see the fundamental character of sin; it causes separation between man and God; perhaps the story also teaches that sin's main motivation is pride. Sin erects a barrier which is not of God's creation but of man's. God does not compel obedience but the biblical writers saw that disobedience always resulted in some kind of punishment; perhaps the hardest and subtlest of all was being cut off from fellowship with God.

All sin is sin against God. When Cain murdered Abel, he sinned against God (Genesis 4:*10*). His brother's blood cried out to God for vengeance. When Potiphar's wife attempted to seduce Joseph, he saw her suggestion as a temptation to betray his master's trust but also to sin against God (Genesis 39:*10*).

Sin is an act hurtful to others
It is equally true that all sin is sin against another person. Abel suffered death as a result of Cain's jealousy and hatred; Joseph suffered the loss of his family and his freedom through his brothers' envy and resentment. And such is the power of sin that not only is the individual affected but also his family, his community and the society in which he lives. Through sinning, a man lowers the level of general conduct and he can become a divisive influence encouraging others to follow his example, especially if he is in a position of authority and leadership.

Sin is destructive of the sinner
The Old Testament also teaches that all sin is sin against oneself: 'but he who misses me (i.e. God's Wisdom) injures himself; all who hate me love death' (Proverbs 8:*36*), and 'by committing a sin a man does wrong to himself' (Ecclesiasticus 19:*4 Jerusalem Bible*). It is possible therefore to define sin as that which brings disharmony and separation; because it disrupts and separates, the individual concerned suffers loss of personhood. By sinning a man diminishes himself and becomes less of a person than he was previously. As God is the source of man's well-being, separation from

God prevents a man from fully realizing all his gifts and potential. Furthermore, the tendency to sin can become a habit which grows until it gets out of control. When sin fully takes hold of a man then 'every imagination of the thoughts of his heart is only evil continually' (Genesis 6:5).

The distinction between moral sin and ritual sin

Ancient man did not always distinguish clearly between moral and ritual regulations. He thought that God demanded animal sacrifice, that he wanted to be worshipped in a set ritual at a specific place, and that the whole apparatus of the priestly office, the prohibitions against certain kinds of food and other minute details concerning outward behaviour found in the law books of the Old Testament were extremely important. It was therefore believed that breaking the ritual law was as much a sin as offending against the moral law. But the great Old Testament prophets saw clearly that this outward observance of patterns of worship was not at all significant to God:

> Has the Lord as great delight in burnt offerings and sacrifices,
> as in obeying the voice of the Lord?
> Behold, to obey is better than sacrifice,
> and to hearken than the fat of rams   (1 Samuel 15:22).

> To do righteousness and justice
> is more acceptable to the Lord than sacrifice   (Proverbs 21:3).

> What does the Lord require of you,
> but to do justice and to love kindness,
> and to walk humbly with your God?   (Micah 6:8).

The debate continued right up into Jesus' day and beyond. Lawyers in the New Testament period counted 613 regulations of the law found in the scriptures. Although some famous rabbis argued that the moral requirements of the law were more important than the ritual, others were adamant that all should be kept equally scrupulously. The lawyer who questioned Jesus on this issue called forth Jesus' brilliant summary of the law in terms of love of God and love of neighbour (Mark 12:29–31): Jesus was quoting from Deuteronomy 6:5 and Leviticus 19:18. He not only agreed with the prophetic approach but felt empowered to crystallize the whole subject of righteousness (i.e. right living) as opposed to sin (wrong living) in the supreme commandment to love. By Jesus' definition, therefore, it is the unloving thought, word and action which is against the will of God, whom he declared to be the loving father of his children.

162

God's punishment of sin

According to the Old Testament, God reacted to sin by punishing it. He banished Adam and Eve from the Garden, he condemned Cain to a nomadic life and he sent the Flood. When the Israelites became settled in Canaan, they turned from worshipping the God of Moses and the patriarchs to the Canaanite gods. The writers of the books of Judges and 1 and 2 Samuel believed that the national disasters which followed—foreign invasions and conquests of Israel—were God's punishment for his people's infidelity. Great 8th-century prophets such as Amos, Hosea, Micah and Isaiah were equally sure that corrupt, unjust and decadent living would inevitably bring about national disaster. God would punish his people by allowing them to be conquered and despoiled.

Of course, one could give a reasonable political explanation for these disasters; the small nation states of Israel and Judah (the northern and southern kingdoms) had little chance of survival among the great powers of Egypt, Assyria and Babylon, unless they were governed by extremely wise and dedicated rulers. The historical causes of the fall of Samaria, capital of Israel, in 721 BC, and of Jerusalem, capital of Judah, in 586 BC, are outside our brief, but the 8th- and 7th-century prophets, particularly Jeremiah, believed absolutely that infidelity to God, in the form of either hypocritical and superficial observance of his moral law or even total disregard of it, would bring about divine retribution.

Christian attitudes to the Old Testament belief in the wrath of God

The whole question of Old Testament beliefs about God's wrath and his punishments is difficult for modern Christians. Jesus taught that nature was neutral. We cannot today believe that natural disasters happen through the direct intervention of a superior, spiritual Being, unless we assume that Being is fickle and liable to change his demands at any time. Such a view goes completely against Jesus' own beliefs. We have also come to realize that any historical situation is extremely complex, that man creates his own history, and that certain actions produce certain consequences. Indeed Amos saw this clearly when he wrote:

> Do two walk together, unless they have made an appointment?
> Does a lion roar in the forest, when he has no prey? . . .
> Does a bird fall in a snare on the earth, when there is no trap for
> it?   (Amos 3:3—5).

But even though we cannot accept the ancient interpretation that God keeps direct and detailed control over human affairs, we can appreciate that on a more profound level the biblical writers are declaring their belief that there is a moral law in the universe. We could call it a law of cause and effect in the moral sphere. Eastern religions recognize the law of Karma, meaning that as a man treats others so he will himself be treated, if not in his present lifetime, certainly in a later one. Paul expresses the biblical concept clearly in his letter to the Galatians: 'Do not be deceived; God is not mocked, for whatever a man sows, that he will also reap' (6:7), and Jesus puts it another way in the Sermon on the Mount: 'You will know them by their fruits. Are grapes gathered from thorns, or figs from thistles?' (Matthew 7:16).

Old Testament sees punishment as a means of bringing repentance and reconciliation

According to the Old Testament the justice of God demands that the sinner be punished for his misdeed. The writers hope that punishment will awaken in the sinner a sense of his error. This will lead to a renewal of his right relationship with God and his neighbour, through repentance and forgiveness. If the sinner himself has gone beyond the hope of reform, then his punishment will awaken others to realize the stupidity and destructiveness of sin. The prophets always taught that punishment was intended to create awareness of sin, thus leaving room for repentance and reconciliation, as we see in the story of David, Bathsheba and Nathan (2 Samuel 12). They believed that God disciplined man for his own sake. The prophets also stated clearly that real repentance was required. Ritual purification was totally inefficient. When many burnt offerings and even the extreme offering of the first-born son were suggested as recompense for sin, Micah answered that what God required of man was justice, mercy and humility (6:1–8).

Punishment, discipline and even national disaster did not always prove effective, for the truth of human experience pointed to the fact that often the wicked man seemed to prosper, at any rate in material terms. How was man to break free from this bondage of sin? What did true salvation mean? The Old Testament offered means for the cleansing of sin and for the renewal of fellowship with God. Where the sin was of a ritual nature, it was naturally believed that ritual purification would remove it, just as a stain on a garment can normally be washed away by soap and water. Israelite ritual, like that of the surrounding peoples, was often a matter of sacrifice. But where the Law demanded sacrifice for sin, it clearly stated that a humble confession of the sin and a truly penitent spirit were also necessary. If the sin had been committed against another, then restitution should also be made (Numbers 5:6,7). On the Day of Atonement, the High Priest made ritual confession for the sins which the community had committed in ignorance of the Law. It was never believed that forgiveness made punishment unnecessary, rather that the punishment awakened the sinner to his need for repentance and forgiveness.

An inner transformation is needed to free man from sin
Although the whole idea of animal sacrifice may be obnoxious to us, we can accept Second Isaiah's notion of self-sacrifice and see how the unselfish action of someone can mitigate (i.e. reduce the severity of) the suffering of others. We can understand how later Old Testament writers realized that sin was so deeply entrenched in man's nature that no amount of punishment could resolve it; some other solution had to be found. Jeremiah looked forward to a new relationship with God; this would create an inner compulsion to obey God's will. You cannot make people good by passing laws and doling out punishment when the laws are broken. Only when they experience some kind of inner transformation can they change their attitude to life. One man may decide not to steal because he is afraid of the consequences; on the other hand, another may simply accept within himself that stealing is unloving, uncharitable and therefore wrong. The first man is obeying the external law of the land, the second man is obeying an inner obligation which he places upon himself as a result of thought and inner conviction. When put to the test the second man will be more likely to withstand temptation than the first. Jeremiah envisaged a day when God would make a new covenant with man and write his laws upon men's hearts (31:*31—34*). Men of their own free will and conviction would choose to do that which was right.

How Jesus saw his mission
The ideas of Jeremiah and Second Isaiah are pointers to Jesus. First, as Jesus summed up the whole of God's law in terms of love, it follows that for him sin was the unloving thought, word and action. Second, there are two passages in Mark's gospel where Jesus states clearly why he has come. In 2:*17* he says: 'those who are well have no need of a physician, but those who are sick; I came not to call the righteous but sinners'. By implication all men, being sinners, need healing from the sickness of sin. And 10:*45* reads: 'The Son of Man also came not to be served but to serve and to give his life as a ransom for many'. This same theme was continued in his words at the Last Supper where he said that his blood was the blood of the covenant which was poured out for many (14:*24*). His

strange sacrificial language would be more meaningful to his Jewish friends than it is to us.

The gospels of Matthew and Luke tell us that before Jesus began his ministry he underwent severe mental conflict in the wilderness as to what kind of a Messiah he was going to be. He rejected every way of bringing in the kingdom of God for all men, except the way of sacrificial love. He also told his disciples that it was the inner motivation which was all-important. The Sermon on the Mount (Matthew 5–7) gives us several relevant examples, but two will be sufficient to illustrate the point. The Law of Moses condemned murder and adultery, but Jesus showed that his teaching went further. He required of his followers a hate-free heart, as hatred and anger so often led to murder. Furthermore, they should not lust after someone else's wife or husband, since lust was the root cause of adultery. When discussing with the Pharisees the nature of religious purity (Mark 7:1–23), he firmly declared that a man could not be defiled by things outside himself, but only by what was in his own heart and spirit. By taking all these ideas together, we can begin to see what Jesus visualized when he talked of overcoming narrow selfishness and unloving motivation, a disease which was so destructive of man's well-being. He believed that his willingness to serve others and even to give his life for them would free them from the tyranny of sin.

Jesus was extraordinary in very many respects, but above all he was free from anxiety about himself. He was compassionate, without regard for himself. True greatness in the kingdom, said Jesus, was humble service. Had Jesus been as self-interested and insecure as most of us, he would have reached some kind of agreement with the authorities and gone off to spend the rest of his days in the wilderness, thus saving his own life. But he decided to go on declaring the truth as he saw it, about the nature of man and his relationship to God, for as long as he could, in the belief that this would bring about other men's freedom: 'and you will know the truth and the truth will make you free' (John 8:32); 'everyone who commits sin is a slave to sin. The slave does not continue in the house for ever; the son continues for ever. So if the son makes you free, you will be free indeed' (John 8:34).

The power of creative love can break the bondage of sin
Jesus actually demonstrated by his own life that it is the creative power of sacrificial love that breaks the bondage of sin. Whatever they did, his enemies found that they could not crush or destroy his compassion and his willingness to forgive them. He refused to become entrapped by the desire for revenge (Luke 23:34). One can interpret the crucifixion on several levels. It was first an act of

great personal courage to die for what he believed to be right. This is an example of profound integrity and as such very relevant for all men. Second, it demonstrated that Jesus could not be prevented from loving, which makes it an act of power, because it released that power for all men. Third, Christians believed that the death of Jesus was not the end of the story. His immediate friends were convinced that he rose from the dead, thus being vindicated by God. Whether this event was spiritual or physical is discussed on p. 177, but whatever else one might believe about the resurrection, there is no doubt that Jesus' first disciples were absolutely sure that in some sense, in some way, his person had gone through the experience of death and had survived it. He was available to them after death. He had a new power he had not possessed before. The risen Jesus was able to awaken in them the same freedom that he had himself—a freedom from self—a freedom for others. So men could look forward with hope to the eventual conquest of evil and the triumph of good.

True freedom

Christians believe that mankind was liberated in the death and resurrection of Jesus, but that each individual must make this freedom his own experience through personal conviction. Paul expressed this truth in terms which were appropriate to his own culture. He wrote about man having a higher and a lower nature, saying that the lesser self must die in order that the spiritual self can fully live: 'We know that our old self was crucified with him so that the sinful body might be destroyed and that we might no longer be enslaved to sin' (Romans 6:6). These may be difficult images for us to appreciate, but it is not difficult to see that one must get rid of hatred and resentment in order to love and forgive, get rid of fear in order to live. We must draw back the curtains to get rid of the darkness, thus letting in the light. If we really desire life, love and light, then we will make these our priorities. Freedom from self-concern means freedom to love. So the finest vision of the men of the Old Testament was realized in Jesus, the Christ.

Discussion and work

1 Look again at the Ten Commandments. You should know them by heart, as well as Jesus' summary of the Law. The last commandment is perhaps the most profound of all because you could summarize all sin as 'I want for myself', which means greed or coveting. According to the teaching of the Buddha, this was the cause of all mankind's trouble. So the Buddha sought freedom from this everlasting craving by extinguishing the self, by walking the eightfold path of right living, thinking and speaking. By

contrast, Jesus thought that the way of freedom from total self-concern was by loving others, so that the self ceases to be our priority, although given its proper place in the sense that loving your neighbour as yourself shows there is a right place for self-regard. Would you agree that our society is dominated by the idea that happiness lies in possessing more and more things? Is it true, however, that wanting more all the time is the enemy of all joy?

2 How would you define sin?

3 Freedom is a commonly used word today. We have freedom fighters, as well as many liberation movements. The theme for the 1975 World Council of Churches was 'Jesus Christ frees and unites'. How true do you think this might be? Do you think it is appropriate to substitute 'freedom' for 'salvation'?

4 Discuss the following propositions:

'You can never be totally free unless you know your own limitations.'

'Freedom is essentially an experience not a feeling.'

'Freedom is being at peace with myself.'

'Love is the way of finding freedom.'

'Universal freedom is necessary, because only if all are free can anyone be truly free.'

'Selfishness is the most evil and imprisoning of vices.'

5 In modern terms, what do you think Jesus' death achieved?

6 Look back to section 2. Do you think it is true that a new type of man must evolve before there can be a new world? If so, how can this new man come into being?

5 The fulfilled life

The biblical vision

As we have seen, the Bible portrays a Creator who is intimately concerned with his magnificent creation and who has endowed mankind with all sorts of gifts and potentialities. It must be clearly stated that both Old and New Testament writers take a positive attitude towards life. They have no doubt that life is good and is meant to be lived to the full. The Bible's realistic approach to the problems of evil, sin and suffering indicates the authors' passionate concern that humanity should find its way back to the source of all true harmony and fulfilment; they dream of a future state when every discord will be resolved and mankind will once more find perfect union with God. Just as the first book gives us the beautiful picture of man's idyllic state in the Garden of Eden, so the last book—Revelation—ends with a vision of a new heaven and a new earth. However strange the images in this final book may seem to us, we cannot doubt the author's intent in saying:

> Behold the dwelling of God is with men. He will dwell with them; he will wipe away every tear from their eyes, and death shall be no more, neither shall there be mourning nor crying nor pain any more, for the former things have passed away
>
> (Revelation 21:*3,4*).

Although it may be variously interpreted by different readers, the Bible as a whole teaches that God is the source of illumination, of life and love. If 20th-century man finds it difficult to visualize a father figure sitting in glory above the world surrounded by his court of angelic beings, he can perhaps accept that God is creative energy or, as Christians believe, creative love. If men and women are to live a fulfilled and purposeful life they must be sure of their priorities. First they have to recognize that they need reconciliation, both with the Source of their being and with each other. Next they must be possessed of an inner spirit or strength which will enable them to put into practice their convictions about the right way to live.

The necessity for obedience

For the ancient Israelite, the real purpose of life was quite simply to do the will of God as defined in the books of the Law and the further declarations of prophetic teachers. The date at which Deuteronomy was written is uncertain and many of its laws belong to a primitive agricultural community whose rituals are alien to us; nonetheless we can appreciate that its main theme is God's love for Israel and Israel's response. It contains the commandment which Jesus emphasized above all others: 'Hear, O Israel: The Lord our God is one Lord; and you shall love the Lord your God with all your heart, and with all your soul, and with all your might' (Deuteronomy 6:*4,5*; cf Mark 12:*29—33*).

Deuteronomy is a passionate call for Israel to demonstrate justice, compassion and mercy in its own corporate life because God is merciful, compassionate and just to his people. All members of the Israelite community were expected to show each other the same loyalty and commitment which God showed towards them. This Old Testament book, however, does accept the over-simple belief that material prosperity is available to those who love and obey God. The doctrine runs:

> If you are faithful in your commitment to Yahweh, then you will prosper, live to a ripe old age and be remembered always by your children and grand-children. Thus any disaster or suffering

169

which comes to you must be God's punishment for your misdeeds and unfaithfulness.

Later generations of Hebrew writers wrestled against this incomplete doctrine of the human condition.

Israel consecrated itself to God at the making of the Covenant on Mount Sinai (Exodus 19:5,6). As a nation it accepted the duty of priestly ministry. It saw this total commitment to God's purpose and his ways as the basis of man's well-being. When a man walked with God, he had a real integrity of character, as the story of Joseph shows. Later on, Jeremiah and others dreamt of God's law being written in men's hearts. The prophet found that God was still with him even though fellow human beings deserted him. Through talking with God he realized that religion was primarily a matter of fellowship with God. When communion with God came first, right living was bound to follow because God's spirit was within.

Worship is essential to the good life

Worship of God was an important part of Israelite life. For several centuries after return from the Exile, the Temple services were extremely significant until the whole system was destroyed by the Fall of Jerusalem in AD 70. By that time the sabbath synagogue service in the local community had become an integral part of Jewish life.

Private and corporate prayer also formed an essential element in the good life, because it is through prayer that a man deepens his relationship with God. Prayer is not just a matter of asking God for something; it involves a man's whole approach to life. Praise and thankfulness to God are as necessary as any other expression of devotion. The Psalms are really prayers, both for the individual and the community. The themes of awe, reverence, wonder and praise run constantly through these poems, as well as consciousness of sin, leading to confession and repentance. Through the institution of the sabbath day of rest and through acts of private as well as public dedication to God, the ancient Israelite (like the modern devout Jew) expressed his conviction that daily communion with God is the first essential of the good life.

Jesus and personal fulfilment

It is against this Old Testament background that we must look at New Testament ideas of the fulfilled life, especially as Jesus has given us fresh insights. In the first place, he is reported as specifically saying that he had come to bring abundance of life (John 10:10). Everything we know about Jesus indicates that he was not speaking solely of eternal life or life hereafter but of this life on earth. He was not anti-social; on the contrary, he attended weddings and parties and was criticized by his enemies for being a glutton and a drunkard (Luke 7:34), a friend of tax collectors and sinners.

In later centuries when Christianity became the established religion of the Roman Empire, many Christians withdrew from the world in protest at corruption within the church. Their disillusionment with society led them to find refuge in the search for personal piety. The spread of the monastic movement is a very important event in the religious and social history of Christianity and the men and women concerned lived a wide variety of lives. However, it was truly a vocation for the few not the many, and it was nowhere implied by Jesus himself. Persecution also coloured the Christian view of the fulfilled life; certain sections of the church were, and still are, content to preach acceptance of poverty and oppression in the hope of a reward hereafter. While these two aspects of Christian thought are historically significant, they do not give the total view. For this we must go back to Jesus himself.

The Sermon on the Mount (Matthew 5—7) begins with nine sayings. Each starts with the words 'Blessed are . . .' or 'How blessed are . . .' hence their name 'The Beatitudes' (Matthew 5:3—12). A beatitude is not quite the same as a blessing. It is really an expression of happiness. Jesus is saying that the man who has a certain quality of life is indeed happy; from it inevitable results will follow. At first sight it seems strange to associate poverty, suffering, gentleness and persecution with any degree of fulfilment, but a closer look at these very enigmatic and concise statements suggests to us that probably Jesus is talking about a way of life that not only refuses to put material prosperity and worldly success first, but also exhibits self-awareness, sensitivity to others and dedication to a noble cause. It is men and women who realize the futility of aggressiveness, who are passionately concerned with justice, mercy and reconciliation, who are truly the children of God and to whom the earth naturally belongs.

Later in the Sermon, Jesus talks about the importance of inner motivation—of the hatred and anger which can lead to murder or to problems from which a man cannot free himself; of the lust which leads to adultery; of the dishonesty which results in perjury; of the desire for revenge which leads on to further retaliation. He talks of the freedom to love and to forgive, which is not weakness but strength. The way of life which he advocates is not ostentatious in the matter of charity, or private and public devotion, or religious and moral acts of self-discipline. He condemns love of money because man becomes the slave to wealth, not its master, if

171

he puts money first. A false perspective about life's values is like physical blindness, and it is just as disabling. Instead of worrying about material things, Jesus advises a certain detachment; this is the attitude that puts peace and happiness above profit or 'getting rich quick'. Love and harmonious personal relationships are the key to a life which can attain freedom from fear and anxiety.

In Jesus' eyes, the Kingdom of God was already a present reality for some men as well as a future hope for all men. Men must seek the kingdom first and then everything else would fall into its proper perspective and place. He demonstrated in his own life the overwhelming power of love and forgiveness and after his death his spirit transformed those who endeavoured to follow in his footsteps.

Paul and 'walking in love': The Apostle Paul knew from his own experience that, although the Law could show a man the good life, it could not make him fulfil all its obligations. Only when he had the Christ nature within him, that is to say when he was governed by the principle of love, could an individual walk the god-like way. Paul's letter to the Romans illustrates his belief that to 'walk in Christ' (12:*3—8*) means to 'walk in love' (12:*9—21*). He uses the phrase 'put on the Lord Jesus Christ' (13:*14*), which in another letter (Colossians 3:*12,14*) becomes 'put on love'. Romans 13 demonstrates that love is the fulfilment of the law and chapters 14 and 15 give a practical illustration of what walking in love should mean for a Christian congregation. Paul has evidently heard that members of the Roman Church are disputing with one another about food and drink. Some vegetarians and teetotallers claim that theirs is the only way; others say that such scruples are unnecessary. They ask Paul to judge which side is right but he lifts the problem on to a different plane of thought. The Kingdom is not really concerned with food and drink but with 'righteousness and peace and joy in the Holy Spirit' (14:*17*). In effect he says live and let live; do not judge or despise others but witness in your own lives the way of love. When Christians live not only for themselves but for others, then reconciliation takes place.

Later Christian experience

For three centuries after their master's death, those first Christian followers experienced suffering and martyrdom. Nevertheless, Luke shows us in Acts that their communal life was marked by a great sense of joy, peace and brotherhood. At certain times and in certain circumstances Christians have had to suffer deeply for their faith, but on the whole they have been called to show that their religion is genuine and valid in the ordinary, everyday affairs

172

of normal living. They should be able to witness to the deep sense of joy and purpose which walking with Jesus brings.

Discussion and work

1 Look up the following passages in Deuteronomy and discuss their implications. How much do you think the spirit of these passages is alive today? Deuteronomy 15:*7—8*; 16:*18—20*; 24:*14,15*; 24:*17—20*; 25:*1—4*; 26:*12—13*.

2 When Job was protesting that he had not deserved the terrible calamities that had befallen him, he listed his good deeds—Job 31:*16—19, 22*. Is this list true of the good person's behaviour today or has the Welfare State removed the individual's sense of personal responsibility for charitable works?

3 Read Hosea 6:*4—6*. What is the role of God's love in creating the fulfilled life?

4 Look up and discuss the following passages from the Psalms: 27:*4*; 8:*3*; 27:*1*; 34:*1*; 103:*1*; 95:*1*; 24:*4*; 143:*10*. What quality of life do these poems portray?

5 Look up and discuss the meaning of the individual Beatitudes in Matthew 5:*3—12*. Do you think Jesus is portraying an idealized character, an impossible ideal? Do you think it was an unconscious portrayal of himself? Do you think these characteristics would lead to a sense of fulfilment in life? Would they produce happiness?

6 Many consider that Paul's ethic, i.e. his basic moral code, is summed up in Romans 12—14. Can you detect which fundamental characteristics in these chapters remind us of Jesus' own teaching in the Sermon on the Mount?

6 Death and the after-life

Old Testament concepts of death and Sheol

Death is a universal experience and man has always yearned for immortality, being unable to accept his own end. In the great Eastern religions the doctrine of reincarnation expressed the cycle of birth, death and rebirth which is found in nature, but the doctrine affirms that through unending lives a man may eventually find permanent union with the Absolute or the timeless peace of Nirvana. The Old Testament Garden of Eden parable tells us that the Tree of Life stood in the garden; this suggests that perhaps mankind was destined for immortality but that he forfeited his chances by disobedience. Adam and Eve were cast out of Paradise: 'Lest he put forth his hand and take also of the tree of life, and eat, and live for ever' (Genesis 3:*22*). As man was now sinful, it would be indeed terrible if he were to become immortal for he would possess powers which he could fearfully abuse. The penalty of Adam's disobedience was death: 'You are dust, and to dust you shall return' (Genesis 3:*19*).

In this way the ancient biblical writers tried to explain both the fact of death and the contradictory longing for eternal life. Nevertheless man and the animals were mortal. Thus in Psalm 89:*48* the Psalmist wrote: 'What man can live and never see death? Who can deliver his soul from the power of Sheol?' 'Sheol', translated in the English bible both as 'grave' and 'pit' was the place of the dead. The Hebrew idea of Sheol may be based upon the Babylonian picture of the abode of departed spirits—the underworld—a great cave or hollow beneath the earth. There was no return from the dead. 'As the cloud fades and vanishes, he who goes down to Sheol does not come up, he returns no more to his house, nor does his place know him any more' (Job 7:*9,10*). It was a shadowy existence, terrible in its emptiness, and some passages even expressed the fear that Sheol was outside God's presence. 'The dead do not praise the Lord, nor do any that go down into silence' (Psalm 115:*17*). 'What profit is there in my death, if I go down to the Pit? Will the dust praise thee? Will it tell of thy faithfulness?' (Psalm 30:*9,10*).

Necromancy
There were other strands of Hebrew belief about the after-life. Many ancient peoples venerated their dead and relied upon them for counsel and advice. From early times until the advent of Marxism, the Chinese were ancestor worshippers; the spirit of the dead parent or grand-parent was considered an intrinsic element of everyday affairs. The Israelites were forbidden these practices because God was the only being worthy of worship (Deuteronomy 18:*9—12*), but from such stories as that of Saul's visit to the Witch of Endor (1 Samuel 28) we can see that necromancy (implying a belief that the dead still existed), witchcraft and what we would call spiritualism were a part of everyday life. Saul asked the witch to summon up the shade of the prophet Samuel, which according to the narrative she was able to do. Samuel's shade prophesied the death of Saul and his sons in the forthcoming battle.

The importance of burial customs
We know from archaeology how important the burial of their dead was to ancient peoples. Mankind appears to be unique in that he troubles to bury his dead with ceremony, believing that this in some way affects the ultimate survival of the dead person. The Hebrews were no exception. It was a wretched thing for the body

to remain unburied. The inhabitants of Jabesh Gilead, who were grateful to Saul, went by night to rescue his body and those of his sons from their ignominious display on the city walls of Beth-shan, and buried them under a sacred tree in Jabesh (1 Samuel 31:*8—13*). The death of Jezebel was all the more terrible because when she fell from her window the dogs consumed her body (2 Kings 9:*34—37*). In contrast, when a patriarch or a king died full of years and honour, it was recorded that 'Jotham slept with his fathers and was buried with his fathers' (2 Kings 15:*38*; 16:*20*).

Survival in one's descendants
Another kind of survival was continuance through one's descendants. A man lived on through his children and family. That was why it was so disastrous to die childless. Hebrew law made it obligatory for a dead man's brother or male next of kin to try to have a son by the widow (Deuteronomy 25:*5—10*) so that this son 'shall succeed to the name of his brother who is dead, that his name may not be blotted out of Israel'. In Jesus' day the Sadducees, the Jewish priestly class and very traditional in outlook, believed only in this kind of survival through the family line. 'For the Sadducees say there is no resurrection, nor angel, nor spirit; but the Pharisees acknowledge them all' (Acts 23:*8*).

Developing belief in more active survival
By analysing the changes in Old Testament thought up to New Testament times, it is possible to trace the development of a gradually growing belief in a more worthwhile survival in another world and/or a belief in a resurrection to life on earth. Hosea's expectation (6:*1, 2*) that the power of God will restore the nation to life, perhaps also implies a hope of individual resurrection. Ezekiel's vision of the valley of dry bones (Ezekiel 37) suggests a similar interpretation. Some scholars consider that a famous passage in Isaiah (26:*19*) shows belief in the resurrection of the righteous dead to life on earth. 'The dead shall live; their bodies shall rise. O dwellers in the dust, awake and sing for joy! For thy dew is a dew of light, and on the land of the shades thou wilt let it fall.' It is Daniel, however, who most explicitly states a belief in the resurrection of the righteous dead. 'And many of those who sleep in the dust of the earth shall awake, some to everlasting life, and some to shame and everlasting contempt' (Daniel 12:*2*). The author was writing during the period of the Maccabean revolt against the oppression of the Seleucid King, Antiochus IV (about 180 BC). Many loyal Jews gave up their lives rather than deny their faith. Daniel expressed the belief that God would establish his Kingdom on earth and vindicate his faithful followers, bringing them back

to life as a reward for their utter loyalty. Equally, the wicked would suffer for their betrayal of God's cause.

Belief in the resurrection of the righteous
In the period between the Maccabean revolt and the New Testament era, belief in the resurrection of the righteous continued to grow. The Wisdom of Solomon (written about 100 years before Jesus) states 'righteousness is immortal' (1:15), and 'the souls of the righteous are in the hand of God, and no torment shall ever touch them' (3:1).

One or two passages in the Psalms suggest a belief in some kind of satisfying life after death. This must not be confused with belief in a bodily resurrection on earth; the latter was part of God's vindication of those who died prematurely in his cause. According to Psalm 49 the wicked go to the place of shades beyond the grave, but the righteous man goes to be with God. 'Like sheep they are appointed for Sheol; Death shall be their shepherd . . . but God will ransom my soul from the power of Sheol; for he will receive me' (v.14,15). Even if the wicked man prospers in his lifetime, he has only the miseries of Sheol to look forward to beyond death. On the other hand although the righteous man may suffer on earth, he can anticipate bliss beyond the grave because he will be with God. The writer of Psalm 73 seems to be saying that both before and after death he has fellowship with God (v.23), an idea which is echoed in Psalm 16.

The teaching of Jesus
Turning to the New Testament period, we find that the Pharisees were the strongest believers in a resurrection of the dead—a question they much debated with the Sadducees who did not share this view. On one occasion the Sadducees challenged Jesus about his own beliefs (Mark 12:23—33), basing their question on verses quoted above (Deuteronomy 25:5—10). Using a passage in Exodus (3:6) to substantiate his view, Jesus stated his conviction that there was a life after death, but pointed out that conditions in that life were very different from this one because the physical body was translated into a spiritual one. Furthermore, Mark reports that several times during the last months of his life, Jesus predicted his own resurrection from the dead (Mark 8:31; 9:9,30; 10:34; 14:25).

Luke's and John's gospels give us further evidence that Jesus believed very strongly in an after-life. The criminal crucified on one side of Jesus was promised fellowship with him in Paradise (Luke 23:43). Before his arrest, Jesus comforted his friends with the noble words:

176

Let not your hearts be troubled; believe in God, believe also in me. In my Father's house are many rooms; if it were not so, would I have told you that I go to prepare a place for you? And when I go and prepare a place for you, I will come again and will take you to myself, that where I am you may be also
(John 14:*1–3*).

Jesus' resurrection

In some way not possible for us to recapture, the first disciples of Jesus experienced his resurrection from the dead. The earliest account of this happening is found in Paul's letter to the Corinthians written about AD 55, some 20 years after Jesus' death. Paul lists six appearances of Jesus; first to Peter; second to the twelve; third to about 500 people, many of whom were still alive when Paul wrote his letter; fourth, to James, Jesus' brother; fifth, to all the apostles; and finally to Paul himself (1 Corinthians 15:*3–8*). It is interesting that he includes his own visionary experience of the risen Jesus on the Damascan road (Acts 22:*6–11*) with the other occurrences. It would seem that he believed Jesus' physical body had been changed or transformed into a spiritual body by the resurrection from the dead. The gospels relate varying kinds of happening: the finding of the empty tomb, angelic visitations and messages and the appearance of Jesus in forms that at first were not recognizable. Nevertheless, Luke records both in his gospel and in Acts that the risen Jesus confirmed the reality of his physical being by eating fish in front of his disciples (Luke 24:*39–43*; Acts 10:*39–41*). John's gospel tells us that Jesus appears first to Mary Magdalene in the garden, although she is slow to recognize him; on another occasion he appears to Thomas. The disciple had doubted his master's resurrection, but now he is shown the wounds of the crucifixion. The last chapter (or appendix) of John depicts Jesus cooking breakfast for his friends by the shore of Galilee and reinstating Peter after his threefold denial.

Those Christians who cannot come to terms with a literal bodily resurrection find it easier to accept a kind of spiritual resurrection through which the disciples became conscious of their Lord's presence among them, even though they did not know him to be there through their five senses. There is no doubt that the gospel writers believed in a bodily resurrection; the experience of Jesus' spiritual presence in their midst was, however, the foundation stone of the early Christian community. A vague hope in an after-life became a most clearly defined faith. Christians were distinguished from their contemporaries by this certainty that those who belonged to Jesus Christ would experience life after death. This enabled them

177

to face martyrdom with great courage and resolution. The Sadducees first persecuted Peter and John because they taught the people that Jesus was risen from the dead (Acts 4:*1,2*). Paul, as a Pharisee, ardently declared his loyalty to his ancestral faith; what distinguished him from his fellow-Jews was the belief that Jesus was the Messiah and that he had been raised by God from the dead: 'With respect to the hope and resurrection of the dead I am on trial' (Acts 23:*6*).

Early Christian beliefs

The Pharisees had believed in a general resurrection from the dead at the End of History. By affirming that Jesus had risen, Christians declared that the End was near and with it would come the resurrection of those who had died before the End.

> But in fact Christ has been raised from the dead, the first fruits of those who have fallen asleep. For as by man came death, by a man has come also the resurrection of the dead. For as in Adam all die, so also in Christ shall all be made alive
>
> (1 Corinthians 15:*20—22*).

In the same passage Paul goes on to describe how he sees this resurrection:

> and we shall all be changed. For this perishable nature must put on the imperishable, and this mortal nature must put on immortality. When the perishable puts on the imperishable, and the mortal puts on immortality, then shall come to pass the saying that is written:
> 'Death is swallowed up in victory.
> O death, where is thy victory?
> O death, where is thy sting?'.

For all New Testament writers, immortality was the gift of God which came to mankind through Jesus the Christ.

The first book of the Bible contains the tragic parable of Adam and Eve's expulsion from the Garden of Eden and their consequent mortality and death. The last book, Revelation, ends with the vision of a new Jerusalem, a heavenly city in which runs the river of the water of life. The tree of life stands by the river 'with its twelve kinds of fruit, yielding its fruit each month; and the leaves of the tree were for the healing of the nations' (Revelation 22:*1—2*). So humanity can be restored to that fellowship with God for which it was first created and for which it has been created anew by the power of the life-giving spirit of Christ: 'The first Adam became a living being; the last Adam became a life-giving spirit' (1 Corinthians 15:*45*). Death was therefore no longer the enemy, but the gate through which it was possible to pass to a fuller, richer, more complete life than anything experienced on earth.

Modern Christian beliefs

The majority of Christians today would reject the very narrow claim that life after death only comes to those who have declared their allegiance to the historic person of Jesus of Nazareth. It is quite inconceivable that a loving God and Father of all humanity should deliberately exclude the greater part of mankind from any hope of immortality simply because nations happen to have been born outside the Christian church's sphere of influence. Increasing knowledge of other great religions has helped Christians to appreciate how God must be at work within the religious life of mankind as a whole.

Christian creeds talk about a resurrection of the body. Belief in this as a literal fact was once common, as we can see from medieval paintings depicting the dead rising from their graves on Judgment Day (cf the 20th-century painter, Stanley Spencer, and his work 'Resurrection in Cookham Churchyard'). Many modern Christians, however, would totally reject this idea while maintaining that there must be survival of some kind of spiritual body. This would be needed to give a sense of continuity after death and a sense of personal identity. If there is no bodily form, these Christians argue, how could we recognize loved ones and how could we experience growth and development?

Other Christians would express their belief in a different way. They point out that eternal life begins here and now. If we can achieve a right relationship with God, through faith, we can experience the quality of eternal life in this world. At the raising of Lazarus, Jesus said to Martha: 'I am the resurrection and the life; he who believes in me, though he die, yet shall he live, and whoever lives and believes in me shall never die' (John 11:25,26). In this sense the person who finds God through faith in Jesus Christ is united to the source of love and life and therefore cannot be destroyed by physical death.

Some Christians may not positively believe in individual resurrection at the moment of death or corporate resurrection on Judgment Day; nevertheless, they are convinced of the immortality of the soul. The latter conviction is common to many different cultures and philosophies and is not necessarily Christian at all. It implies that within humanity itself are the seeds of immortality. A Christian who accepts the idea of immortality, however, sees mankind—the creation of God—as possessing great potential. Man has an inherent ability to survive physical death, but much depends upon the quality of life he leads, on the use or misuse of his gifts. Regardless of his faith or lack of it, if he walks the way of love and compassion which Jesus exemplified, then his spiritual essence or soul will develop and realize its full potential, thus equipping him for the different kind of existence which lies beyond the grave.

Discussion and work

1 It has been argued that man's implicit and unquenchable belief in some kind of survival beyond death is proof that it must be so. Do you agree?

2 The first Christians believed that their master would soon return in glory to judge all humanity and then establish his kingdom forever. Does the fact that their time-scale was wrong make you doubt their other convictions about a future life?

3 Is there any truth in the idea that the carrot of heaven beyond the grave has been used to make people accept a less equal and just life on earth?

   Find out which political philosopher was most famous for launching this attack on Christian concepts. Should the idea of life after death alter one's conduct and one's attitude to life on earth?

4 The Apostles' Creed states: 'I believe in the Communion of Saints'. What are your views on the matter, bearing in mind that 'Saints' refers to the community of past Christian believers and does not only mean the outstanding men and women of past centuries?

5 The practice of spiritualism, i.e. the belief that the living can communicate with the dead, was forbidden in the Old Testament. Writers declared that it was against God's will to meddle with spirits who might influence man for evil as well as for good. Modern investigations (The Society for Psychical Research) into the claims of 20th-century spiritualists have simply returned a not proven verdict.

   What arguments would a Christian advance against going to a seance or taking part in a table-turning session? In what sense might a Christian believe that it was possible to have some link with a loved one who has died?

Appendices

1 Preamble to the United Nations Charter

We the people of the United Nations determine

to save succeeding generations from the scourge of war, which twice in our lifetime has brought untold sorrow to mankind, and

to reaffirm faith in fundamental human rights, in the dignity and worth of the human person, in the equal rights of men and women and of nations large and small, and

to establish conditions under which justice and respect for the obligations arising from treaties and other sources of international law can be maintained, and

to promote social progress and better standards of life in larger freedom,

and for these ends

to practise tolerance and live together in peace with one another as good neighbours, and

to unite our strength to maintain international peace and security, and

to ensure, by the acceptance of principles and the institution of methods, that armed force shall not be used, save in the common interest, and

to employ international machinery for the promotion of the economic and social advancements of all peoples,

have resolved to combine our efforts to accomplish these aims.

Accordingly, our respective Governments, through representatives assembled in the city of San Francisco, who have exhibited their full powers found to be in good and due form, have agreed to the present Charter of the United Nations and do hereby establish an international organization to be known as the United Nations.

2 Summary of The United Nations Universal Declaration of Human Rights, 1948

Protection of the person Section: 1—3

All human beings are born free and equal in dignity and rights. They are endowed with reason and conscience and should act towards one another in a spirit of brotherhood. Everyone is entitled to all the rights and freedoms set forth in the Declaration without distinction of any kind. . . . Everyone has the right to life, liberty and security of person.

4. No one shall be held in slavery or servitude . . .

5. No one shall be subjected to torture or to cruel, inhuman or degrading treatment or punishment.

6. Everyone has the right to recognition everywhere as a person before the law.

7. All are equal before the law . . .

8. Everyone has the right to an effective remedy by the competent national tribunal for acts violating the fundamental rights granted him by the constitution or by law.

9. No one shall be subjected to arbitrary arrest, detention or exile . . .

Legal procedure

10. Everyone is entitled in full equality to a fair and public hearing . . .

11. Everyone charged with a penal offence has the right to be presumed innocent until proved guilty . . .

Right to privacy

12. No one shall be subjected to arbitrary interference with his privacy . . .

Freedom of movement

13. Everyone has the right to freedom of movement. . . . Everyone has the right to leave any country . . .

14. Everyone has the right to seek and to enjoy in other countries asylum from persecution.

Nationality

15. Everyone has the right to a nationality . . .

Marriage and the family

16. Men and women of full age, without any limitation due to race, nationality or religion, have the right to marry and found a family. They are entitled to equal rights as to marriage, during marriage and at its dissolution . . .

Property

17. Everyone has the right to own property . . .

Religious toleration

18. Everyone has the right to freedom of thought, conscience and religion . . .

Freedom of Expression

19. Everyone has the right to freedom of opinion and expression . . .

Assemblies and Associations

20. Everyone has the right to freedom of peaceful assembly and association . . .

Political rights

21. Everyone has the right to take part in the government of his country, directly or through freely chosen representatives. . . . The will of the people shall be the basis of the authority of government . . .

Social and industrial welfare

22. ⎫ . . . Everyone has the right to work, to free choice of employ-
and ⎬
23. ⎭ ment, to just and favourable conditions of work and to protection against unemployment . . .

24. Everyone has the right to rest and leisure . . .
25. Everyone has the right to a standard of living adequate for health and well-being. . . . Motherhood and childhood are entitled to special care . . .

Education, science and the arts

26. Everyone has the right to education. . . . Education shall be directed to the full development of the human personality and to the strengthening of respect for human rights and fundamental freedoms . . .
27. Everyone has the right freely to participate in the cultural life of the community . . .

Safeguards for human rights

28. Everyone is entitled to a social and international order in which the rights and freedoms set forth in this Declaration can be fully realized.
29. Everyone has duties to the community . . .
30. Nothing in this Declaration may be interpreted as implying for any State, group, or person, any right to engage in any activity or to perform any act aimed at the destruction of any of the rights and freedoms set forth.

The United Nations Covenants on Human Rights

After many years work the General Assembly in 1966 adopted two international covenants designed to transform the provisions of the Declaration of Human Rights into international law. Both covenants came into force in 1976 and are now legally binding on the nations who ratified them—about 45 in number, including Britain.

Responsibility for United Nations work concerning human rights is entrusted to the Economic and Social Council which reports to the General Assembly.

3 The Helsinki Agreement and the European Convention for the Protection of Human Rights

At the 1975 Helsinki Conference on Security and Co-operation in Europe 35 nations, including the USA and the USSR, agreed to maintain basic human rights. The agreement set up a programme of rights, including the reunification of families, marriages between citizens of different states, travel, tourism, circulation of information, cultural co-operation and so on. Attempts to check how far the USSR was keeping to the agreement have involved Russian dissidents in a great deal of trouble.

The signatories to the Helsinki agreement held extended meetings in Belgrade during 1977 and 1978 to discuss putting the Final Act into practice. They met again, this time in Madrid in 1980. On that occasion questions were asked in the British parliament about how far the Soviet Union was keeping the letter and the spirit of the agreement. These questions arose from information that psychiatry in the Soviet Union was being abused for political purposes and that those who had criticized the Soviet government for not observing the agreement were being imprisoned.

Further review conferences will probably take place. The United Kingdom government believes that it is worthwhile to continue these contacts despite the difficulties that arise, as the discussion gives an opportunity to bring abuses to the public eye.

The European Convention for the Protection of Human Rights and Fundamental Freedoms was adopted by the Council of Europe in 1950 and came into force in 1953. The Convention provides an international guarantee for basic rights and freedoms and is closely linked with the Universal Declaration of Human Rights. Any member state which seriously violates the Convention's principles may be asked to withdraw from the Council or may be expelled.

4 The Rights of the Child

In 1959 the United Nations General Assembly adopted a Declaration of the Rights of the Child, believing that mankind owes to the child the best it has to give.

Here are the first clauses of the Ten Principles adopted:
1. The child shall enjoy all the rights set forth in this Declaration
. . .

2. The child shall enjoy special protection, and shall be given opportunities and facilities, by law and by other means to enable him to develop physically, mentally, spiritually and socially in a healthy and normal manner and in conditions of freedom and dignity.

3. The child shall be entitled from his birth to a name and nationality.

4. The child shall enjoy the benefits of social security.

5. The child who is physically, mentally or socially handicapped shall be given the special treatment, education and care required by his particular condition.

6. The child, for the full and harmonious development of his personality, needs love and understanding. He shall, wherever possible, grow up in the care and under the responsibility of affection and of moral and material security. A child of tender years shall not, save in exceptional circumstances, be separated from his mother . . .

7. The child is entitled to receive education, which shall be free and compulsory, at least in the elementary stages.

The best interests of the child shall be the guiding principle of those responsible for his education and guidance.

The child shall have full opportunity for play and recreation.

8. The child shall in all circumstances be among the first to receive protection and relief.

9. The child shall be protected against all forms of neglect, cruelty and exploitation. He shall not be the subject of traffic in any form. The child shall not be admitted to employment before an appropriate age.

10. The child shall be protected from practices which may foster racial, religious and any other form of discrimination . . .

5 The International Year of the Disabled, 1981

The General Assembly of the United Nations proclaimed the Declaration of the Rights of Mentally Retarded Persons in 1971 and the Declaration of the Rights of Disabled Persons in 1975. It then declared 1981 the International Year of Disabled Persons. The United Nations set out five principal objectives for the Year:

1. Helping disabled persons in their physical and psychological adjustment to society;

2. Promoting all national and international efforts to provide disabled persons with proper assistance, training, care and guidance,

to make available opportunities for suitable work and to ensure their full integration in society;

3. Encouraging study and research projects designed to facilitate the practical participation of disabled persons in daily life, for example, by improving their access to public buildings and transportation systems;

4. Educating and informing the public of the rights of disabled persons to participate in and contribute to various aspects of economic, social and political life;

5. Promoting effective measures for the prevention of disability and for the rehabilitation of disabled persons.

The keynote theme of the year was 'full participation and equality'.

The problem of disability is far more widespread than is generally realized. In any community one person in 10 has some kind of disablement. Two-thirds of the disabled live in developing countries where poverty and lack of medical and social assistance add to their difficulties. In fact the greatest single cause of disablement is poverty leading to malnutrition and disease.

As part of its contribution to the International Year, the Snowdon Working Party on Integration of the Disabled published a summary of its findings to distribute to schools in the United Kingdom. In this report the Earl of Snowdon said:

> Disabled people must have equal opportunities and equal rights as the rest of us. The right to go to work, the right to enjoy their leisure time to the full, and to go where they want, when they want. . . . I hope that this publication will serve as a permament reminder to everyone of how far we still have to go in integrating the disabled. For their need is to be consulted, and treated, as far as is conceivably possible as an important section of the community who have a great deal to contribute to our society.

6 The United Nations and Refugees

The Second World War created an enormous number of refugees all over Europe. With their problems in mind, the 1951 United Nations Convention defined a refugee as follows:

> Any person who owing to well-founded fear of being persecuted for reasons of race, religion, nationality, membership of a particular social group or political opinion, is outside the country of

his nationality and is unable, or owing to such fear, is unwilling to avail himself of the protection of that country; or who, not having a nationality and being outside the country of his former habitual residence, is unable, or owing to such fear, is unwilling to return to it.

The Convention also recognized that persons having more than one nationality could apply for refugee status.

The Protocol of 1967 amended the document so that in future all refugees, and not just those resulting from World War II, were automatically entitled to the protection of the 1951 Convention.

In 1969 the Organization of African Unity (OAU) drafted additional recommendations and procedures for dealing with the growing problem of refugees in Africa. As a result, individuals who may be fleeing from war or civil disturbance or escaping violence of any kind in Africa are recognized as refugees. The spirit of these resolutions is:

that every person is entitled to freedom from persecution and that he or she will receive recognition and assistance from the international community in order to effect that freedom.

The UNHCR seeks to protect the legal rights of refugees and to provide them with food, shelter and a new home. It relies heavily on the support of voluntary agencies to alleviate the plight of the 10 million refugees throughout the world.

7 The British Council of Churches Autumn Assembly, 1980

Nuclear Weapons and Disarmament

On a private member's motion moved by The Rev. Dr Kenneth Greet—This Assembly registers the following judgements:
1. The continuing escalation of nuclear arms threatens the very security which the weapons are held to guarantee.
2. The development and deployment of nuclear weapons has raised new and grave ethical questions for Christians. Because no gain from their use can possibly justify the annihilation they would bring about and because their effects on present and future generations would be totally indiscriminate as between military and civilians, to make use of the weapons would be directly contrary to the requirements of the so-called just war. The doctrine of deterrence based upon the prospect of mutual assured destruction

is increasingly offensive to the Christian conscience.

3. The resources devoted to military expenditure of all kinds are desperately needed to tackle the world-wide and domestic problems of poverty, hunger, ignorance and disease. Military budgets make demands which are denials of Christian understandings of how resources are to be used.

4. The time has come for a more resolute involvement of Christians in the current debate about defence and disarmament and in the taking of new initiatives for peace. Such initiatives must include attempts to use and increase contacts between Christians in the West and in Eastern Europe and the Soviet Union.

5. Therefore, this Assembly, calls upon all Christians to support the World Disarmament Campaign as one way of advocating the multilateral or unilateral approach towards disarmament, by signing the petition and encouraging others to do so.

(This motion was discussed on 24 November 1980, and carried overwhelmingly.)

8 Letter launching the World Disarmament Campaign, 1980

World Disarmament or World Death

Disarmament has never been more necessary. It is accepted that existing weapons could destroy all life on earth. *But it is also true that there has never been an opportunity as now to achieve disarmament.*

This is the fact: The Special Assembly of the United Nations has instructed the representatives of forty nations at Geneva, including all the nuclear powers, to:

(1) recommend practical measures to abolish all armed forces except those needed for internal security and a UN Peace Keeping Force, and

(2) meanwhile prepare proposals for the reduction of arms leading to complete disarmament.

At the Special Assembly of the United Nations all Governments pledged themselves to co-operate in seeking disarmament. The British Government gained the support of fifteen nations in submitting radical proposals to Geneva; President Carter has declared for reducing nuclear arms to zero when the SALT II treaty is ratified; and President Brezhnev has advocated the destruction of all weapons of mass destruction.

These are the statements of Governments, but experience has

shown that the hopes of Governments are not fulfilled unless there is pressure from peoples. In 1932 President Hoover prepared drastic disarmament, and there were high hopes, destroyed seven years later by the Second World War. That may happen again if peoples across all frontiers do not now make clear their demand for peace.

We call on all peoples who desire disarmament to unite in a campaign within Britain and world-wide to achieve it. Those who called for disarmament in the past were called Utopians. The UN Special Assembly and the Geneva discussions to implement its recommendations make us Realists. If Governments mean what they say disarmament *can* be achieved. The alternatives make action imperative: World Disarmament or World Death.

We sign this letter as individuals, though a number of us have the support of many associated with us.

With good hope,

Yours sincerely.

Lord Philip Noel-Baker, Lord Fenner Brockway, Hugh Montefiore, Bishop of Birmingham, Victor Guazzelli, Bishop of East London, The Rev. Dr Kenneth Greet, Chairman of the Executive of the British Council of Churches and Secretary of the Methodist Church, Rabbi Hugo Gryn of the West London Synagogue, Professor A.J. Ayer, Oxford, Member British Humanists Association, Jack Jones, Trade Union Leader, Moss Evans Secretary of the Transport and General Workers' Union, Alfred Lomas, MEP, Political Committee of London Co-operative Society, Frank Allaun, MP, Chairman Labour Party, 1978–79, The Rt Hon. Judith Hart, MP, Ex-Minister for Overseas Development, Richard Body, MP, Conservative, Holland with Boston, Christopher Brocklebank-Fowler, MP Conservative, Norfolk North West, The Rt Hon. David Bleakley, Ex-Minister of Community Relations, Northern Ireland Parliament, Lord Gerald Gardiner, Ex-Lord Chancellor, Lord Taylor of Gryfe, Chairman, Economic Forestry Group and Scottish Railway Board, Lord Bruce of Donington, Ex-Reporter, Budget Committee of European Parliament, Lord MacLeod of Fuinery, Founder of the Iona Community, ex-Moderator of The General Assembly of Churches of Scotland, Professor Sir Richard Doll, Warden Green College, Oxford, Professor Eric Burhop, London University, Trevor Phillips, President of the National Union of Students, Glenda Jackson, OBE, John Arlott, OBE, TV Commentator and *Guardian* Correspondent in Cricket, James Cameron, World Journalist, Lord Wade. Brian Clough.

Some Useful Addresses

For ease of reference I have listed the addresses under section headings, but where the work of an organization overlaps different sections, as in the case of the Salvation Army, I have only given one reference. It is impossible to give a comprehensive list of voluntary organizations here, but I have included the names and addresses of several publications which will be useful sources of further reference.

Where possible it is better to contact the local office of an organization but in case of difficulty, the national address is given below.

Section A—The Individual

Family Welfare Association,
Denison House, 296 Vauxhall Bridge Road, London SW1

Family Service Units,
207 Old Marylebone Road, London NW1

Family Planning Association,
Margaret Pike House, 27–35 Mortimer Street, London W1

Catholic Marriage Advisory Council,
Clitherow House, 15 Lansdowne Road, London W11

National Marriage Guidance Council,
Herbert Gray College, Little Church Street, Rugby,
Warwickshire CV21 3AP

National Council for One-Parent Families,
255 Kentish Town Road, London NW5 2LX

Gingerbread,
35 Wellington Street, London WC2E 7BN

National Association of Citizens Advice Bureaux,
115 Pentonville Road, London N1

Manpower Services Commission,
Selkirk House, 166 High Holborn, London WC1V 6PF

Workers Educational Association (WEA),
9 Upper Berkeley Street, London W1H 8BY

Samaritans Incorporated,
17 Uxbridge Road, Slough SL1 1SN
The National Council for Voluntary Organizations (NCVO) in
1981 published a report on the work of the Manpower Services
Commission entitled 'Work and Community: A report on MSC
Special Programmes for the Unemployed' by Richard Grover with
Stephen Hopwood, Trevor Davison and Rosemary Allen, Bedford
Square Press.

Section B—The Community

The Elderly:
  Age Concern,
  60 Pitcairn Road, Mitcham CR4 3LL

  British Red Cross Society,
  9 Grosvenor Crescent, London SW1X 7EJ

  Help the Aged,
  318 St Pauls Road, London N1

  National Association of Leagues of Hospital Friends,
  44 Fulham Road, London SW3 3HH

  National Corporation for the Care of Old People,
  Nuffield Lodge, Regent's Park, London NW1 4RS

  Salvation Army, 101 Queen Victoria Street, London EC4P 4EP

  St John Ambulance, 1 Grosvenor Crescent, London SW1X 7EF

  Women's Royal Voluntary Service,
  17 Old Park Lane, London W1Y 4AJ

The Disabled: Many of these societies are specialist concerns but a large number of them are members of the Royal Association for Disability and Rehabilitation, 25 Mortimer Street, London W1N 8AB

British Council for the Rehabilitation of the Disabled,
Tavistock House South, Tavistock Square, London WC1

Central Council for the Disabled,
34 Eccleston Square, London SW1

Leonard Cheshire Homes,
26 Maunsel Street, London SW1

National Association for Mental Health (MIND),
22 Harley Street, London W1N 2ED

Multiple Sclerosis Society of Great Britain,
4 Tachbrook Street, London SW1 1SJ

Muscular Dystrophy Group,
26 Borough High Street, London SE1

National Society for Mentally Handicapped Children,
Pembridge Hall, Pembridge Square, London W2 4EP

Royal National Institute for the Blind,
224 Great Portland Street, London W1N 6AA

Royal National Institute for the Deaf,
105 Gower Street, London WC1E 6AH

Spastics Society,
12 Park Crescent, London W1N 4EQ

The Deprived:
Catholic Housing Aid Society,
137 Holland Road, London W14

Child Poverty Action Group,
1 Macklin Street, London WC2B 5NH

Shelter National Campaign for the Homeless,
157 Waterloo Road, London SE1 8XF

National Cyrenians
13 Wincheap, Canterbury, Kent CT1 3TB

Children at risk:
Church of England Children's Society,
Old Town Hall, Kennington Road, London SE11 4QD

Dr Barnardo's,
Tanner's Lane, Barkingside, Ilford, Essex

National Children's Bureau,
8 Wakley Street, London EC1V 7QE

National Society for the Prevention of Cruelty to Children,
1 Riding House Street, London W1P 8AA

National Children's Home,
85 Highbury Park, London N5 1UD

Violence and prejudice:
Women's Aid Federation (England),
374 Grays Inn Road, London WC1

Commission for Racial Equality,
Elliot House, 10–12 Allington Street, London SW1E 5EX

Institute of Race Relations,
247 Pentonville Road, London N1 9NG

Minority Rights Group,
29 Craven Street, London WC2N 5NT

National Association for Multi-Racial Education,
Northbrook Centre, William Penn School, Penn Road, Slough
SL2 1PH

National Council for Civil Liberties,
21 Tabard Street, London SE1 4LA

The Runnymede Trust,
37A Grays Inn Road, London WC1 8PS

British Council of Churches Community and Race Relations
Unit,
2 Eaton Gate, London SW1W 9BL

Society of Friends Community Relations Committee,
Friends House, Euston Road, London NW1 2BJ

Alcohol and drug abuse:
Alcoholics Anonymous,
11 Redcliffe Gardens, London SW10 9BQ

Churches Council on Alcohol and Drugs,
4 Southampton Row, London WC1B 4AA

Institute for the Study of Drug Dependence,
1–4 Hatton Place, Hatton Garden, London EC1N 8ND

Christian denominational concern with social problems:
Baptist Union Christian Citizenship Committee,
4 Southampton Road, London WC2

Catholic Commission for Social Welfare,
1A Stert Street, Abingdon, Berks.

Church Army,
184 Marylebone Road, London NW1

Church of England Board of Social Responsibility,
Church House, Dean's Yard, London SW1

Toc H,
15 Trinity Square, London EC3

United Reformed Church Social Responsibility Department,
86 Tavistock Square, London WC1L 9PT

Unitarian Social Service,
Great Trenches Park, Copthorne, Crawley Down, Sussex

Quaker Social Responsibility and Education,
Friends House, Euston Road, London NW1 2BJ

Law and order:
Criminal Injuries Compensation Board,
Russell Square House, Russell Square, London WC1B 5EN

Howard League for Penal Reform,
125 Kennington Park Road, London SE11 4JP

National Association for the Care and Resettlement of Offenders (NACRO),
169 Clapham Road, London SW9 0PU

A copy of the annual report of NACRO can be had from the above address. It deals with NACRO's work in the areas of accommodation, employment, education, day centres, juvenile offenders, crime prevention, training, research and public education.

Advertising:
Advertising Standards Authority,
15 Ridgmount Street, London WC1

National Consumer Council,
18 Queen Anne's Gate, London SW1H 9AA

Service by youth for the community:
Board of Information on Youth and Community Service,
67 York Place, Edinburgh EH1 3JD

British Youth Council,
57 Charlton Street, London NW1 1HU

Community Service Volunteers,
237 Pentonville Road, London N1 9NJ

Duke of Edinburgh's Award,
5 Prince of Wales Terrace, London W8 5PG

Friends Work Camps Committee,
Friends House, Euston Road, London NW1 2BJ

King George's Jubilee Trust,
39 Victoria Street, London SW1H 0EE

National Council for Voluntary Organizations,
26 Bedford Square, London WC1B 3HU

National Council for Voluntary Youth Service,
26 Bedford Square, London WC1B 3HU

National Youth Bureau,
17–23 Albion Street, Leicester LE1 6GD

National Union of Students,
3 Endsleigh Street, London WC1

Task Force,
Clifford House, Edith Villas, London W14

YMCA,
640 Forest Road, Walthamstow, London E17 3DZ

YWCA,
Hampden House, 2 Weymouth Street, London W1N 4AX

For Overseas volunteering, see Section C.

Publications:
Voluntary Organizations: An NCVO Directory, A National Council
of Voluntary Organizations publication.

Sparing Time-The Observer Guide to Helping Others, by Elizabeth
Gundrey, Unwin Paperbacks. This book is written to explain the
preliminaries of getting involved, the range of volunteers that
can be accommodated and the scope of the work that is
available.

*Voluntary Social Service-A Handbook of Information and
Directorate of Organizations,* A National Council of Social Service
publication.

Section C—The World

As Section C covers an extremely wide field of study, I have listed
the societies in alphabetical order, adding a brief description of
their activities.

Amnesty International (British Section), 1 Easton Street,
London WC1X 8DJ
World-wide organization focussing strictly on prisoners of con-
science who have neither used nor advocated violence.

Catholic Institute for International Relations (CIIR), 22
Coleman Fields, London N1 7AF
Non-denominational. Particularly active in Third World volun-
teer work and campaigning for social change.

Central Bureau for Educational Visits and Exchange, 43–45 Dorset Street, London W1
Source of information about voluntary work and studying abroad.

Centre for Alternative Industrial and Technological Systems, North East London Polytechnic, Longbridge Road, Dagenham, Essex.
Based on the Lucas Aerospace Combine Shop Stewards Committee.

Centre for World Development Education, 128 Buckingham Palace Road, London SW1
Major source of teaching materials on world hunger and development.

Christian Aid, P.O. Box 1, London SW9 8BH
Largest Christian aid agency, with education department.

Conservation Society, 12a Guildford Street, Chertsey, Surrey KT16 9BQ

Friends of the Earth, 377 City Road, London EC1V 1NA
World-wide environmentalist society.

Intermediate Technology, 9 King Street, London WC2E 8HW
Active in promoting and researching small scale, appropriate technology, especially in Third World.

International Voluntary Service, 53 Regent Road, Leicester LE1 British branch of Service Civil International. Aims to bring international groups together in peace and practical work. Workcamps throughout Europe and the United Kingdom.

Oxfam, 274 Banbury Road, Oxford OX2 7DZ
Largest British voluntary agency, with excellent teaching material for schools on world development.

Save the Chidren Fund, Mary Datchelor House, 17 Grove Lane, London SE5
Dedicated to relief of children in distressed areas.

Standing Conference of British Organizations for Aid to Refugees,
26 Bedford Square, London WC1B 3HU

United Nations Association, 3 Whitehall Court, London SW1A 2EL
The UNA International Service specializes in sending volunteers overseas.

War on Want, 1 London Bridge Street, London SE1
Voluntary aid agency with good educational material available.

World Development Movement, Bedford Chambers, Covent Garden, London WC2E 8HA
Campaigns on Third World issues and fairer trading links.

World Wildlife Fund, Panda House, 11 Ockford Road, Godalming, Surrey
An international organization committed to conservation projects in all parts of the world.

Voluntary Service Overseas, 9 Belgrave Square, London SW1X 8PW
Largest British volunteer agency.

For anyone thinking of voluntary work, the publication *Thinking About Volunteering?* is a useful guide. Obtainable from: 1 Amwell Street, London EC1R 1UL.

British Volunteer Programme, 22 Coleman Fields, London N1, is an umbrella organization incorporating CIIR Overseas Programme, IVS, UNA International Service and VSO.